D1555301

COMMUNICATION STRATEGIES
in EVALUATION

NEW PERSPECTIVES IN EVALUATION

Series Editor: Nick L. Smith

Northwest Regional Educational Laboratory

THE BOOKS IN THIS SERIES reflect an emerging awareness among evaluation practitioners and theorists that evaluation involves *more* than conducting an experimental study in an applied setting. Evaluation is increasingly recognized as a highly complex technical, economic, political, and social activity requiring the skills of many professionals—lawyers, economists, artists, and scientists, in addition to psychologists, sociologists, political scientists, and other applied social research specialists.

The purpose of this series is to deepen methodological discussions of evaluation and to improve evaluation practice. Beginning with Volume 1, this series strives to provide readers with new ways to view the evaluative enterprise and innovative tools compatible with these emerging perspectives. Written by some of the field's most creative theorists and practitioners, these volumes will share the adventure of uncovering new approaches to an exciting young discipline and disseminate useful guidelines for the expansion and improvement of its practice.

BOOKS IN THIS SERIES:

Additional titles in preparation

COMMUNICATION STRATEGIES in EVALUATION

Nick L. Smith, editor

NEW PERSPECTIVES IN EVALUATION
Volume 3

AZ
191
.C65
West

*This volume published in cooperation with
the Northwest Regional Educational Laboratory*

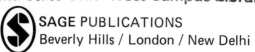

SAGE PUBLICATIONS
Beverly Hills / London / New Delhi

For information address:

SAGE Publications, Inc.
275 South Beverly Drive
Beverly Hills, California 90212

SAGE Publications India Pvt. Ltd.
C-236 Defence Colony
New Delhi 110 024, India

SAGE Publications Ltd
28 Banner Street
London EC1Y 8QE, England

Printed in the United States of America

Library of Congress Cataloging in Publication Data

Main entry under title:

Communication strategies in evaluation.

    (New perspectives in evaluation ; v. 3)
    Includes bibliographies.
    1. Evaluation—Addresses, essays, lectures.
2. Communication—Methodology—Addresses,
essays, lectures. I. Smith, Nick L. II. Series.
AZ191.C65   001.4'33   82-698
ISBN 0-8039-1821-6   AACR2

FIRST PRINTING

CONTENTS

Preface

Evaluators are increasingly recognizing that they must clearly communicate the purpose, procedures, and results of their evaluation work if it is to be useful. This book is about communication in evaluation and the ways that evaluation information can be communicated with greater clarity, impact, and variety. The purpose of this volume is to change the way evaluators think about the role of communication in evaluation as well as to change the nature of the communications they produce.

Most evaluators have adopted a narrow, quantitative view of the programs they evaluate, and have communicated their work primarily through technical narrative reports that rely heavily on quantitative representations. But long discursive passages and multiple tables of numerical results seldom capture the imagination of evaluation audiences—even audience members with the training and experience to understand such technical reports rarely use them for little more than occasional reference documents. The effort and resources required to conduct meaningful evaluations, as well as the importance of evaluation findings, demand that evaluators use more effective means than these technical reports in communicating with interested clients and publics.

The ways in which evaluators seek to communicate about their work influences not only the evaluators' methods, but also their fundamental perceptions of the programs and policies being evaluated. Alternative ways of conceiving of programs are presented in the four chapters of Part I of this volume, including discussions of how understandings can be represented in songs, stories, and pictures. Part II of the book contains ten chapters on alternative techniques for communicating evaluation information, including research briefs, graphic display procedures, stem and leaf displays, operational network displays, geographic displays, oral policy briefings, briefing panel presentations, adversary hearings, committee hearings, and television presentations. Although there is a natural flow to the sequence of the chapters, with those of Part I being more theoretical and methodological, and those of Part II being more pragmatic and procedural, the chapters were designed as independent, stand-alone contributions. For example, readers may wish to use Part II of the volume as a reference guide in planning improved communication procedures for particular evaluation studies.

While many of the examples used throughout this volume are from educational evaluation, the chapter authors have included examples from a variety of fields. The insights and techniques presented here are clearly applicable in many areas of social science evaluation, including health, criminal justice, social welfare, housing, community development, and federal oversight, as well as in education. The book is intended for evaluation theorists interested in alternative forms of communication in evaluation and for evaluation practitioners desiring pragmatic techniques to increase the reception and use of their work. To promote this broad, practical appeal, I have selected authors from a variety of work settings. These seventeen authors, who all have firsthand knowledge of and experience with the procedures they discuss, represent evaluation work in local education agencies (2), a state education agency (1), federal agencies (2), research and development centers (2), private industries (2), and universities (8). From the breadth of experience of these authors comes an increased awareness of the forms of communication possible in evaluation as well as practical procedures for implementing fresh approaches to evaluation reporting.

The material presented in this volume has resulted, in part, from a programmatic effort to improve the practice of evaluation through the development of new evaluation methods. This work was performed under the direction of the Research on Evaluation Program of the Northwest Regional Educational Laboratory in Portland, Oregon, and was supported by funds from the National Institute of Education. It is with pleasure that I acknowledge the support given this work by the National Institute of Education staff, especially Daniel Antonoplos and Charles Stalford, who have provided sustained interest and encouragement. The work has also benefited greatly from the helpful guidance of the Research on Evaluation Program's National Advisory Panel, which consists of

Adrianne Bank, University of California at Los Angeles
Joan Bollenbacher, Cincinnati Public Schools (Ret.)
Egon Guba, Indiana University
Vincent Madden, California State Department of Education
Jason Millman, Cornell University

Stacy Rockwood, New Orleans, Louisiana
Blaine Worthen, Utah State University

I also wish to thank the Program staff members who assisted in successfully completing this work, including Vicky Kerr for her excellent secretarial assistance, Judy Turnidge for her superb supervision of all editorial and manuscript preparation details, and Darrel Caulley for his thoughtful reviews and helpful commentaries on the material in the first part of the volume. My very special thanks go to my wife, Denny, for her steadfast support and her persistent proddings toward excellence in my work.

To these individuals and the many others who also assisted in the successful completion of this work, I give my sincere appreciation.

Nick L. Smith
Portland, Oregon

Acknowledgments

We are grateful for the kind permission granted by the following publishers and individuals to reprint or reproduce from their original works portions of text in this volume:

Sing Out! The Folk Song Magazine, Vol. 25, No. 1 (505 Eighth Avenue, New York, NY 10018).

Kenneth Goldstein, *A Guide for Field Workers in Folklore,* Folklore, 1964, 199 pp. (Copyright © 1964 by Folklore Associates, Inc.; reprinted here by permission of Gale Research Company).

A. L. Lloyd, *Folksong in England,* Lawrence and Wishart, London, 1976.

EVALUATION AS THE REPRESENTATION OF REALITY

This book is addressed to a more fundamental issue than the recognition that varied presentations are more entertaining and will consequently promote more effective use of evaluation results. The underlying theme of this volume is that the nature of our understanding, indeed, what we seek to understand and how we share that understanding with others, is directly related to the forms of sensation in which we seek reality and the forms of representation we use to communicate that reality.

This theme is presented in detail in the first chapter of Part I, "Conceiving and Representing: Implications for Evaluation," by Elliot Eisner. Eisner discusses how alternative forms of representation in words, pictures, songs, and the like affect our understanding of phenomena. He argues that not only do evaluators unnecessarily restrict their ability to communicate with audiences by relying only on quantification and narrative discourse, but that they seriously misrepresent those elements of reality that require alternative forms of representation for adequate understanding. The three other chapters of Part I illustrate and extend Eisner's position.

One of Eisner's major arguments is that the form in which we find reality shapes the form of inquiry we use and the nature of our understanding. An excellent illustration of this point is the chapter by George Madaus and John McDonagh, "As I Roved Out: Folksong Collecting as a Metaphor for Evaluation." Madaus and McDonagh investigate the collecting of folksongs (ethnomusicology) in which reality (i.e., the "data") are auditory, nonvisual, and nonrecorded. The investigation of reality represented through song requires procedures far removed from traditional methods of controlled studies and formal testing. These authors point out, however, the many similarities between folksong collecting and various forms of naturalistic evaluation, suggesting a ready application to evaluation of techniques from folksong collecting.

A second major argument of Eisner's is that the form one wishes to use to represent reality shapes the nature of our inquiry and understanding. Edward Wachtman and Patricia Templin both provide illustrations of this point. Wachtman, in "Storytelling: The Narrative Structure of Evaluation," discusses how evaluators are storytellers, not because they create fictional accounts, but because, like all people, they rely on narratives to create ordered and sequential relationships and to illustrate the meaning of events within a chronological framework. He suggests that by recognizing the narrative quality of their work, evaluators can become more effective storytellers, profiting from the long history of the use of story in communicating among diverse groups.

In "Still Photography in Evaluation," Templin provides an extensive review of the use of photographs in evaluation. Drawing on the existing use of this form of representation in sociology and anthropology, she identifies the ways in which evaluators can broaden their repertoire of representational techniques. Her presentation includes a discussion of the practical as well as the theoretical concerns in the use of visual data from still photography in evaluation.

ELLIOT EISNER
Stanford University

CHAPTER *1*

Conceiving and Representing

Implications for Evaluation

Elliot Eisner is Professor of Education and Art at Stanford University and Director of Teacher Education at that institution. For the past decade he and his students have been exploring the use of art criticism and aesthetic theory in the field of educational evaluation. These studies have resulted in a dozen Ph.D. dissertations and in Dr. Eisner's most recent book, Cognition and Curriculum: A Basis for Deciding What to Teach *(Longman, 1982).*

The Current Context in Education

The nature of knowing and the character of the forms through which what is known is made public has not been a salient theme in the training of educational evaluators. This chapter is an effort to identify and discuss the processes of conception and representation, and to examine their implications for practice and theory in evaluation. To put this discussion into a context that will be meaningful, it will be useful to start with a detour. We start not with cognition, but with the context in which the schools find themselves today. Theory, or if a more modest term is more appropriate, perspectives, should in some way relate, as Dewey suggested, to the problems of men. They should relate to the problems with which people cope, or should illuminate problems that through present perspectives go unseen. My aspiration is to contribute to the realization of both goals: to provide some leads that can be used by those in the schools who must evaluate the processes and consequences of classroom life, and to identify issues and to describe problems that are often unrecognized. Neither this chapter nor those that follow pretend to provide answers or blueprints for the solution of educational problems. We regard our work more in the spirit of heuristics than algorithmics. Its value is to be tested in what it suggests rather than what it resolves.

Anyone familiar with American education circa 1980 cannot help but conclude that whether warranted or not there is a feeling on the part of the American public that the schools of the nation are not as educationally effective as they once were. From various quarters one hears that high school students' math skills have seriously declined, that "bonehead English" is oversubscribed, even for those admitted to universities, that the recruits to the armed forces cannot use the manuals necessary for operating even simple military equipment because their reading skills are so poor, and that test performance has been dropping for over a decade.

One finds the covers of major magazines such as *Time* exclaiming that teachers are no longer able to teach because student discipline is so poor, and that many teachers, cannot spell well enough to make what they teach worthwhile (Time, June 16, 1980, p. 54). One hears on CBS Walter Cronkite, one of America's most respected commentators, hosting programs titled "Is Anyone Out There Learning?" The fact that the question is raised in the first place is tacit condemnation of the educational quality of the schools.

What are the facts of the case? Has the quality of education declined? Are schools no longer as educationally effective as they once were? How adequate must the data be to make such judgments? To those steeped in educational theory, answers of a definitive nature are very difficult to provide. The quick, cocky answer in matters such as these can lead to "solutions" that create greater problems than the ones they were originally intended to resolve.

Yet, test scores, particularly at the secondary level, *have* been dropping, and not in one indicator but in many. Harnischfeger and Wiley (1975) report that the drop in test performance has occurred not only in the much publicized Scholastic Aptitude Test, but in measures designed specifically to assess achievement in the so-called "basic skills." The drop in test scores has been one source of concern for that great mass called the American public. But it is by no means the only source of concern. Since the 1960s America has undergone a period of enormous social change. During the sixties many young people made it quite clear that conventional values and lifestyles were not necessarily sacrosanct. A great many were not willing to participate in what they regarded as an immoral war. They and other minorities wanted to have more than a token voice in shaping social policies. It was in the sixties that the civil rights movement was tested, it was in the sixties that the innovative federally funded programs of the Great Society came into being, and it was in the sixties that the traditional view of the American family as the hub of American life was brought into question, first by the young and then later by Margaret Mead (1980) who, as an anthropologist, reconceptualized the way in which "family life" could be led.

Such developments are not, I believe, unrelated to the current drift of American education. The challenge to conventional values has been to a great many people a source of puzzlement and difficulty. The student whose school gives him an opportunity to design his own secondary school program presents something of an anomaly to parents who fully believe that the school authorities know best *and* that they should, therefore, prescribe what students should study. Schools without walls, educational parks, flexible scheduling, open education, team teaching, schools within schools are regarded by many as forms of educational exotica that are in part responsible for what they believe to be a decline in the quality of education. When these forms of educational innovation are combined with the social upheavals that pervaded so much of the sixties—the challenge to conventional values, the redefinition of social aims, the emergence of a strong civil rights movement, the exploration of new forms of communal life—it becomes understandable that a return to a more conventional life in and out of schools should seem attractive.

America seems to want to go "back to the basics." "Back to the basics" is significant as a slogan in at least two senses. First, because it calls for a return to the past rather than for an expedition into the future. What is needed is a retreat to older values, a return to what has been lost. One moves ahead by going backward. Second, the back-to-the-basics slogan calls attention to something that is believed to be basic in education, and for most people what is basic is no mystery: the ability to read, the skills of arithmetic, and the competencies needed to write clear prose, in a word, the three Rs. What "back to the basics" signifies is, I am suggesting, not simply an educational prescription designed to raise test scores, but a symptom of a larger social malaise. People seem to be seeking the stability of the familiar in the context of the present in order to stabilize what appears to many a destabilized social life in America. The manifestations of this movement backward emerge in the politics of the day, in the rise of evangelical religious fundamentalism,[1] a fundamentalism that is increasingly active in the political arena, in the reinstitution of capital punishment,[2] in the fiscal conservatism that is so general in the nation, in the failure of the Equal Rights Amendment, and in the nostalgia for the 1920s on the one hand and the growing interest in nature, natural foods, health care, and the like on the other. We seem, as a nation, to be yearning to recapture a life that never was for most of us, while at the same time we are captivated by the dazzling possibilities and accomplishments of scientific technology. We are a nation that seems to want once again to sit with good friends close to a warm fire, drinking our favorite brand of beer, while our meal is being cooked in a microwave oven in the next room.

The combination of these factors, both historical and technological, has set the tone for the schools of America in the 1980s. I say tone because the practices and prescriptions that have emerged in American schools during the past decade are an offshoot of a more general *Weltanschung*; there is a basic continuity between the way the nation goes as a whole and what it expects of its schools. When conventional values are threatened, when the divorce rate approximates the rate of marriage, when the adolescent suicide rate increases tenfold over the decade, when the nuclear family is no longer for many the accepted model of family life, people seek a rock on which to stand, something to provide stability in the flux and flow of social change. And they look to the schools as one such rock, as a bastion of stability, a kind of haven in which the young can be socialized in the older, more familiar ways. The consequences for schools are predictable. Consider its impact on curriculum.

When the public demand is for a return to the basics, and when the basics are defined as the three Rs, it is not likely that significant amounts of time and attention will be devoted in elementary schools, in particular, to subjects that are not directly related to student performance in reading, writing, and arithmetic. Teachers who once operated on the assumption that children need a balanced curriculum—even though the concept of balance itself was not well defined—would with good conscience plan field trips, encourage projects in science, plan group activities in the social studies, develop art and music programs in their classes, pay significant attention to the social and emotional well-being of their students. Many teachers still do. However, such teachers swim upstream. Teachers who once devoted as little as five percent of their formal classroom instructional time to art or music in the elementary school curriculum do so today at the risk of being regarded as frivolous. Such a use of time would not be positively sanctioned by a great many school principals who know, as do teachers, that student growth in the fine arts, even if it should develop by spectacular leaps and bounds, would not show up on the tests that are now used to assess the quality of education. And what principal can endure the emnity that would flow from a community that believed the school was wasting their children's time or jeopardizing their chances for educational mobility by paying so much attention to what is "nice but not necessary," to quote Harry Broudy's (1979) telling phrase? The answer is all too clear: only a few. Time cannot be devoted to support programs that are consistent with one's philosophic commitments when one knows that one is to be evaluated on other criteria.

Support for a restricted array of curriculum content comes also from researchers who have focused on what is called "time on task." During the past decade a great deal of educational research has focused on the use of time in school.[3] Researchers have asked questions about the ratio of time devoted to formal instruction and time devoted to problems of management and discipline, to questions dealing with the amount of time devoted to each of the subjects taught in school, and to questions dealing with time allocated by the teacher in relation to the time in which students are actually engaged in the time that has been allocated. Perhaps the major single general conclusion that can be drawn from such studies is that the amount of time allocated to particular content areas within the curriculum has a significant bearing on the level of achievement students attain. Put more prosaically, children who are given an opportunity to learn something are more likely to learn it than those who are not.

What the results of such research have suggested for some researchers is summed up by Barak Rosenshine (1976) as follows:

> The message in this section seems clear. The stronger the academic emphasis, the stronger the academic results. Time spent on reading and numbers is associated with growth in those areas, whereas time spent in other areas appears to detract from growth in reading and mathematics. Furthermore, there are *no* nonacademic activity [sic] that yielded positive correlations with reading and mathematics achievement. This finding is somewhat surprising, since it has frequently been argued that some of these other activities contribute to reading achievement by motivating students or by providing additional stimulation or practice. Such indirect enhancement was not evident in this study [p. 345].

Neither in this quotation nor in the article in which it appears is there any discussion of the implications of such research conclusions for a more generous conception of education than is implied in the quotation. No discussion is provided of the possible benefits of exposure to other curricular areas, no analyses of the possible tradeoffs among the things learned in different content areas, and no examination of the ways in which skills acquired in some fields emerge in others. The conclusion, to the contrary, is straightforward. "The stronger the academic emphasis, the stronger the academic results." What occurs here is the legitimation from the research literature of curriculum practices that limit what children have access to in school. Without adequate interpretation of the educational implications of the research, it is easy to continue to move toward a restrictive view of curriculum content, and this in the name of improved educational quality.

The impact of current cultural concerns is in no way limited to what schools emphasize. While the character of curriculum content is a fundamental influence on what students learn (the surest way to reduce the probability of learning something is to eliminate opportunities to learn it), the manner in which students are taught also significantly influences what they will learn. In artistic terms, form is content: *How* one teaches has a significant bearing upon *what* one learns. Or in Dewey's (1938) words, "It is one of the major educational fallacies that a student learns only what he is being taught at the time" (p. 49).

In what sense have teaching practices changed, and what is their impact on what students learn in school? How do changes in practice relate to the context or social ethos in which the schools function? It is to these questions that we now turn.

One development that has emerged in America during the past decade is a desire for educational accountability. Not only are goals to be defined with precision; methods should be employed that will provide evidence of their accomplishment. To be accountable is to give an account of what has been attempted and what has been accomplished. Not an unreasonable expectation. Teachers and school administrators should have aims, they should know where they are headed, and they should be able to provide evidence regarding what the students have learned. Yet the spirit of the move toward educational accountability does not stop with general goals or with informal evidence regarding the consequences of teaching. Goals need to be precise; they need to specify the behaviors the student is to display; according to some they need to identify criterion levels to be achieved, and the means through which they are assessed need to be objective and replicable. More of these matters will be addressed later, but here let us focus upon the consequences of this view upon teaching.

Teachers often come to believe that to have precise goals, the description of small units of behavior are more appropriate than descriptions of behavior at general levels of abstraction. The more global a goal, the more complex is its assessment. Teachers also come to believe that if they are to be held accountable for the achievement of goals that they formulate, it is prudent not to formulate goals that might be difficult to achieve. The payoff for the teachers who function within this system is the achievement of the goals they select, not necessarily the achievement of complex or difficult ones. Teachers also come to realize that the achievement of goals that are related to small units of material to be learned makes it possible to keep an account record for each child's progress. For some teachers such accounting takes the form of contracts between student and teacher; for others it is handled through workbooks. Programs are laid out in advance, they are individualized for each child, and the teacher-cum-accountant records student achievement on small units of material that is behaviorally defined and criterion referenced. The assumption is that these small units can eventually be aggregated into complex wholes.

The practical consequences of this approach to teaching and learning for students and teachers are several. First, the prediction and control of student behavior looms as a prime virtue. The goals specified in advance become a contract between teacher and school district and between student and teacher. The exploration of unexpected learning opportunities that emerge during the course of the school year are often given short shrift; they are not a part of the original scheme of things. Second, pupil-teacher planning diminishes, since to give students a meaningful role in the formulation of curriculum, goals, and activities is to risk taking directions that do not coincide with the goals originally formulated. Third, in a great many classrooms the benefits of group deliberation and class planning also go by the boards. In the name of individualization virtually all students proceed down the same paths toward the same ends but at different rates of speed. Fourth, because students do not participate in the conceptualization of ends, their role is limited to the execution of means instrumental to the achievement of ends defined by others. Conception is separated from execution, means are severed from ends, and meaning in the intrinsic sense is often relinquished by the use of artificial incentives designed to motivate the student's activity.

But in such a system standardization is possible, and with standardization uniform achievement standards can be formulated and their attainment assessed. Surprise, ingenuity, discovery, the sense of play and exploration have little place in such a scheme. Put another way, schools become increasingly academic and decreasingly intellectual. They become more concerned with achievement than with inquiry.

Seldom in the consideration of educational innovations is the question asked: "But what is in it for the teacher?" For many teachers the accountability movement and the consequences I have identified have dissipated the satisfactions they sought and once had from teaching. The same constraints that limit students to prespecified goals and preformulated workbooks also constrain the teacher. The elementary school teacher whose major source of professional satisfaction was in developing with children projects in the social studies that would take on a life and momentum that might pervade the classroom for a week or two, now feels unable to allow this to occur. The teacher hears from *Time* and from Walter Cronkite, from the Gallup and from the Harris polls, from businessmen and from Navy recruiters that students cannot read, write, or cipher. Teachers know that they will be held accountable for the scores their students receive. In such a climate the personal joys in teaching must be set aside for the "real" business of the schools. In the meantime, school truancy becomes a national problem and school teachers—some of the best of them—leave teaching to take positions where the pay is larger and the criticism smaller.

The reduction of the scope of the curriculum and the fragmentation of what is taught are two general consequences of the effort to rationalize educational practice within the scope of an educational accountability paradigm. These consequences are not trivial; collectively they shape an educational way of life. Yet as important as they are, it is the assumptions about evaluation and objectivity that constitute the heart of the accountability movement. The logic of the movement looks something like this.

Student performance as measured by a variety of achievement tests has been falling, thus providing *prima facie* evidence that schools are not as educationally effective as they once were. To make them more effective, greater attention must be paid to the teaching of basic skills. But attention in terms of more time, while laudatory, is not enough; goals for each grade level in the basic skill areas must be specified. Furthermore, they must be specified in a way that makes them amenable to objective evaluation. To be objectively evaluated they must be stated in a form that makes measurement possible, since through measurement objectivity is maximized. Once statements of goals are translated into testable items of performance, criteria defining acceptable standards for performance must be defined. Once defined with tests constructed to measure the achievement of behaviorally stated goals, students are to be tested to provide evidence of the effectiveness of the instruction they have received. Once such data are secured, information can be provided to the relevant publics so that they may know how effective the schools have been, which schools and which teachers should be rewarded, which need assistance, and which need a change in personnel. Through the monitoring of student perform-ance the educational productivity of the school and of teachers can be appraised and the public informed about what it is receiving for its investment in education.

At first glance the logic seems impeccable. Objectivity, if one means by that term the ability to replicate observations, can be increased when conventions are defined and specifications for the use of those conventions provided. What then are the problems? What makes the evaluation prac-tices used to assess competency less than satisfactory, and what makes a less than satisfactory process so widely used in the schools?

One reason the process of evaluation, as defined through what is essentially a testing approach to evaluation, is so significant in shaping practice is because evaluation results have a public status that neither curriculum nor teaching have. The results of evaluation practices are public results, they can be inspected and appraised by principals, by other teachers, by parents, and by the community at large. Goals formulated for the curriculum are, by comparison, vague and general. They are statements having to do more with intentions than with results. Furthermore, the criteria through which their adequacy can be appraised are not well known. Many parents and unfortunately even many school administrators do not know what questions to ask when appraising educational goals or curriculum content. When evaluation results are quantified they can be rank ordered, schools and classrooms can be compared, and the data can take on an aura of precision that leads easily to the conclusion that the higher the students or schools score, the higher the quality of educational practice. Such a conclusion simply cannot by itself be defended.[4] Thus, one reason why evaluation is at the heart of the accountability movement is because evaluation procedures yield consequences that often are sub-stantially more significant in affecting the status of the school or the teacher than are other aspects of educational practice. It is not the goals that drive the system as much as it is the way in which the system is to be evaluated: The form of the evaluation and the content to which it attends *become* the operational goals of the system.

A second source of difficulty with evaluation procedures used to measure competencies deals with the limits of measurement and the assumptions that are held about the nature of objectivity. These limitations are several. First, the use of a measure applied to a group consisting of individual events, say the performance of 30 students on some task, results in a description of those events on a common scale applied to dimensions that cut across the individuals in that group. For example, in evaluating writing skills, say in the area of composition, the features that constitute excellence in composition are treated as common across all compositions evaluated and the scores assigned are derived from a common scale. The results of procedures based on such assumptions is that (1) characteristics not included in the dimensions are neglected, and (2) the qualities that uniquely constitute excellence in one composition as compared to another might be entirely different, but because the score assigned is derived from a common scale, unique features of particular compositions are obfuscated. It is erroneously implied by such procedures that two or more compositions are of high, medium, or low quality for the same reasons, on the same dimensions, when in fact the reasons and the dimensions may be radically different.

A third problem deals with the fact that numbers simply cannot convey all that can and often needs to be said about the qualities that constitute educational objects or events. Numbers are reporting devices. Their meaning derives from two sources, the scale of which they are a part and the referents they represent. To know what a number means one needs to know its position on a scale and the qualities it is selected to represent. It is in the latter area that number is severely limited. No number looks like its referent; numbers are conventions, and the transformation of qualities into such conventions *never*, without the ability to imagine the qualities referent, can "contain" those qualities. As surrogates, numbers are not self-explanatory. They do not necessarily portray, even though by convention the operations that lead to certain scores are replicable and, hence, regarded as objective.

Among the most vivid examples are those found in IQ testing and in grading. An individual may be given an IQ test and as a result receive a score of, say, 116. What does such a score tell about the individual's intelligence? We have some sense of where that individual stands in relation to a group, but we do not know the particular ways in which his or her intelligence is manifested, we do not know the areas of performance in which his or her score might have differed simply because the areas in which the student is most able might not have been among the areas tested. We know nothing of the individual's level of motivation, and the prospects of getting a large enough array of measurements to portray the intelligence of individuals as they function in particular situations is very dim. The score is a useful, but limited indicator. It describes the location of an individual within a distribution more than it tells us about the particular qualities of a person.

Grades have similar characteristics. Students can receive the same grade for very different reasons. Knowing that a student received a B+ in a course, by itself, tells us very little about the character of the student's work. We tend to trade in symbols, even when their meaning is far from clear. Thus, while we have an objective representation of a set of qualities, the objectivity is a function of the process of replication rather than a function of the re-presentation of the qualities the number stands for. It is only when one can imagine the referent to the numbers that we can know the meaning behind the numbers. For educationally relevant qualities this is often extremely difficult to do. Indeed, even the same scores on subtests may be the result of different patterns of performance on those subtests, not to mention the comparability of total test scores or means among groups.

Because objectivity is seen as such a prime virtue in evaluation, qualities that are difficult to measure reliably are often neglected in evaluation altogether. The so-called affective areas of learning are familiar examples. Because a rationalistic orientation to procedure provides the baseline criterion that method must meet, those aspects of educational life that are more easily susceptible to measurement command the most attention. What occurs is that methodological commitments influence the character of evaluation procedures and evaluation procedures influence the character of curriculum priorities. Curriculum priorities, in turn, influence the opportunities students will have access to, which in turn shapes the kind of mental skills they are able to develop. Put another way, at present our culture embraces a systematic and objectified approach to knowledge that emphasizes the use of methods that yield conclusions that are replicable. Because quantification is the paradigm for conventional description, it is regarded as a necessary condition for achieving objectivity. The ethos of the time supports an epistemology that regards with suspicion the idiosyncratic and those aspects of educational life that are difficult to objectify through measurement. What results is an overly restrictive assessment of the very life we are trying to understand and improve.

At the beginning of this chapter I said we would need to get into questions about the nature of conception and the forms humans use to make their conceptions public by way of a detour. That detour has moved through some of the terrain that constitutes the context for current practices in American education. I have taken this detour because I believe that the methods we employ and the aims we seek are a part of a larger social ideology. To understand what we do we need to know not only what goes on in schools, we need also to peer below the surface of school practices in order to uncover the assumptions on which they rest and to see how those assumptions relate to the social ideology of the time in which we live. In the course of my reading I have come across the work of a German sociologist, Ferdinand Toennies,[5] who has provided a pair of concepts that elegantly differentiates two major modes of social life, one of which seems to characterize quite nicely our current situation in America and in American schools. The distinctions that Toennies makes are between what he calls *Gemeinschaft* and what he refers to as *Gesselschaft*. According to Toennies social arrangements can be characterized by the extent to which they emphasize two different styles of life. Gesselschaft is that style that emphasizes objectivity in human relations, moral detachment, order defined by rationally articulated rules. It is a social order in which explicitly developed criteria for defining status, role, and function are the guide to proper action, and in which order, regularity, and a disposition toward abstract values are salient.

Gemeinschaft is characterized by organic rather than formal or mechanical relationships, where status emerges from and varies with the context in which individuals function. It characterizes a social order whose prime value is in the establishment of community and group identity as contrasted to Gesselschaft, which emphasizes society and individuality. According to Toennies, modern industrialization has led to personal anonymity to, as Robert Nisbet puts it, "deprivation of the sense of organic relatedness to others." Writing of Toennies' work, Nisbet (1976) says

> The kind of society that had for Adam Smith, David Ricardo, and other prophets of the industrial system, carried the promise of a higher freedom for modern man, carried something quite different for Toennies: Not freedom, but increasing anonymity, displacement and deprivation of the sense of organic relatedness to others. . . . The important point here, however, is the image that Toennies' classic acquired almost from the day of its publication and retained thereafter, of being profoundly negative in its representation of modern society as Gesselschaft, which for Toennies meant the whole complex of impersonal, abstract, and anonymous relationships which characterized capitalism, nationalism, and all the forces of individualism, bureaucratization, and secularism, which he could see eating away at the social fabric.

Conversely, no reader can remain blind to Toennies extremely positive treatment of Gemeinschaft and of the social structures and forms of human mentality associated with it. In kinship, religion, village, and social class, overwhelming in their medieval forms, Toennies found that kind of society which he thought organic and vital and which had been largely destroyed or greatly diminished under the impact of modernity [pp. 119-120].

Summarizing his views on the distinction he has made, Toennies writes "*Gesselschaft* deals with the artificial construction of an aggregate of human beings which superficially resembles *Gemeinschaft* insofar as the individuals live and dwell together peacefully. However, in *Gemeinschaft* they remain essentially united in spite of all separating factors, whereas in *Gesselschaft* they are essentially separated in spite of all uniting factors" (Nisbet, 1976, p. 120). What strikes me as I think about the two modes of social life that Toennies has described is the fit of Gesselschaft to our schools and society. At the same time, groups emerges intent on establishing communities within the Great Society that can lead the kind of life that Toennies describes as Gemeinschaft.

The formalization of goals, the bureaucratization of evaluation procedures, the stress on individualization, the need for objectified evidence, the faith in hyperrationalization of activity, the use of contracts between teachers and students and teachers and school boards as a way of defining responsibility, the preoccupation with hierarchical relationships, the prescription of status all fit the image of Gesselschaft that Toennies has described. And at the same time, we see television commercials portraying the warmth of communal life in order to sell McDonald's hamburgers, of male camaraderie in order to sell Budweiser beer, of the recall of tradition in order to sell Mazola oil. There seems to be a deprivation that the ad agencies have recognized, and like the astute merchants that they are, they have exploited our sense of deprivation to sell their wares.

Lest there be doubt about the relationship between the context I have described and theory and practice in educational evaluation, I shall make these relationships explicit here. Conceptions of educational practice, including practices in evaluation, are not natural entities; they are constructions of mind. Such constructions are influenced by the leading values of the society in which practitioners function. In our society we have developed a faith in the power of scientific rationality to help us resolve problems that we confront and to enable us to realize the values we aspire toward. At present our society appears to have an especially acute need to find stability; the world has changed in ways that are unsettling, the young appear to question older values, the schools do not appear to be effective. Stabilization is to be achieved, some say, by going back to older values, recapturing them as it were, and by instituting standardized methods of assessment that address themselves to publicly stated goals that can be objectively appraised to determine the extent to which the goals have been attained. The character of the assessment procedures are such as to place great reliance upon quantification, thus increasing the replicability of the results. What is suspect in education are processes that are exploratory in nature, that value surprise, that cultivate idiosyncrasy and ingenuity, that depend for their assessment on the sensibilities of individuals and that use reporting procedures that require personal interpretation and judgment. In a word, Gesselschaft dominates our approach to the improvement of educational practice and to the ways in which we believe we should assess its consequences. The general aim of this book is to provide the grounds for using other modes of evaluation, not as a replacement for conventional ones, but in order to secure a fuller, more balanced understanding of what goes on in schools. The task is both theoretical and practical. The theoretical is not yet complete—and never will be—and the examples provided are simply that, examples of leads that need refinement. Let us therefore examine the basis for seeking new modes of evaluation in the first place, and then later turn to some of the efforts that have been made to develop these modes in the practical order.

Conception, Representation, and the Evaluation of Educational Practice

The previous section described the context for educational practice in America and linked the ethos of the nation at this particular period in its history to beliefs about the curriculum, about teaching, and about educational evaluation. The aim of the section was to make clear the fact that these aspects of practice are not immune to social ideologies. I have argued that Gesselschaft characterizes quite well the style in which America functions at present and that our efforts to systematize practice and to insure the effectiveness of schools has led to a neglect of content areas that do not lend themselves to such methods. I have argued that such methods neglect the cultivation of certain modes of thought, and limit in significant ways the data we can use to understand schools, classrooms, and the kind of life that students and teachers lead within them.

In this section I turn to evaluation in particular; as I have indicated, it constitutes the heartbeat of the accountability movement, it drives the priorities of the school, and it reflects the view of mind and the conception of knowing that is socially dominant. To secure a foothold on that terrain on which a wider and more adequate view of evaluation can be built we will start not with extant theories of evaluation but with an examination of the nature of mind and of the forms it uses to represent what it has come to know.

The fundamental question that any adequate theory of evaluation must address is not what can be evaluated, or how, or whether or not objectives have been achieved, but how it is that humans come to know in the first place. Second, it must ask: How do humans represent what they know to others? Without a conception of the ways in which knowing occurs and the forms through which it is represented, the assumptions about cognition that are now salient are likely to continue and the possibilities of broadening the dominant view of knowing, and thereby extending the grounds and methods of evaluation, are diminished. New conceptions of evaluation, I am arguing, need to be grounded in new views of mind.

The starting point of my discussion is the starting point for experience: the interaction of the individual with the environment. It is this interaction that elicits what in educational and psychological circles is referred to as cognition. Although cognition is often regarded, indeed defined by some, as thinking that is mediated by language—as a kind of inner speech—cognition is a process far wider in scope. Cognition is a process through which the organism achieves awareness. To engage in cognitive activity is not simply to think about the world through words or number, but in the first instance to be aware of the qualities of which it is constituted. This awareness is what we mean by cognition. If the *Dictionary of Psychology* is any guide, it is the way in which cognition is defined. Cognition depends upon experience, and experience depends upon our ability to discern qualities, either those that emanate from the world or those that we generate as images in the privacy of our psychological life. What we cannot experience, we cannot know.

Why has cognition been identified with speech and number? Several reasons commend themselves. First, in the literature in education and psychology rather tidy distinctions have been made between cognition and affect. The former refers to thinking while the latter to feeling. Thinking is associated with symbolic mediation, not directly with experience. Hence, language and number are regarded as the chief mediators of thought. Like buying and selling, one cannot do one without the other. For example, one writer on cognition describes the situation this way:

> When we adopt the monistic standpoint, we reject the claim that language and thinking can exist separately and independently of one another. Of course, we are talking about specifically *human* thinking, in other words about *conceptual* thinking. Thus we assert that in the process of cognition and communication, thinking and using a language are inseparable elements of one and the same whole. Integration is so perfect and interdependence is so precise that neither element can ever occur independently, in a "pure" form. That is precisely why the functions of thinking and language may not be treated separately, let alone contrasted with one another [Schaff, 1973, p. 118].

What we see here is a view that conceives of cognition—human cognition at least—as requiring discursive mediation, a view which incidently even one so steeped in the role of language in mentation as Noam Chomsky (1973) rejects.

A second reason for conceiving of cognition in terms of linguistically mediated thought is because of our conception of abstraction. Concepts are regarded as general (which they are), and that to be general they must be abstract (which they must be), and to be abstract they must be linguistic (which they need not be). Thus, what is not linguistic is not cognitive and what is not cognitive must belong to lower realms of human functioning, the realm of the senses, of feeling, of the subjective, in other words to the noncognitive aspects of human life. Indeed, it is not for nothing that mathematics, the subject considered the most abstract and the least dependent upon sense data, is also regarded as "the queen of the sciences," the apotheosis of human cognition.

A third reason is that in language there are rules of procedure. There is among formal languages such as those used in science and mathematics a logic and a grammar that increase the degree to which common meanings can be secured among a community of readers. Contrasted with expressive forms that have no comparable rules or criteria, meanings are personalized, they are less amenable to consensual validation, and they appear to be related in greater degree to the subjective, personal, and imaginative life of particular individuals. Activities using such forms make verification tasks difficult. Since cognition is identified with knowing, and since knowing is wedded to "truth tests," "warranted assertion," and other forms of verification, processes that do not use language as a mediator or vehicle for expression are not regarded as cognitive.[6]

These views of cognition have a long history, one going back at least as far as Plato.[7] It is a tradition that has separated mind from body, thought from emotion, feeling from knowing, cognition from perception. Cognitive activity is widely regarded as a process so abstract that sense data are never considered a part of it. Sense data are considered particular, whereas thinking requires concepts and concepts are general. Sensory awareness is believed to be immediate, whereas cognition requires mediation. I find such views naive and wish to argue a wholly different case. I wish to argue that thinking always requires a content—we must think about something—and that at base that content is sensory. Put another way, I wish to argue that the senses play a crucial role in thinking, that we cannot think without the content that they provide, and that the senses are biologically given "information pick-up systems" through which that content is made available.

To say as I have that the senses play a crucial role in picking up information about the environment is not to suggest that the individual is merely a block of moist clay upon which the world impresses itself. Individuals *construe* the world; their prior history, the frames of reference they can use, their needs and purposes perform a selective function in their interactions with the world. But without a fully functioning sensory system the qualities of the world are mute, and in silence the content for reflection is unavailable.

If we examine how the senses function, it becomes clear that they are designed so that they are sensitive to some but not all of the qualities that constitute the environment. The world is made up of qualities and the extent to which those qualities can be experienced depends upon the acuteness with which each of the sensory systems can function. Thus, with vision we are able to see those aspects of the environment that are visual, but we cannot with our eyes hear the sounds of the world. Through audition we are able to hear, but we cannot see. Through our ability to taste, the gustatory qualities of the world can be experienced, but not heard. And so it goes. We are biological creatures designed to be able to experience the features of the world in which we live. What we know about those features depends initially on what our sensory systems make available.

The significance of the senses in our developing awareness of the world might be illuminated by imagining for a moment that a red filter were placed over our eyes. What would we be able to see? Under such conditions the visual features of the world would not be eliminated, but the variety of qualities we could experience would be radically curtailed. We would experience no colors other than red and its value gradations:

Whatever we would be able to see would fall within a highly restrictive color range. If we were congenitally blind, even the limited range of color would not be available. Thus it is with all of the senses; if any are impaired or not functioning, the kind of information we receive from our contact with the world is reduced. In this sense the kind of consciousness we can achieve is dependent upon (1) the acuteness with which our sensory systems can function and (2) the variety in the qualities that constitute the environment we inhabit. When certain qualities are absent or restricted, the possibility of achieving certain levels of consciousness is also curtailed, as much as if the sensory systems were impaired. The ability to achieve any form of consciousness depends upon the interaction of the sentient being with a qualitative universe.[8] If sentiency is diminished, or if the qualities of the world are restricted, the character of consciousness is affected. Should this occur, the basis for knowing is also restricted.

Human experience is not limited to what the organism can experience directly. Human organisms have the capacity to recall and to imagine. Recall may be regarded as the retrieval of reconstructed experience secured when the organism was in direct contact with the qualitative environment. We can remember what we ate for breakfast because we experienced breakfast only a few hours ago. Imagination is the creative reconstruction of recalled images so that experience is created that never was secured directly. We are able to picture ourselves eating a hearty breakfast consisting of foods we have seen but never tasted in a setting in which we have never been. Through imaginative processes we can construct events that are made up of elements of more prosaic experiences. The difference between recall and imagination is one of degree; in all recall there is alteration, no recalled experience—even a so-called eidetic image—is identical with the experience from which it was originally secured.

The utilities of recall and imagination are considerable. When we are not in the presence of one of Bach's Brandenberg concerti we can hear it for ourselves as we walk to our office; when we are far from home we can recall our family and imagine sitting with them in the comfort of our living room. Our imagination—the central term of which is image—allows us to create experiences, to achieve modes of consciousness that are built upon the information that the senses provided in the first place.

To talk about the role of the senses in knowing and to relate sensory information to cognition may appear to some as incongruous. Sensory data has for decades been separated from cognition through the differentiation of sensation, perception, and cognition. My effort here is simply to emphasize that among the most sophisticated work in cognitive psychology, perception and cognition are no longer separated or regarded as independent processes. Ulric Neisser (1976), a leading cognitive psychologist, states, "Perception is a cognitive event." And 40 years earlier Dewey (1938) himself pointed out the intellectual aspects of perceptual activity.[9] Piaget (1971) underscores the transactional relationships among the processes involved in adaptation, relationships that depend upon the use of schema for purposes of accommodation and assimilation. To disregard the selective and adaptive character of the individual's interaction with the environment and to regard sensory information a function of some mindless process is to underestimate the organic relationships occurring with a living system. It is to continue the separation of body and mind. The senses provide, I am arguing, the "stuff" from which experience is secured; and experience is what is required for consciousness to arise. I am arguing further that because the nature of experience is directly related to the kind of information the particular senses pick up, when the senses are impaired or underdeveloped, or when the qualities to which they can react are unavailable, the form of consciousness that would otherwise have been secured will not be achieved. Further, that when such qualities are unavailable, the imagination will have little, *in that mode at least,* with which to work.

Given that the senses always interact with particular qualities of the environment, how is it that concepts that are general are formed from such particular interactions? The process of concept formation that Aristotle described moved from sensation, to experience, to memory, to generalization; it was a process that was inductive in character.[10] Other philosophers, most notably Mill, argued that concepts were mental constructions that were then tested in the empirical world. The argument offered by Mill, Locke, and most recently by Popper (1980) is deductive rather than inductive in character. The separation of mind from body, whether through a deductive or an inductive view of mind, does not appear to be satisfactory. The organism to be sure has genetically defined intellectual capacities, but these capacities require commerce with specific qualities in order to function. Kittens, for example, deprived of light from two to twelve weeks of age will be blind even after being put in an environment in which light is available after twelve weeks.[11] In the case of the kittens, what is latent cannot become manifest without certain forms of stimulation, in this case light. In humans the capacity to form general concepts is necessary for survival. But to form concepts the qualities of the world must be available to the organism. In the transaction between particular events, the individual forms patterns that allow what has been experienced in one context to be applied to the next. Thus, a face seen from one angle, in one light, in one context will be recognized in another context; the individual child does not have to learn to cope with each situation as if it were entirely new. In this sense *every* concept formed, insofar as it represents the grasping of the structural features of particulars, is a vehicle through which generalization occurs. That is why in the vernacular we say we learn through experience, not because we structure our lives to yield generalizations or because we randomly sample events from a universe through a table of random numbers, but because we recognize that the significance and meaning of particulars is not necessarily limited to the experience secured from the particular at the moment. Particular events leave a residue that forms structures that are necessary for anticipating the future. Concepts that are formed through the images that the senses make possible provide the forms that are later named first through metaphor, later through vernacular language, and later still through the formal language of science. These initial concepts are the schema to which other experiences are assimilated: The universe is likened to a great machine and later to a cloud; the heart is first seen as a furnace and later as a pump. It is the basic structures or principles within particular machines, clouds, furnaces, and pumps that we use to make our world comprehensible, and it is our experience of them—how they look, sound, feel, taste that provides the basis for the primary conceptual image.

The argument presented thus far aims at calling attention to the role that the senses perform in providing contact with the qualities of the world. But even more, I have argued that conception itself depends upon the information provided by the senses. We form our concepts, the images that organize or structure our conception of the world, through the information that each of the senses makes available. Because the content the senses provide is qualitatively specific, that is, because each of the senses provides information limited to different qualities of the world and because these qualities as experienced create different forms of consciousness, the character of our experience is directly related to what our senses make possible. Once available we can both recall and treat imaginatively these qualities, qualities that take shape as images. Thus conception depends upon sensory information but is not limited to the specific information that arises from particular contacts the individual has with the qualitative world. Through imagination we can recombine, extend, vivify, delete, and create images that insofar as the world is concerned never were—hence, unicorns, twenty-first-century spaceships, models of mind, theories of motivation, and tunes you can whistle. Even more, conventional conceptions such as "infinity," "truth," "virtue," and "the double helix," are the fruits of the imagination. The content the imagination provides constitutes much of the subject matter of our reflective life.

Thus far I have tried to sketch a picture of the unity of sensation and cognition. Perhaps it would be useful to list the major points of the argument here.

- The senses provide the means through which the qualities of the environment are experienced.
- Each sensory system is sensitive to some, but not all environmental qualities.
- The information picked up through the senses provides the basis for concept formation.
- Once concepts are formed they can be recalled and treated imaginatively.
- Conception, born of sense material, provides the basis for knowing.
- The kind of knowing that is achieved depends upon the kinds of concepts formed which in turn depend upon (1) the sensory system employed and (2) the qualities available to the individual in the environment in which one functions.

These six points focus upon the relationship of the sensory systems to conception, but concept formation is a private affair; it exists as an experience in the possession of an individual. If humans did not have a need to express and communicate what they have conceptualized, we would need go no farther than to pursue in greater depth the nature of conception. But humans fortunately do have a need to make public what they have conceptualized. Through the public articulation of conceptions our environment itself is enriched and the sources for our own concepts are broadened. Through the process of communication we are able to share what we have come to know. This public sharing constitutes a significant aspect of culture. Our problem now is to identify the means through which such sharing takes place, and for this task we turn to what I have called the *forms of representation* that humans have invented to make public privately experienced conceptions.

Forms of Representation

Human conception is a private affair; it occurs within the experience of an individual. Because of the human's social nature, the individual has a need to express and to communicate what has been conceptualized to himself and to others. I say "to himself" because expression is a process not only through which conceptualizations are brought forward, but that

itself shapes conception and provides the conditions that make its modification possible. To make public what is private some vehicle must be
employed; these vehicles are forms that are used to represent the conceptions that have been achieved or that are formulated through the process
of expression, a process that is one of transformation. How shall experience, that is, say, tactile experience, be conveyed or made public in a way
that does not vitiate its content? How does one move from the qualities of
a particular experience into the public realm without destroying the
meaning that the experience provided in the first place? Humans have
always had to cope with such a task, the task of inventing vehicles that
make such transformation possible. One way to achieve this transformation is to employ a form that, itself, shares features of the initiating
conception. If the conception is visual, one may employ a visual analog in
the public realm. But the use of public qualities that are veridical with the
visual conception are not the only means through which such transformation and communication occur. Forms can be used that are not themselves
visual, but which suggest visual features or convey the feeling that those
features possessed. Music is one example. Program music often suggests
visually through sound, while romantic music sounds like the feeling that
the composer wishes to convey. Distinctions among *modes* of treatment
will be discussed momentarily, but for now the point is that forms of
representation must be invented to make public what is private, and these
forms, if we examine the culture at large, are designed to present patterned
qualities that are picked up by the sensory systems. Although forms of
representation often combine information so that several senses are
appealed to—cooking, film, drama, for example—forms of representation
are often constructed so that they appeal dominantly to one or two of the
senses at one time. Thus painting is, in general, more visual than auditory
or kinesthetic; music more auditory than visual; dance more visual than
auditory, gustatory, or olfactory. These forms exist—including poetic,
literary, and propositional language—because if what has been conceptualized is to have a public status, the use of such forms is necessary.
Musical conceptions cannot be conveyed without an auditory form of
representation.

What shall we regard as a form of representation? The examination of
the culture will be instructive here. It tells us there can be no definitive or
exhaustive list because forms of representation are human inventions and
the inventions through which expression and communication occur have
not been nor are they likely to be exhausted. Yet, some forms of
representation have special social significance and have had a very long

history. For example, speech and writing in its several forms, poetic, literary, and formal; visual art; music; dance; cooking; mathematics; and comparatively recently, film and holography. Such forms serve as crucially important means through which conceptions are publicly articulated, and because they appeal to different sensory systems, the kind of experience they make possible differs. There is every reason to believe that as technological developments occur, the forms of representation that individuals will have access to will also expand. The development of new devices for combining sound with tactile experience, of integrating words with color, and the use of devices that are now not even imaginable will surely broaden the repertoire of such forms. Even new developments within existing forms of representation, the invention of day-glow color, for example, adds new possibilities in the use of visual art for conveying conceptions that previously could only be dimly suggested.

Once again the point here is that the senses are the vehicles through which information about the world is picked up. Forms of representation are devices that appeal to the senses; they capitalize on their sensory specificity and exploit their potential to bring to consciousness the conceptions held by others. Through their use communication is expanded.

Consider the converse. Suppose it was the case that the government placed a moratorium on the use of all forms of representation except the formal use of discursive language. All that we wish to communicate, say for a period of a year, must by law be conveyed through this form and this form alone. What would we want to say that we could not express? What frustrations would we experience? What kind of conceptions would remain buried in our cortex? And what would eventually happen to the capacities of our brain?

Such speculation highlights the utilities of the forms we have access to and use with varying degrees of skill. Prose is not translated poetry, a visual image is not a substitute for a sonata, a mathematical proposition cannot be translated to poetry. Forms of representation are nonredundant, and their nonredundancy is what has commended themselves to us over the years. They make different kinds of experience possible, and from different kinds of experience flow different kinds of meaning. Indeed, the character of our consciousness is affected largely by the forms of representation with which we interact: A musical consciousness requires music, a mathematical consciousness, mathematics—although if Einstein is any example, a visual and a kinesthetic one as well.[12]

For the field of evaluation the implications of this thesis are several. We do not need to have a government moratorium on the use of forms of representation to have restrictions on how we communicate. Tradition, entrenched groups with vested interests to protect, and ignorance of alternatives can be almost as restrictive. Yet, with a restricted range of expressive vehicles the content of our conceptual life is also restrained. This restraint impedes not only what we are able to express, but what we seek when we inquire in the first place. Conventional methods and expectations in educational evaluation provide us with comforts that can diminish our ability to understand.

I indicated above that the forms of representation that we have become accustomed to not only influence what we can convey, but also shape the questions we ask and the information we seek. The way forms of representation affect conception need at least some further explanation.

It was E. H. Gombrich, the noted art historian, who observed that artists did not paint what they could see: They saw what they were able to paint. The skills they had acquired within the form of representation called visual art became, in a way, templates through which they perceived the world. Thus the interest of a Monet in qualities of light reflecting off of haystacks, church facades, and lily ponds were fundamentally different from those of a Constable or a Wyeth, whose interests were directed to matters of texture and mood. The artist who comes to a small fishing town looks for the scenic, the quality of the fog as it surrounds the houses and trees and that seems to rise, slowly from the ground. He looks for color and value, for compositional arrangements that are interesting, and seeks complementary fields of color that can be transformed into visual images on canvas or paper. The sociologist, with his tools, looks for the social structures within the town, how groups are formed, what statuses exist, in which context, the role of the local tavern and filling station as a source of information and social contact for the town's people. He tries to bring the particulars of his data within the power of sociological theory. He is after propositional explanation.

Each inquirer, the artist and the sociologist, have different backgrounds, they have acquired different skills, they use different media, they raise different questions, they seek different data, and have different things to tell us about the "same" place. Their training in the use of the tools of their respective trades becomes for each a salient frame of reference for construing a small piece of the world, and it is because the vividness that the images each creates are telling ones, that we learn to experience the town in different ways. When these images are particularly compelling, as they are when made by people of genius, the images become a paradigm or structure to which other experiences are assimilated. By creating the compelling images of ego, superego, id, and the mechanisms of defense, or of surplus value and the alienation of labor, Freud and Marx have provided the world with images of wide scope that do much more than simply convey the ideas they had; these images shape our conception of man and society. The same is true of dance, visual art, music, and theater. Those skilled in these realms look at the world through the terms the forms they use command. In turn, the work they produce within these forms directs our attention to the dimensions of the reality that those forms have portrayed. Through a multiplicity of forms we begin to appreciate the multidimensionality of experience and the complexity of the qualities through which that experience is secured. Evaluators have much to learn by studying the uses people make of the forms of representation employed within the culture. The very existence of such varieties should be clue enough that they perform important functions in helping us conceptualize and convey what we have experienced.

Modes of Treating Forms of Representation

The conceptualization of forms of representation as vehicles through which conceptions are externalized does not, by itself, describe the particular ways in which such forms can be treated. Given a form of representation, say visual art or discursive language, how might such forms be treated so that they represent what one has come to know? To label this activity, the term *modes of treatment* has been formulated. Any form of representation can be treated in one or more of three ways. These modes of treatment are *mimetic, expressive,* and *conventional.*

The mimetic conveys through imitation, that is, it represents by replicating within the limits of the medium employed the surface features of some aspect of the qualitative world. There are throughout human history numerous examples of mimetic modes of treatment, from the use of hieroglyphics and pictographs that were used to imitate the basic structural features of the visual world to the most advanced forms of pictography and holography. Just what is it that mimetic modes of treatment do? Simply stated, they extract the salient features of some aspect of the world and represent them as an image within some medium. Thus, the images of animals drawn on the walls of the Lescaux caves were due to early man's interest in representing his observations of the world. It seems reasonable to assume that members of his community knew when they looked at these drawn images that they were representative, that they were intended to portray running animals. In the use of hieroglyphics we have not only the abstracted visual representation of human figures, animals, furniture, and so forth, but we have them in a time sequence, a visual narrative that individuals are able to read. Hieroglyphics exemplify man's ability to combine both spatial experience (the visual image) and temporal experience by sequencing visual images in a form that not only parallels the individual's visual experience at a particular point in time, but over time as well.

If we look at a more modern example of the ways in which mimetic modes of treatment occur, it is vividly apparent in the use of highway signs. Particularly in Europe, one will find signs that tell the driver what one can expect to encounter as the car moves down the highway; a curve in the road, a dip, animals crossing, zigzags, castles nearby, turnoffs, and the like. In each case the image created shares some structural similarity with the object or situation it is designed to represent. Even though the form of representation is highly schematized, it presents the driver with as much information as is necessary—and probably as much as can be handled at 70 miles per hour.

Consider also paintings and photographs. Suppose you wanted to know what the south of France looked like, or the Chartres Cathedral, or your long-lost cousin Beatrice. You could, of course, read descriptions of such places and people and perhaps, if the writer were very skilled, it might be possible to gain a fairly good idea of their features. But a photograph or a painting will usually do the job much better. The spatial features of these places and people are more likely to be represented in a medium and form of representation that is, itself, spatial than one that is not. If we are trying to find someone disembarking from an airplane we have never met before, we would probably do better if we had a photograph than if we had a verbal description or a set of numbers describing the person's height and weight.

Perhaps the most telling example of mimetic modes of treatment are to be found in the use of fingerprints. Here what one has is a direct visual imprint of a textured surface. The prints duplicate the configurations of the surface of the fingers. Indeed, the correspondence is so close that among several million examples of prints on file in the FBI offices in Washington, no two are identical. One print is structurally isomorphic with the finger or fingers of a particular individual.

It is curious to me, therefore, to encounter Nelson Goodman's (1968) assertion[13] that "a Constable painting of Marlboro Castle is more like any other picture than it is like the castle" (p. 5) or that "none of the automobiles off an assembly line is a picture of the rest" (p. 4). I find these statements curious because we do, in fact, expect a portrait to represent, that is to say, to look like the sitter. If it does not, we are disappointed. And if we go into an automobile showroom, select a car, and ask the salesman to order the same car except in a different color, we are in fact using the car on the showroom floor as a model that we expect our car, when delivered, to duplicate. If we find that another model has arrived instead, or that the grill has been altered, or that another motor has been installed or different tires affixed, we would not only have cause for complaint, but for canceling our order as well.

Or consider still another example: the use of a prototype in the production of automobiles. It is standard practice to build a prototype automobile which in every respect is to be reproduced on the assembly line. Cars coming off the line are copies of these prototypes, which themselves are representations of the designers' and engineers' conceptions. When a car coming off the line does not possess the features of the prototype, there is or should be a call-back: Something has gone amiss.

Such practices are examples of mimesis, the prototypical model being the standard against which other cars are to be appraised. In this way, as well as through the pictures and specifications provided in sales brochures, a mimetic function is performed. Like the highway signs, the prototype automobile presents to us what is to be found when the journey is completed. It "pictures" in detail, ideally as a perfect replica, what the efforts of the workers, the buyers, and the management are to find when the work has been completed. In this sense one car does indeed stand for another.

It is true that in some respects a painting of a car is more like *any* other painting than it is like any other thing. But that is true only if we shift context and disregard the function of representation. A scientific formula—H_2O—is more like any other formula—CO_2—than it is like water. We can always choose to disregard the central function of a form if we are intent on doing so, and for some purposes to do so is functional. But the argument that imitation is largely irrelevant to representation is, I believe, not sound. Man has for thousands of years represented through efforts of mimesis. Indeed techniques such as perspective were invented to make more credible the representations attempted. This is not to say that paintings and even photographs are simply copies, the way in which fingerprints or death masks are copies. Idiosyncratic expression and interpretation are always present to some degree. It is to say that we have learned how to read abstracted and interpreted images, and that for a great many kinds of information we do not require the degree of mimesis that fingerprints provide.

Most of the examples I have used thus far are visual, but mimesis occurs not only in the visual but in other forms of representation as well. Music can be composed to imitate the sound of thunder, running brooks, riders on horseback, and the like. Words can be onomatopoetic. Smells can be created to imitate a wide range of other smells, and so forth. The point here is that the imitation of selected features of the empirical world within an available material has been and is one of the major means through which representation occurs.

There is another point about the mimetic mode of treatment that is so obvious that it is often neglected. That is, for the purposes of mimesis the closer the form is to the content represented, the closer the mimesis is likely to be. Thus, to represent what is visual, forms of representation that appeal to the visual sensory system are likely to be more revealing than forms that emphasize the use of other systems. To know how something sounds, forms of representation that emphasize the auditory are more appropriate than forms that emphasize the visual. To know what someone said, a duplication of the words is more appropriate than a picture. This is not to suggest that transformations of experience from one sense modality to representation in forms that emphasize another do not or should not occur. To do so would be the demise of literature. It is to suggest that mimetic functions operate most successfully when the sense modality emphasized in the form of representation is like that which it aims to represent.

One other observation. In many situations the meaning of an experience is not simply the function of the experience secured through one of the senses, but due to the interaction among the several senses. Consider discourse. When people talk, the meanings conveyed are simply not due to "what is said" but how they say what they say, that is, the intonation and emphasis they give to the words they use, the gestures they make while speaking, their expression, the context in which what they have to say is said, what preceded in the conversation, and so forth. The absence of these features in transcripts of discourse can radically alter the meanings that, in fact, were conveyed when the discourse took place. To pick the varieties of information that accompany the discourse itself—if indeed one can talk about the "discourse itself," since it is never by itself—a variety of sensory systems must operate and one must know how to read the meanings that the content they make possible provide. The ability to reconstruct varieties of information through sound and sight, tempo and context, is one of the virtues of film. Perhaps that is one of the reasons why film is so captivating and compelling. The absence of such contextual information in so much research on teaching might be one of the reasons why it has been, in the main, so uninformative.

A second mode of treatment that is used to shape forms of representation is called expressive. By expressive I mean that what is represented is not the surface features of an object or event, but rather its deep structure. Consider the movement of a jet plane speeding down a runway about to take off. The plane moves along very slowly and gradually increases its speed, its speed continues to increase and about three-quarters down the runway its nose rises and, like a duck leaving a lake, it lifts off the surface of the earth. Such an experience, if we were standing on the roof of an airport building, would be auditory as well as visual. We would experience a stark white form accelerating and gradually becoming nothing more than a small speck against the vast expansive blue sky. It is this movement, this graceful takeoff, the sound of the jet engines gradually diminishing in volume, the gradual reduction and size as the plane moves into the sky that a dancer or a visual artist might create. Such creations have less to do with mimesis than with creating the experience of acceleration, with the gradual increase in speed and with the experience of a slow rise into the atmosphere. How these expressive qualities might be represented is precisely what the artist has to create: There are no codified formulas for producing such expressive forms. What the artist wants to do is not to imitate the surface features of a moving plane, but to capture its essential properties, that is to say, its expressive character. Here a kind of imitation is also at work, but it is not imitation of things seen, but rather of things felt. The form of representation is treated expressively rather than mimetically. The analogic relationship is not through the imitation of appearance, but through the creation of a form that generates the expressiveness of slowly accelerating movement.

Why have artists been interested in such a task? Why should such efforts occupy such a central place in the history of the arts? At least a part of the reason is because much of what is most important in human experience is not what is apparent, but rather what is felt about what is apparent. Things are not always what they appear to be on the surface, but in the kind of emotional life that they generate; the sense of curiosity displayed by a very young child exploring a new toy or the fear of an old man anticipating his imminent death are not simply physical movements, but appearances that possess a pervasive quality that convey to the sensitive perceiver the character of curiosity and fear. The behavior is read by looking below its surface features. Just how forms, whether human or not, convey such qualities of life is not altogether clear. Gestalt and associationist theories hold competing views, and it is not necessary for explanations of these theoretical views to be given here. What is important is to recognize that the expressive treatment of forms of representation does occur and does shape our experience.

If to know about the character of life in a school or classroom, suburb or ghetto, requires one to know not only about their surface appearances, but also about the character of life within them, then it is imperative that those who wish to make such knowledge public use means that can embody the qualities they seek to express. It is here that expressive modes of treatment are crucial. In literature and in poetry the artistic achieve-ment is realized in the expressive character of the forms created, not because such forms are necessarily beautiful or pleasant, but because without them the very content that the artist wishes to convey could not be expressed. The expressive mode of treatment is, therefore, not simply a pleasant affectation, a dressing up of content to make it more palatable, but is itself part and parcel of the content of the form of representation. When descriptions of situations that are emotionally loaded for individuals are presented that do not possess the emotionality that they hold for those who live in those situations, a significant form of bias and distortion results. To use a form of representation of the Buchenwald or Dachau concentration camps that leaves out of its content the character of life as experienced by the inmates, is to render less than a partial view of those camps: It is to mislead.

A third mode of treatment is conventional. By conventional, I mean simply that as individuals are socialized within a culture they learn that certain conventions such as discursive language, traffic signs, bells and alarms of one kind or another, stand in the place of something else. A red light, the flag, the almost wholly arbitrary vocabulary of our discursive language are examples of the conventional mode of treating forms of representation. Usually words and colors are neither mimetic (although at one time they might have been) nor expressive (although they might be used expressively as words are used in literature and in poetry). The relationship between the form and referent is arbitrary. "Pain" in English means something like a sharp, uncomfortable feeling, while in French it means bread. There is nothing in the word per se to commend it to one rather than to the other referent. What matters is that within a culture there is an agreement among those who use its conventions that the referent for each is so and so. Conventions do, of course, have variability in interpretation by different individuals. However, in the conventional mode the range of the variance is generally far narrower than in either of the other two modes of treatment.

There is, of course, an important and interesting difference between the mimetic and expressive modes of treatment and the conventional mode. In both the mimetic and the expressive analogic relationships operate. In each case what is created parallels some aspect of the form being represented. In conventional modes of treatment this is not the case. A table does not look like how it sounds. For the word or the sentence to have meaning, the individual must be able to imagine the referent for the term or terms employed. This does not mean that for every word used there is a corresponding image. We have so mastered discourse that we do not need to visualize a referent in order to speak or write. However, if we are unable to imagine the referent for a discursive term that we encounter we cannot have a conception of what it means. Thus language in the ordinary sense of the term may be said to function as a surrogate for an image. If the surrogate is to have meaning, we must be able to imagine the referent to which the term refers. This is why when children do not understand a word, we try to help them by providing examples.

The distinctions I have made between the mimetic, the expressive, and the conventional should not be taken to mean that a form of representation uses only one mode of treatment. The three are often combined. For example, much visual art, particularly painting, uses mimetic, expressive, and conventional elements within the same work. Literature and poetry employ the mimetic in the way in which the sound of events are emulated, the expressive in the way in which the structure of the prose penetrates the surface features of the events portrayed, and the conventional through the standardized use of language and symbol.

Perhaps the most vivid example of a form of representation that combines modes of treatment is to be found in film. The modern film not only lets us see how something looks or sounds, but when artistically successful, also enables us to experience the various structures underlying the events and places portrayed. Films such as "Breaking Away" give us a glimpse of a part of middle America, its streets, people, and the stone-cutting plant in which Indiana limestone is cut. It also makes it possible for us to participate vicariously in the race between the "Cutters" and the campus cycle team. Furthermore, the conventional and unconventional use of language serve as vehicles through which we understand the interaction among the characters. Indeed, it is the "Italianization" of the English language from which so much of the film's comic quality emerges. In addition, the use of camera angle, the character of the film's music, and the skillful editing all combine to convey (through all three modes of treatment) the meanings that constitute the film itself. We not only acquire some sense of what Bloomington, Indiana looks like; we also get some sense of the relations between "town" and "gown." We not only encounter five adolescent males discussing their ambitions and fantasies; we are helped to identify with them and to experience their triumphs and defeats. The film is an extremely potent form of representation that can employ different modes of treatment. It is the awareness of this potentiality that directors, writers, and actors exploit to inform us about the events of the people that they portray.

The Syntactical Structure of Forms of Representation

Forms of representation are forms whose elements are arranged in a pattern. This arrangement is what is here called a syntax. The term syntax is typically used in dealing with spoken and written language, but the term is not restricted to these forms of representation. The term "syntax" emanates from the Latin "sintaxis" which means "to arrange." A syntax is an arrangement of parts within a whole; thus, in visual art there is an arrangement called a composition, in music compositions are arranged by composers or arrangers. There are arrangements in dance, architecture, cooking, in any sphere of human activity in which patterns are produced.

The design of these patterns in different forms of representation is guided or controlled by different criteria. If the bases for arrangements are examined, it becomes clear that some are controlled by clearly defined conventions whose violation yields expressions that are either wrong or without meaning. Consider arithmetic. To be able to create an arrangement that is correct within arithmetic an individual must know how to combine elements within the canons of arithmetic procedure. If these canons are incorrectly employed, answers to arithmetic problems will be wrong. The correctness or incorrectness of the answers can be determined without difficulty and with virtual unanimity by those who know the rules. Indeed, the criteria are so clear that human judgment is not necessary: A machine can perform the same functions.

Spelling and punctuation are similar, but are not quite as rule-governed. Nevertheless, in American English, words misspelled can be identified without difficulty by matching them to conventionally accepted standards. Punctuation also, in somewhat lesser degree, is highly rule-governed and can be determined to be correct or incorrect by applying the rules of punctuation to the statements in question. The point here is that some forms of representation are highly *rule-governed* in nature, and the results that are achieved by the use of such forms can be appraised with little difficulty by comparing them with standardized expectations.

At the other end of the continuum are those forms of representation whose elements are arranged not by obeying codified rules of procedure but by trying to create a figurative coherence or by juxtaposing elements within a whole so that productive novelty and meaning result. This end of the continuum we shall call *figurative*. The use of a figurative syntax is epitomized in the arts. There is no such thing as an incorrect or correct poem, painting, musical composition, because there are no codified standards or rules that such forms must meet. A poem might be more or less coherent and cohesive, but that judgment is made by appraising the relationships among the qualities it possesses, not by looking for isomorphism between the arrangement and an acceptable standard. The task requires judgment and uses criteria, not standards. It is a deliberative activity, not a calculative one.[14] Thus, when one selects a form of representation, one also selects the kind of criteria that will be used to appraise the results of one's work. A level of precision can be secured in mathematics and spelling that is simply impossible to achieve in film or music.

Although the arts emphasize the use of a figurative syntax, there are "rules" and criteria that guide artists in the course of their work. A novelist who wishes to write a romantic novel functions within the criteria called "the novel" and within the form called "the romantic." A painter who wishes to create a painting that participates in an impressionist genre works within the historical exemplars of impressionism: the work of Monet, Vuillard, and Bonnard. These painters have established some of the parameters within which the work must fit. The images these and other works present to the world define their style, and establish the grounds that artists, composers, writers, architects, and others must work within or depart from. In *this* sense there are "rules" in the arts, and in *this* sense artistic forms of representation are rule-governed.

But the rules I have identified are fundamentally different from those used in forms whose syntax is at the rule-governed end of the continuum. As I said, arithmetic, and mathematics more generally, are paradigm cases. Here the canons of procedure are publicly articulated and codified, they can be explicitly taught, a machine can be programmed to produce correct arrangements and to identify incorrect ones, truth and falsity can be determined unambiguously and finally, rules of equivalence can be applied, and translation—in the literal sense—is possible without loss of information: Five plus three times two means exactly what ten plus one means, no more, no less. There is no comparable translatability in those syntaxes that are figurative. Their meaning emanates from the *particular* configuration among the elements the form possesses. When that configuration is altered, there is an alteration in meaning.

It is both interesting and significant to note that during the primary years of schooling, and even beyond, the use of forms of representation that emphasize rule-governed syntaxes is quite dominant. The three Rs are classical examples. There are probably several reasons for this. The use of forms of representation that are rule-governed does increase the precision of communication. By emphasizing conformity and obedience to convention, children develop skills for simple decoding, writing, and basic computation. Such skills are of undoubtable importance in dealing with many of the messages received within the culture. Furthermore, because school curriculum to a very large degree requires the use of such skills, a self-fulfilling prophecy occurs; the needs of the future in school define the skills to be acquired in the present. If the skills needed in the future were those that made the imaginative treatment of music important, the skills emphasized at present in school would be quite different.

It is also noteworthy that performance in rule-governed forms of representation is simple to evaluate compared to performance in those forms that require the use of judgment. Teachers need to have skills that are far more complex and subtle in order to judge the quality of a poem compared to determining whether the words that the student has used are spelled correctly. Even factually oriented material in the social studies and in science can be used to evaluate student responses on a matching basis that is not possible in evaluating student work and performance in music and in art. There is, after all, a back of the book to which teachers can turn for correct answers that are simply unavailable in the fine arts.

One cannot help but wonder about the meta lessons children, especially young children, learn when forms of representation that emphasize rule-governed syntaxes are used so overwhelmingly in school.[15] One lesson that it seems to me is unavoidable is that problems—at least the kind they encounter in school—usually have correct and incorrect answers, that the teachers know what the answers are, and that the students' task is to work in a way that will lead them to the correct answers. Ambiguities, matters of judgment, tradeoffs among competing alternatives, holding conclusions in abeyance until more evidence comes in—these are not very significant features of classroom life. We emphasize by both what we teach and how we evaluate that there is a right and a wrong answer to virtually everything. The student's task is to arrive at the correct destination. In school, as in the movies, we are a nation of happy and unambiguous endings.

Such an emphasis is curiously incongruous with a school concerned about helping the young prepare for the future. The future, and indeed the present for most people, is riddled with ambiguities, tradeoffs, dilemmas, competing alternatives, and conflicting answers. It is far from clearcut. There are very few problems the solutions to which can be determined once and for all by adding up the columns of pluses and minuses. Yet we seem to prepare the young, in school at least, in a way that provides little practice in dealing with such problems and we reinforce the significance of right answers that hint of no ambiguity by the ways in which we evaluate. The multiple-choice test leaves no room for doubt. Again, not only our evaluation practices but the forms of representation and syntaxes they employ support and reflect a social ethos where rule, prediction, control, and standardization appear to be pressing social needs.

Some Practical Implications for an Impractical World

Do discussions of the relationship of the senses to conception and of the forms used to represent them have any bearing upon the practical problems of educational evaluation? It seems to me that they do in several ways. In the first place, if concept formation is, as I have argued, based upon information provided by the sensory systems, then any representation of those concepts requires various degrees of translation. Words and sentences, for example, are surrogates for what is known in nonverbal ways. In translation there is always a loss or change of information. Second, the extent to which the qualities of the environment are known in the first place depends upon the extent to which the sensibilities are able to pick them up. When the senses are dulled, ill-developed, disregarded, or in other ways diminished in importance, the qualities of the environment to which those neglected sensibilities are related are not likely to be experienced. To the extent that those qualities go unexperienced, to that extent at least is our information partial and incomplete. Third, the traditional restriction to particular forms of representing information that have been conceptualized has led to two egregious faults. First, it has restricted attention to aspects of the environment most amenable to the forms of representation that are permitted. Second, it has limited severely what has been rendered, even about those qualities to which the forms themselves may be related.

Given such limitations why is it that certain conventional forms, namely language and number, have received so much attention in the social sciences, and more particularly in educational research and evaluation. Part of the reason is that our conception of objectivity is rooted in replicability. Replicability breeds confidence in the conclusions that the methods that meet such criteria yield. Replicability and rule-governed procedures fit quite well with our need to stabilize a rapidly changing world. With such procedures we believe we are more likely to be able to predict and control our environment. Finally, an entire professional constituency exists that has spent a great deal of time and effort in developing the skills needed to use such methods. This group does not play an insignificant political role in maintaining the status quo.

To expand the range of legitimate approaches in the evaluation field is an epistemological problem, a political problem, and an educational one. It is an epistemological problem because the philosophical grounds for claims that forms other than discursive ones can provide knowledge needs to be justified. Such justification requires work of the kind presented in this book. It is a political problem because, as I have already indicated, vested interests exist. People do what they know how to do. Few professionals are eager to be displaced by others having different skills and working with different assumptions. The politics of university life and of professional associations, of journals and of schools tend to support the status quo, although it is reassuring to see some change occurring in all four arenas. It is an educational problem because the development of the sensibilities upon which consciousness depends is not an automatic consequence of maturation. To be able to pick up what is qualitatively specific and subtle requires training. Universities can play an important role here. To be able to skillfully use nondiscursive forms of representation requires intuition. Each form of representation is a kind of language. Its structure needs to be learned. One must know when and how to take and read photographs or to speak poetically about classrooms, schools, or the qualities of an individual student's work. Such skills are difficult ones to acquire, but they can be acquired. We now train doctoral students interested in educational research and evaluation by requiring that they take courses in statistics, measurement, research design, and evaluation theory. These courses typically neglect using forms of representation that are neither quantitative nor propositional. Indeed, the *idea* of their use, with the exception of only a few evaluation courses that I know of in the nation, simply never become a part of the conversation.

In attempting to contribute to the construction of a wider approach to educational evaluation, I have risked overstating the case for nonquantitative and nondiscursive forms of representation. I have taken this risk because quantitative and propositional forms are presently very strong and highly refined. Let me say explicitly that what I have tried to convey is not the need to replace existing methods, but rather the need to expand the methods that can be used. Propositional discourse and number have no substitute. They, like other forms of representation, make unique contributions to our understanding. But they do not tell the whole story. In restaurants in Japan examples of the variety of food being served are placed in the window outside the restaurant. Passersby can look at these plates and get an idea what the food is like. The Japanese recognize that words on a menu provide limited information about what will be served, and so they represent what they serve with a mimetic form of representation. We can take a cue from the Japanese. There is much to be learned about classrooms, teaching, and the quality of student work by seeing what it looks like, by hearing what it sounds like, by reading literary prose that illuminates its subtleties as well as by reading the scores the students received on standardized tests. No single form of representation will do justice to everything.

The ways in which diverse forms of representation can be used in educational evaluation constitutes an area of work that is only just beginning. The other chapters in this book present some of the initial forays. To me they provide useful leads. If these and other beginnings take root, as I hope they will, the next quarter century should see a much richer array of tools available to educational evaluators for the evaluation of educational practice.

Notes

[1] The membership of churches that can be described as fundamentalist and evangelical in their orientation is documented in the *Yearbook of American and Canadian Churches,* various years.

[2] At the present time, 36 states have statutes that provide for capital punishment. Council of State Governments (1978).

[3] For a discussion of research that has been conducted on "time on task," see B. V. Rosenshine (1978).

[4] Higher scores can be achieved in some subjects by neglecting other equally important subjects, thus lowering the overall quality of education.

[5] For a discussion of Toennies' work, see Robert Nisbet (1976).

[6] Perhaps the classic example of this view is provided by Alfred Jules Ayers (1946).

[7] See for example, Plato's *Republic,* especially Books Six and Seven.

8For a brilliant discussion of the role of the senses in the achievement of consciousness see Herbert Read (1955).

9John Dewey, *Art as Experience* (1934), especially Chapters 3 and 4.

10Rudolph Arnheim (1969, pp. 8-12) reviews Aristotle's thoughts on sensation, perception, and cognition.

11Stephen W. Kuffler and John G. Nicolls (1976), especially Chapter 19.

12Albert Einstein is quoted as follows: "The words or the language, as they are written or spoken, do not seem to play any role in my mechanism of thought. The physical entities which seem to serve as elements in thought are certain signs and more or less clear images which can be 'voluntarily' reproduced or combined. . . . But taken from a psychological viewpoint, this combinatory play seems to be the essential feature in productive thought—before there is any connection with logical construction in words or other kinds of signs which can be communicated to others. The above-mentioned elements are, in my case, of visual and some of muscular type. Conventional words or other signs have to be sought for laboriously only in a secondary stage, when the mentioned associative play is sufficiently established and can be reproduced at will (Holton, 1967-1968).

13For a very full treatment of the concept of symbol systems, see Goodman (1968).

14The distinction between the deliberative and the calculative is Aristotle's. See, for example, J. L. Acrill (1973, pp. 114-122).

15The concept "meta lesson" is related to notions concerning the hidden curriculum. It is also related to the older notion of concomitant learning. Stated more simply, it underscores the idea that students learn more than one thing at a time, and that the syntactical structure of the forms that are used in school curricula instruct in many unexpected ways.

References

Acrill, J. (Ed.). *Aristotle's ethics.* London: Faber & Faber, 1973.

Arnheim, R. *Visual thinking.* Berkeley: University of California Press, 1969.

Ayers, A. *Language, truth and logic.* New York: Dover, 1946.

Broudy, H. Arts education: Necessary or just nice? *Phi Delta Kappan,* 1979, 60, 347-350.

Chomsky, N. Foreword. In A. Schaff, *Language and cognition.* New York: McGraw-Hill, 1973.

Council of State Governments. *The state book* (Vol. 22, 1971-1979). Kentucky, 1978.

Dewey, J. *Experience and education.* New York: Macmillan, 1938.

Dewey, J. *Art as experience.* New York: Minton, Balch, 1934.

Goodman, N. *The languages of art.* Indianapolis: Bobbs-Merrill, 1968.

Harnischfeger, A., & Wiley, D. *Achievement test score decline: Do we need to worry?* Chicago: CEMREL, 1975.

Help! Teacher can't teach! *Time,* June 16, 1980, p. 54.

Holton, G. Influences on Einstein's early work in relativity theory. *The American Scholar,* 1967-1968, 37.

Kuffler, S., & Nicolls, J. *From neuron to brain: A cellular approach to the function of the neuron systems.* Massachusetts: Sinovar, 1976.

Mead, M. *Aspects of the present.* New York: Morrow, 1980.

Neisser, U. *Cognition and reality: Principles and implications of cognitive psychology.* San Francisco: Freeman, 1976.

Nisbet, R. *Sociology as an art form.* New York: Oxford University Press, 1976.

Piaget, J. *Biology and knowledge.* Edinburgh: Edinburgh University Press, 1971.

Plato's *Republic* (Francis MacDonald Cornford, trans.). New York: Oxford University Press, 1951.

Popper, K. *The logic of scientific discovery.* New York: Harper & Row, 1980.

Read, H. *Icon and idea.* Cambridge, MA: Harvard University Press, 1955.

Rosenshine, B. Academic engaged time, content covered, and direct instruction. *Journal of Education,* 1978, 160, 38-66.

Rosenshine, B. Classroom instruction. In *75th yearbook of the national society for the study of education, The psychology of teaching methods* (Pt. 1). Chicago: University of Chicago Press, 1976.

Schaff, A. *Language and cognition.* New York: McGraw-Hill, 1973.

Yearbook of American and Canadian churches. Nashville: Abingdon, various years.

GEORGE F. MADAUS
Boston College

JOHN T. McDONAGH
Archdiocese of Dublin

CHAPTER **2**

As I Roved Out

Folksong Collecting as a Metaphor for Evaluation

George F. Madaus is Professor of Educational Research and Evaluation and Director of the Center for the Study of Testing, Evaluation, and Educational Policy at Boston College. His primary interests are in the administrative use of tests in public policy, program evaluation, and minimum competency testing. • John T. McDonagh recently received his Ph.D. from Boston College. He is currently working for the Archdiocese of Dublin. His interests include program evaluation, epistemological issues related to evaluation, and the evaluation of religious education programs.

FOR OVER SIXTEEN YEARS, as part of his vocation, the first author has conducted evaluations and has studied, taught, and written about various aspects of evaluation. During that same period, his avocation has been the study, collection, and enjoyment of the folksongs and music of the English-speaking world. He never saw any connection between the two activities until he received from the Evaluation Center at Western Michigan a paper in their Occasional Paper Series by Terry Denny entitled, "Story Telling and Educational Understanding" (1978). As he read the Denny paper, he experienced a vague feeling of déja vu that he could not quite place. That evening he put on a folk record and began to work on cataloging songs, when it hit him that Denny's description of his field work experiences were remarkably similar to Pat Carroll's (1974) description of the work of the Irish folksong collector, Tom Munnelly. A comparison of the Carroll and Denny papers prompted an awareness of the affinity between naturalistic inquiry as it is being explored by evaluators and the naturalistic inquiry of the folksong collector.

In recent years the evaluation field has seen a growing divergence from the positivistic/quantitative approach to evaluation, typified by the works of Tyler, Provus, Popham, and others. More recent theorists have advocated a phenomenological/qualitative approach to evaluation. Typical of the latter school would be Guba's "naturalistic inquiry," Eisner's "connoisseurship evaluation," Stake's "responsive evaluation," Parlett and Hamilton's "illuminative evaluation," and Denny's case study or "storytelling" approach. The differences in the way evaluation is conceptualized arise not merely from methodological considerations, but more basically, reflect ideological differences that underpin the respective approaches. Evaluation is not, of course, the only discipline that experiences this ideological split on how best to seek "truth" in the human enterprise. Indeed, it may be seen as but one instance of what Lewis Thomas (1979) described with respect to science in general:

> Much of today's public anxiety about science is the apprehension that we may forever be overlooking the whole by an endless, obsessive preoccupation with the parts [p. 6].

In the light of these divergent approaches to evaluation, the authors acknowledge that they come from the more traditional school. At the same time, both have enjoyed the interchange in the literature between those advocating the "naturalistic" approach. Both authors have also enjoyed a lifelong interest in folkmusic. The Denny and Carroll articles generated a resonance at the level of personal avocation and prompted heuristic inquiry at the level of personal vocation.

A long and rich tradition from the world of the folk collector prompted an exploration of folk collecting as a metaphor for naturalistic inquiry in educational evaluation. From a conceptual viewpoint the metaphor related to three aspects of the evaluation field as we know it. First, it throws light on a naturalistic approach to evaluation. Second, the history of the collecting field throws light on the positivistic/phenomenological debate in the evaluation field. And third, we found that practitioners in both fields share many conceptual problems and practical decisions.

We shall first describe some of the metaphors to evaluation that we found in the folksong/folklore literature. In doing so, we will rely heavily on quotes from collectors, since we feel they convey the metaphors more lucidly than we could ever hope to do through paraphrase. Second, we shall discuss differences between the enterprises of folksong collecting and that of educational evaluation. Finally, while the dominant concern of this chapter is conceptual, we shall describe briefly some typical methods and techniques of the collector that lend themselves to use in a naturalistic educational evaluation.

Evaluation Metaphors from Folksong Collecting

The Collector's Personality

Naturalistic evaluation shares many of the established features of folksong collecting. Perhaps the single most important feature in common is the personality requirements necessary to engage fruitfully in either enterprise. The famous American collector of folklore and folksongs, Kenneth Goldstein, in the Introduction to his book, *A Guide for Field Workers in Folklore* (1964), writes:

> A methodology is only one of the requirements for successful collecting. More important is the individual who would become a collector. If he does not have the inclination, temperament, or personality for collecting, he will not become a successful field worker merely by using methods and techniques [p. 9].

An aspect of this necessary personality is the ability not only to collect, but to live with the frustrations and discomforts peculiar to this type of research. Goldstein (1964) alludes to this personality dimension and to costs associated with personal investment in collecting:

> Primary among these costs is personal discomfort. Under the strain of constantly accommodating himself to others, of living in the public spotlight, of having his good nature taken advantage of, of playing a role and living up to the status it carries, of not being able to indulge in his own idiosyncrasies while forced to tolerate those of others, of continually being careful to avoid untoward incidents, and then having to deal with them as they inevitably arise—under the strain of all these and more, the collector's patience is sure to be strained. Emotional stability will only delay the strain. His personal discomfort resulting therefrom must eventually affect his field work [p. 75].

Bela Bartok, the great Hungarian collector, graphically describes the frustrations associated with field work in an August 1907 letter to a friend:

And so da capo al fine from morning to night, Monday to Sunday (day after day)! I can't bear it any longer. Impossible!

Endurance, perseverance, patience . . . to hell with you all . . . I'm going home.

I can't do with this farce for more than 6 weeks at a stretch. Even in my dreams I hear: "Jesus keep you. . . . Is she at home? . . . She's gone mowing . . . holy songs. . . . Round is the forest . . . it doesn't fit in my pocket."

Terrible! Good-bye to you, high plateau of Tyergyo, I shall not see you again until Easter [Demeny, 1971, p. 74].

Already we can note in the experiences of naturalistic evaluators chords resonant to the strains of Goldstein and Bartok. Denny (1978) adverts to "the precious prattlings about the lush rewards that await the fieldworker" and adds:

That's not what happens to me. It is a job. I love it; but it *is* often dull stuff and I regularly reach a point in my work where I contemplate fleeing to Guadalajara under the assumed name of Nick Barf [p. 15].

For the individual with temperament and skills, who is willing to undergo these discomforts, the experience of collecting and of naturalistic evaluation can be rewarding not only personally, but to the field of inquiry. The Irish folk collector Tom Munnelly, listening to Jack Horan sing for him in a dark, smoky Kerry pub, made all his travel, separation from family, long hours, bad food, numerous pints of stout, and hard, often dull, work worth it:

"You know," said Tom, "that ballad has never been collected from oral tradition in Ireland before. There was a manuscript version turned up in Cork in 1928 but aside from that, no evidence that the song existed in this country" [Carroll, 1974, p. 8].

What the "folk collector" metaphor suggests here is that personality factors are critical to the success of naturalistic evaluation. As an aside of this suggestion, the extent to which the present lack of dialogue between some traditional evaluators and their naturalistic counterparts is grounded in the personality differences that underlie respective group membership, is worthy of consideration but not explored here. The metaphor does not suggest that all those presently engaged in evaluation must down tools and follow. It does suggest that the evaluation field open itself to the possibility of "different strokes for different folks," as Denny (1978) puts it.

Different Types of Collectors

In the evaluation literature an important distinction is made between the roles of internal and external evaluators. Both are important, but each role carries with it a unique set of opportunities, pressures, and limitations. It is significant that we can find a ready metaphor for this role distinction in folksong collecting.

Folksong collectors, like evaluators, can enter the community from the outside (external evaluator)—or be part and parcel of the landscape of the community (internal evaluator) (Henderson, 1964). The latter, if good at the job, can become "an integral part of tradition, a chronicler and remembrancer of the culture and therefore has no need to assume a role because his role is obvious for all to see" (Henderson, 1964, p. ix).

The external collector (evaluator) can be of two types. The first is analogous to the naturalistic evaluator. This is the "Quiet Man" collector of the sort who eschews a conspicuous posture and is capable of recovering a rich lore of material for further analysis. The field worker stays in the community for an extended period and returns after establishing and maintaining rapport with informants (Henderson, 1964).

The second type of external collector is the person who collects folklore transiently. For legitimate reasons this type of collector does not become deeply involved with informants. Like the test-pretest survey evaluator, the transient collector stays only a few days in a community "collecting from hundreds of informants, making casual relationships, getting a story in a barber shop here, a bus stop there . . . not particularly concerning him/herself with the problem of motivating informants" (Goldstein, 1964, p. 160). This kind of transient folklore, like test score data in evaluation, is important and should not be denigrated. However, such a collector (evaluator) will rarely be able to find out what that informant's stories or songs (program and teaching) mean to the person. To do this as Goldstein (1964) points out, the collector would have to collect the singer as well as the folklore.

All three types of collectors (evaluators) can recover rich, but quite different material. The nature of the problem to be addressed, and the material to be collected to answer it, determine which mode of collecting (evaluating) is most suitable in each context. The personality factor we have already addressed, and the skills of the collector (evaluator) will help decide the role type to be exercised.

Different Stages in Folksong Collecting

Like evaluation, folksong collecting has also gone through different chronological stages in its development. Evaluators are familiar with the chronology of their field. At the risk of oversimplification, we can identify a series of focal points. The first was the objectives-based, pretest/posttest, approach. The second was a series of revisions to this model that point out the limitations of an exclusive focus on product and increment to the exclusion of process. The third stage saw arguments for naturalistic inquiry, illuminative evaluation, and connoisseurship evaluation. Proponents of this stage were attending to modes of inquiry and forms of knowledge that were neglected in the previous two stages. It is to this final stage that the metaphor from modern folk collecting is particularly applicable.

When we turn to an overview of folksong collecting we find a corresponding evolution marked by a dialectic between an established approach and a search for a more adequate approach. The first wave of collectors, beginning in the eighteenth century, concentrated almost wholly on the poetry and texts of the songs (Kennedy, 1974), due in no little measure to the lack of a good system of notating music. An old laborer who knew many folksongs, sums up this approach: "If you can get the words, the Lord Almighty will send you the tune" (Williams, 1974, p. 19).

This first stage was replaced in the mid-nineteenth century by collectors whose emphasis was primarily on the air and secondarily on the text. Kidson (1970) typified this approach, where the text was the vehicle for the air (melody). In commenting on the song, "White Hare," he observed "a fine and sterling old air. I wish I could say as much for the words" (Green, 1970, p. ix).

The third phase began in the late nineteenth century when collections began to appear with equal emphasis on both text and melodies. Here it's not an "either-or" matter. In this respect, this stage offers an interesting comparison to what we identified as the second generation of evaluation models which emphasized the need to examine both process and product.

But it is modern folksong collecting that offers the strongest metaphor to the most recent conceptualization of evaluation. It may be best to let Peter Kennedy (1974), a famous British collector, describe this fourth stage in folk collecting:

> Although I had already been won over by the lilting rhythms of folkdance music, performance of folksong had always left me cold. So when I first heard a traditional singer roar out his salt-sea chanties with a strong, rhythmic vitality, I knew that the printed page would never contain either his robust and ribald verses, nor convey the subtleties of his performance. In fact, the importance of the tradition was not so much what he sang but the way he sang it [p. 3].

Or consider this quote from the Ulster collector, Robin Morton, which bears striking resemblance to the concerns and approach to evaluation expressed in the writings of Guba, Eisner, Stake, Denny, Parlett, and Hamilton.

> The opinion grew in me that it was *in* the singer that the song becomes relevant. Analyzing it in terms of motif, or rhyming structure, or minute variation becomes, in my view, sterile if the one who carries the particular song is forgotten. We have all met the scholar who can talk for hours in a very learned fashion about folksong and folklore in general, without once mentioning the singer. Bad enough to forget the social context, but to ignore the individual context castrates the song. As I got to know the singers, so I got to know and understand their songs more fully [Morton, 1973, p. 11].

Thus, Morton's book on the great Ulster folksinger, John Maguire, or Bob Copper's (1971) book on the various generations of his famous singing family are interesting and illuminating—it is nice to have the text and music in print. But it is only when you actually hear Maguire sing or hear the close harmony of the Coppers that you truly appreciate living folkmusic. Often even a recording is not enough. Anyone into folkmusic can tell you of the singer who just does not come across on a recording; the vinyl disk or tape just does not do justice to the performance. Some singers you must *see* and *hear* performing before a live audience, whether in a living room, a pub, or concert stage, to appreciate the vitality, humor, sadness, anger, and so on inherent in their performance.

The strength of modern folk collecting is that it moves beyond words and notes and attends to subcultural meanings, embracing elements of personality and style:

> How else account for Alan Lomax's tale of how city children listening to an Aunt Molly Jackson program likened her singing to a cat's yowling, whereas children in Enid, Oklahoma, wrote that it was the most beautiful music they had ever heard on the air? As Charles Seeger has pointed out, a singing style "consists of a complex of dispositions, capacities, and habits build into the bodily processes and personality of the individual carrier of a song tradition when he is very young by the social and cultural environment into which he is born and by which he is nurtured" [Wilgus, 1959, p. 341].

The critics of more traditional evaluation approaches make a similar argument. Test scores and answers to questionnaires simply cannot convey the subtleties, complexities, and idiosyncracies of educational programs. Instead, the richness of the program must be captured and described to participants in a way that helps them better understand the program and their place in it.

Communication Problems in Collecting

A by-product of the wealth of data attended to both by the modern folksong collector and the naturalistic evaluator is a range of communication problems. The printed word often is not enough to convey such richness and complexity; recordings or videotapes of actual performances are often much more powerful modes of communicating. And folk collectors, like evaluators, when they are forced to use the printed word, face a serious translation problem.

The famous team of Iona and Peter Opie, who specialized in the lore, language, and games of school children, describe this language problem in their own field of collecting when they commented on Norman Douglas' book on London Street Games, published in 1916:

> Written by a fastidious literary craftsman and based on genuine research amongst young cockneys, it records the secret joys of the gutter in a finely printed limited edition of the book . . . which

might have become a success if it had not been almost incomprehensible to anyone but a street Arab. It is a skillful prose-poem fashioned out of sayings and terminology of Douglas' urchin friends; and we must admit that it was only after several years, when we ourselves had become familiar with the argot which the kids still speak in London's alleyways and tenement courts, that we appreciate the book's finer points [Opie & Opie, 1959, p. v].

How many "limited edition" evaluation reports are incomprehensible to anyone but an evaluation "Arab"? Incidentally, before leaving the Opies we should point out that their work documents the strong oral tradition that exists among school children. Tapping this tradition could tell an evaluator much about the feelings of children toward their school, specific teachers, unpopular children, examinations, discipline, tardiness, and so forth.

A folk collector, reporting his findings, may do so in a way that reflects how fully he wishes to convey his collecting experience. He may present an oral or written account, a sound recording or perhaps a video sound recording. One mode will capture more adequately than another the original experience. The collector too, must weigh the implications of using the various recording techniques in the field setting. He must ask such questions as how intrusive a factor the introduction of all video recording equipment may be, especially when it is a novelty in the field setting. We shall address the reactivity factor again later, but here note that specifically in relation to choosing an appropriate reporting technique the collector must weigh the reactivity factor against the report adequacy factor. It is not sufficient to address only the reactivity of the individual performer. To illustrate this point, one frequently finds in a relaxed setting, the folk custom of a person handclasping a folksinger and rhythmically guiding the singer's expression in performance. Yet, in video recording, where the focus on individual performance is enhanced, this fascinating audience interaction is often lost. The collector must weigh the implications of various modes of recording on various modes of reporting and on the total context of the situation. Evaluators, too, share this concern for careful judgment in the relationship between recording, reporting, and reactivity.

One notes too that folk collectors meet a differential set of needs in those who attend to their work. A video recording may indeed convey one's experience most adequately to the public. On the other hand, professional folksingers who wish to include one of the collector's songs in their repertoire will more likely appreciate the words and the music score, while a fellow collector may only attend to a single stanza previously unrecorded, or to the scholarly discussion of sources in oral tradition. The responsibility of attending to a variety of audience needs in evaluation reports is a well established concern in the evaluation field.

Another aspect of reporting shared by both collectors and evaluators deals with the political constraints that lead them to color or modify their presentations. This pressure can come from ethical, cultural, social, financial, and future prospect considerations. Lloyd (1967) asks the question: "Why did the English collectors habitually modify the texts of erotic songs before publishing them?"

> Sometimes they want to protect polite people from being offended by the notions of rougher men and women. Then, too, working without support or subsidy they had to rely on popular publications and concert performance if they were to get even a meagre financial return for their labours in the field . . . most important, the need to tread carefully in the presence of the Establishment, if one was going to get folksong accepted officially and returned to the mass of people [p. 184].

Societal changes have eased the climate of constraints on reporting erotic songs for collectors. However, in the case of evaluators, while the concerns are far from erotic, the constraints on reporting constitute one of the major difficulties in an increasingly commercial and political enterprise.

Different World Views in Collecting

As the brief description of the four stages of collecting described above illustrates, the background and world view that the collector (evaluator) brings to the task colors not only what is collected (evaluated), but what is done with the raw material collected. Some collectors, like evaluators, deplored a lack of uniformity in their data, and felt that there had to be some means of getting at the tune unhampered by individual idiosyncrasies (Hugill, 1969; Green, 1970). Thus, a collector like Sir Richard Runciman Terry, who worked in the 1920s, is described by Hugill (1969) as working "patiently at sorting out from various deviations what, in his view, was the real tune of each shanty which he then transcribed on paper forever" (p. 110). These collectors (evaluators) are "not concerned with specific performances of an air, so much as with an ideal or standardized form" (Green, 1970, p. xii).

The "pen and ink" folk collector, with the goal of standardized folk-music and folklore, came out of a more literary, classical music experience without the "benefit of the cottage kitchen, hop field or four-ale bar" (Lloyd, 1967, p. 58) and consequently failed to appreciate, as do the more recent school of collectors (evaluators), that the song (educational program) cannot be separated from the singer (teacher) and context (classroom). Modern collectors are well aware that it is precisely in variation that the power of the song and singer lay:

> A song that lives by word of mouth is always to some extent in a state of flux. There is no printed notation to which it can be referred and by means of which it can be stereotyped. Thus in the nature of things there can be no single or correct version. Some versions are more pleasing than others, and that is all we can say. Each singer will repeat the song substantially as he learned it, but nearly always he will make slight variations which he introduces more or less unself-consciously. Incidentally, he will always maintain that his is the "correct" version, even though he may never sing the tune twice in exactly the same way [Karpeles, 1973, p. 5].

This sort of variation is also true of most educational programs. The effort in the sixties to build "teacher proof" materials that would reduce variation among teachers was doomed to failure. Often there is as much variation between classrooms following the identical educational programs as there is between different programs. The naturalistic evaluator tries to capture the richness of this variation rather than trying to reduce performance to standardized form. A. L. Lloyd (1967) comments on the subtle nature of variation, and the difficulty many collectors had in capturing it:

> The singer would convey the mood of the song by a small alteration of pace, a slight change of vocal timbre, an almost imperceptible pressing or lightening of rhythm, and by nuances of ornament that our folklorists, with the exception of Percy Granger, have consistently neglected in their transcriptions; more's the pity [p. 78].

Lloyd captures the dichotomy between the two world views:

> One afternoon in a sombre room of the Ethnographical Museum in Budapest a well-known folklorist, colleague of Bartok and Kodaly,

played his visitor a recording of a Csagno-Magyar ballad singer from Moldavia. Her song was tragic and she performed it with a fine contained passion, in a way that showed she was totally immersed in the sense of the song. The visitor remarked on the poignant quality of the rendition and the learned professor gave him a sharp look and said: "Surely by now you know that the sound of folkmusic is meaningless? It's not until we have it down in precise notation and can see what's happening inside the mould of the melody that it comes to have any significance at all." For him, what the song meant to the singer was irrelevant; that it brought her almost to tears was a detail not worth inquiring into; the woman was a mere accessory and her heart, mind, voice were superfluities, unnecessary to take into account; pitch and duration were all that mattered. He was a good man for Kelvin's principle: What we measure can be understood [p. 17].

This episode is a perfect metaphor for the evaluator who tries to reduce everything to numbers for statistical analysis by computer. Part of the problem is that the school of collectors (evaluators) who emphasize the pen and ink, standardized (output, objective) approach to collecting (evaluating) did so because of their background and training. They were:

often thrown into confusion, faced with tonal language contrary to the one they had been taught; they imagined the singers were singing out of tune, and felt it their duty to "correct" the notations, for instance, to reduce them to standard major or minor shape, before putting them before the public. Cecil Sharp, Ralph Vaughan Williams and Percy Granger were among the first in England with a sensitive appreciation of the modal and rhythmic character of traditional song, and even they were baffled by some of its features [Lloyd, 1967, p. 33].

When faced with recordings of a live folksinger, the pen-and-ink standardizers were baffled and considered the singing odd. Lloyd's observations about the closed mentality of some collectors applies equally well to evaluators who are ill at ease with the naturalistic approach to evaluation.

They [folk melodies] are not oddities at all. We only think them so because we live in a literate civilization whose artistic conventions have become more and more inflexible and we ourselves have grown increasingly unreceptive towards other conventions [Lloyd, 1967, p. 33].

The concerns that Lloyd expressed in the world of folkmusic may be extended to the world of evaluation. The pursuit of excellence within any of the evaluation ideologies commands respect. However, the field of evaluation will suffer if it is marked by polarization, inflexibility, and an increasing unreceptiveness to the approaches to the task of evaluation that are other than one's own.

While there are important ideological differences among evaluators holding different conceptualizations of evaluation, there are also important differences among those who purport to hold the same conceptualization of evaluation. Here again we can explore folksong collecting as a metaphor for the variety of approaches within a single conceptualization of evaluation. Folksong and folklore collecting is a discipline that is as purely naturalistic as any, yet there are various approaches to the field. One scholar has described seven approaches and the only thing they share in common is that they are concerned in some way with the materials of the oral tradition (Goldstein, 1964). How the folk collector deals with materials, in fact what materials are collected in the first instance, will depend on whether the collector is interested in a comparative analysis, in the literary aesthetics, or in the social psychological meaning of the data. In short, the collector (evaluator) brings the totality of personal history and background specialization to the work. One example from Goldstein (1964) should suffice:

> The theory of folklore which treated the materials as survivals resulted in the collection of great masses of materials removed from their context and catalogued for the purpose of comparison and identification. Similarly, a theory of folklore that treats the materials as oral forms will result in the statement of the problem leading to the collection of materials in their fullest social and physical context [p. 18].

Goldstein sums up the problem of various approaches to collecting (evaluating) very nicely when he writes:

> The validity of either of these approaches is beside the point. What is significant is that though the methods and the kinds of materials collected differ, the differences were traceable to the body of theory which inspired the collector. Both types of collector started with problems framed in terms of their respective schools of thought, and both obtained the data considered relative to the solution of those problems. Theory is sometimes condemned by the unenlightened as

involving "preconceived ideas." It involves rather preconceived problems [Goldstein, 1964, p. 15].

The evaluator interested in naturalistic inquiry needs to be aware of the
various approaches within that mode. When working within the broad
label of naturalistic inquiry, the evaluator needs to make explicit the
theory or framework that will guide definition of the evaluation problem
and the material sought to address the problem.

Finally, it is to be noted that some collectors are ill at ease with the
place of intuition in collecting. But intuition can play an important part in
both collecting and evaluating:

> So that just as a numismatist can tell true coins from false by their
> rough or soapy feel, the folklore specialist may "instinctively" tell
> the authentic folk creation from, say, the vaudeville song sung in the
> same company [Lloyd, 1967, p. 15].

Intuition emerges from the collector's personal history, training, world
view, and practical experience. It also can be a treasure in the storehouse
of the evaluator.

Differences Between the World View of the Collector and the Singer

Part of the difficulty in folksong collecting—as in evaluation—is that the
collector often fails to appreciate the world view of his informants. In fact
the two world views can be not only antithetical but at times antipathetic.
This antipathy can often result in an unpleasantly condescending attitude
toward the informant (Green, 1970). For example, Kidson apologizes for
the texts, whose absurdities, he implies, are excused by the beauty of the
airs, and points out that they were meant to satisfy the tastes of a "simple
audience" (Green, 1970). One commentator describes this antipathy as
follows:

> The discipline of folklore has suffered much from the ideas of
> scholars who at heart dislike the materials they are working with
> almost as much as they dislike the bearers of that material whom, if
> ever they meet them, they find disconcerting, baffling, embarrassing
> [Lloyd, 1967, p. 58].

This antipathy can be a two-way street:

> Commonly, the bourgeois collector anticipates deviousness in the countryman's mind, and the countryman suspects the motives of the bourgeois (how often, in prewar Eastern Europe, the folklorist was taken for a tax-inspector in disguise!). Such tenuous contact, lack of mutual confidence, downright misunderstanding, has severely restricted folklore study in the past and inhibited the search into such matters as the origin of songs [Lloyd, 1967, p. 18].

Often the collector and singer "tended to be rather less than candid because, however civil, each approached the other gingerly across a social chasm" (Lloyd, 1967, p. 18). Lloyd gives the following examples of this chasm when he describes the activities of Miss Laura Smith who in the 1880s visited Tyneside boarding houses in search of sailors' songs:

> Her harvest was scanty and pallid, partly because, as Captain Whall says: "If a lady goes around sailors' boarding houses and attempts to copy down the words and music of Shanties from the men, she is bound to fail. First, sailors are shy with ladies. Second, few of the songs have words which a seaman would care to sing to a lady in cold blood" [p. 18].

Lloyd continues:

> But the difficulty is not so much a matter of sex as that of social difference. Old Mr. Grantham, the Sussex carter "knew a many songs which he wouldn't even sing to a gentleman," saying: "They be outway rude" [p. 18].

There is a remarkable similarity between Lloyd's description of the social chasm between collector and singer and the ideological chasm that Jackson (1968) argues exists between the objective/testing mentality of the evaluator and the softer service-oriented world view of the classroom teacher. The differences Jackson describes are ideological and that chasm is as difficult to bridge as is a social one. This is not to say that there are not social chasms between evaluators and the subjects of the evaluation. An evaluation of parental participation in a Title I program is an obvious case in point. There are many chasms between evaluators and the various publics they wish to serve.

The establishment and maintenance of rapport (which will be addressed later) is partly a function of the collector's (evaluator's) conscious recognition when this chasm between world views arises. It need not always arise. Building rapport across this chasm when it does arise is not an easy task. It calls for:

> sympathy without condescension and an ability to step over the gulfs separating class from class, both qualities in short supply among scholars though some improvement shows [Lloyd, 1967, p. 17].

Often the chasm can only be bridged by building up a personal bond between the collector (evaluator) and his informants, which can lead to a diminution of detachment or objectivity.

> But the scientific collector is also a human being and his greatest value to his discipline is the fact that he is not an electronic computer which classifies and categorizes and comes up with nonhuman (and frequently anti-human) responses and solutions. The collector feels and senses things, and this is as important as seeing and reporting only facts. Because of his scientific training he is able to separate the facts from his feelings when his analysis calls for that, or to mix them in various proportions when that is called for, and is thereby enabled to solve the essentially human problems involved in the process of folklore. Nor should the scientific collector ever feel that he has to deny (even to himself) the love and high regard which he has for his informants as friends and people [Goldstein, 1964, p. 165].

This leads however to another consideration in folksong collecting and naturalistic inquiry in evaluation, namely reactivity.

Reactivity in Folksong Collecting

In describing naturalistic inquiry Guba (1978) points out that one of its hallmarks is that neither dependent nor independent variables are manipulated by the investigator. However, while naturalistic inquiry evaluation eschews each manipulation, it cannot avoid another form of reactivity, namely that induced by the very presence of the evaluator. This type of reactivity is a well recognized phenomenon in folksong collecting.

> The collector must also be aware of a fundamental fact: his very presence changes to some degree every situation in which he partici-

pates. Though full awareness of this fact will assist the collector in the objective evaluation of his data, it does not enable him to erase it as a factor. He participates as an outsider, which fact is an important element in interactive relationships with his informants. To obtain total naturalness in any social situation, the collector would be forced to remove himself wholly from the situation, thereby making it impossible for him to participate, observe, or enquire. Even an experienced collector, utilizing the full range of techniques at his command, can at best only minimize his own effect on the situation [Goldstein, 1964, p. 73].

When songs are collected in a natural context (music sessions, baptisms, wakes, weddings, or at a specific time of the year, e.g., Christmas, May Day), the presence of the collector can alter the performance in subtle ways. Reactivity can be kept to a minimum if one has taken the time to establish proper rapport and is unobtrusive in one's recording. But collectors often cannot wait for natural contexts and are forced to set up artificial or induced contexts. For example, Tom Munnelly found Mr. Horan at his farmhouse during the afternoon and took him to a nearby pub for the recording session. It was the middle of the day, it was not a real session, there were only a handful of customers present, and there had not been time to establish a deep rapport. This artificial situation is quite different than that experienced by Kennedy collecting from Sarah Makem, who could "best remember the old songs when she was working and it meant following her around with the microphone, verse by verse, from the kitchen sink to the kitchen range and back to the sink again" (Kennedy, 1974, p. 1). Both situations were reactive but the former was much more artificial than the latter. Incidentally, both resulted in the collection of a beautiful song, "Lord Thomas and Fair Elinor" from Mr. Horan and "As I Roved Out" (among others) from Mrs. Makem.

Goldstein (1964) gives us an excellent example of how reactivity works in naturalistic inquiry. It is an example that has direct transfer to evaluators interested in observing and recording the work and dialogue of teachers. He writes:

One of my Scots informants was a fine stylist both as a singer and as a storyteller. In natural contexts her performances never failed to hold her audiences spellbound. When performing in the artificial collector-informant context, she was able to retain a high degree of artistry in singing, but became a commonplace or even poor performer of tales. But even her song performances in the artificial context were not the same order as her natural context performance of the same pieces. Her performance in the artificial context involved slower tempos and highly dramatic hand and body gestures and facial expressions, none of which were present to the same degree in her natural context performances. When asked to explain the differences in her performance style, she stated that since there was going to be a permanent record made of her performance, she wanted to show herself at her best; and to her, her best meant "hamming-up" the performance. In the case of storytelling the difference was even more marked. During formal collector-informant sessions she became overly careful of her enunciation and grammar, resulting in stammering and a visible degree of nervousness with a concomitant loss of effectiveness in her storytelling art. To have described her performance styles on the basis of the observations made in an artificial context would have been ridiculous, as well as doing an injustice to her great talents [p. 87].

This is also an example of the naturalistic model of inquiry having its own set of methodological problems as complex and as tough to resolve as those associated with the experimental model. Untrained or naive evaluators who wish to employ naturalistic methods must be aware of the problems endemic to this mode of inquiry if their data are to be valid and reliable in terms of the problem of investigation. But then Denny, Guba, Stake, and others never promised evaluators a rose garden.

Creativity: Collecting and Evaluating

If one is to anticipate that folksong collecting is to be a useful metaphor for evaluation, it seems important to attend to their respective relationships to the folksinger on the one hand and the teacher on the other. When we find that there are striking parallels between the folksinger and the teacher, it suggests an added and important dimension to the metaphor. There is an important aspect of creative performance to which both collector and evaluator must attend. Both the folksinger and the teacher engage in a dialectic between the music or the curriculum convention on the one hand and an individual personal interpretation and style on the other. A. L. Lloyd (1967) describes this dialectic from the folksinger's point of view. Lloyd uses the specialized terminology of *maqam:*

which is but a tune pattern, a melody formula, based on one or other modal scale and having certain stereotyped, more or less obligatory moments and passages, but otherwise allowing great freedom of treatment. In short, the *maqam* is a kind of skeleton or, better, scaffolding of melody which the musician, observing certain rules, is able to fill in for himself according to his fantasy and the mood of the moment. For westerners, the clearest, most familiar example of the maqam principle is provided by the Blues, always the same yet always different, a well-known, well-worn frame apt for any extemporization, baffling to strangers, and listened to by fans not simply as a tune but as a traditional exercise at once achingly familiar and arrestingly fresh. The Blues is an extreme example, but in some measure all folk tunes in the natural state, unfixed by print or other control, nourished by constant variation, having no single "authentic" form but somewhat altering from singer to singer and even from verse to verse, are made on the maqam principle, with its balance of constraint with freedom, fixed model with fluid treatment, communal taste with individual fantasy, traditional constancy with novel creative moments, sameness with difference [p. 63].

Teaching, like folksinging or jazz, has its obligatory moments and passages, its well established skeletal frame, around which the teacher, as long as certain rules are observed, is free to extemporize and create. It is precisely this "maqam" of teaching that makes the art of classroom observation a worthwhile exercise. However, appreciative observation and reporting demands familiarity with the creative possibilities in the interaction between the maqam (curriculum) and the singer (teacher). Phil Jackson (1968) and Terry Denny (1978), among others, describe the limitations of preordained observational instruments that perhaps can capture the obligatory conventions and form of the curriculum (maqam) but that fail completely to capture the constant variation and fluency of teaching. How evaluators can best capture and convey such variations is at present not at all clear. Certainly Denny's storytelling is an effort in the right direction.

Teaching, like folksinging, is a performance and the evaluator (collector) is often interested in variations between performances and performers. A. L. Lloyd (1967) puts it nicely:

The idea that somehow all folkmusic performers are on the same footing, and that folkmusic is something produced as naturally as a bird sings on the bough, is a myth. Traditional performers, no less than the performers of fine art and music, show varying degrees of skill, talent, taste, and imagination. Some are expert musical hands and acknowledged as such by their neighbors, while others are mere novices nobody wants to listen to [p. 64].

Extending this idea to the community of teachers throws light on the problem of treatment or curriculum implementation that is a particular concern of evaluation. Consider this description again from A. L. Lloyd (1967).

> It is not only in the inventive performance of the individual folk-singer that the "maqam spirit" shows itself, it is also in the way the collective, the community, works on the song.
>
> But social determinism is not the only factor in the life of the song because after it has come into being, a multitude of other singers are likely to get to work on it, altering it about, decomposing and recomposing it, producing sometimes richer, sometimes poorer versions of the original; now deepening the emotional and ideological content, now making it more shallow; now bringing the tune into sad decay, now recreating and renewing it happily. In a flourishing folk tradition, work on an already-created song never ceases [p. 65].

Teachers, in dealing with a curriculum, like a singer with a song, are constantly recomposing, adapting, changing the material, processes and even content they receive from the curriculum developer. Differences between "master" teachers covering the same material can be as striking as differences between a Donegal and a Sligo fiddler's treatment of "Scatter the Mud." Karpeles (1973) reminds us of how the process works in the world of folkmusic:

> One has to remember that the folksinger is not tied to the printed page and so it is the idea of tune, its general shape and feeling, that he wants and not a series of fixed notes. And it is the same with the words. The singer will not find it necessary to tell the story word for word as he got it, provided that he gives the sense of it. It is the small changes made by the singer that gradually lead to development and the emergence of new forms [p. 67].

The study of the process of adaptation, as in the case of collectors, is a rich one for evaluators to explore and understand. This process of adaptation can enrich the curriculum or impoverish it.

Differences Between Folk Collecting and Educational Evaluation

If the folk collector metaphor for evaluation is to be usefully explored, one must also acknowledge its limitation. While an evaluator may learn from the tradition of the folk collector, there are important differences in the history and purpose of their respective enterprises. To ignore such differences could lead to an unrealistic estimation of the power of the folksong metaphor. While differences alert us to difficulties of translation from one field experience to the other, they may also raise questions of alternative possible directions in educational evaluation studies.

The Place of the Government in Collecting and Evaluation

The history of folk collecting has a rather charismatic vocational character. One senses that folk collectors do what they are born to do, with little room for compromise with popular demand and the marketplace of mass culture. Their charisma is exercised, often with little regard from society, in a lifestyle of willing vagrancy. The state has played a small part and one that, of its nature, at the same time differs from its role in the history of evaluation. State-commissioned folk collectors are recognized by the state for their personal gifts and joy in the work, regardless of its hardships. For example, in the work of Tom Munnelly or of Seamis Ennis for the Irish Folklore Commission, it was never a matter of a tailor-made proposal but rather a recognition of personal genius that prompted the Commission to employ them. The piper, Ennis, armed with a phonograph, pen, and paper, cycled his way through the villages of Ireland and Scotland before the war. He lives his latter days in a humble simplicity, while all around him, the modern record industry broadcasts the music of a world he entered with great sensitivity and respect. The music he sought was neither highly valued nor commercial then, but his life's work was one for which he was uniquely gifted.

In contrast, state initiative in the 1960s has been vital to the growth and development of the evaluation field. Indeed, it has set the climate for what is, in effect, an evaluation industry. Characteristically, over the past two decades evaluation companies and centers within universities have engaged in the ritual of competing for public funds. This ritual helped enshrine the ideology and technology of practitioners, who initially and understandably held a quantitative orientation. The climate afforded by government concern for evaluation of its social programs and the money made available for that task, have colored the history and nature of educational evaluation. It has emerged as an industry. Within this framework evaluators are faced with the moral, legal, and ethical responsibilities to society, with the demands of clients, and with the enormous responsibilities for people and programs that may follow from their work. Other differences between the worlds of the folk collector and the evaluator are inherent in their respective tasks.

Differences in Collecting and Reporting Data

When a folk collector returns from a field trip with a set of songs, stories, or other folk artifacts, each item in the collected set will have a relative significance within the framework of the collector's approach. A song may have variant significance, depending on whether it is seen from an historical, a cultural anthropological, a musical, or a social psychological standpoint, and categorization of materials rests on the expressed theory, often quite personal and interdisciplinary, that underlies that collector's work. In collecting data and categorizing findings, the focus of the collector is on each item collected. It is not a matter of simple inventory, in which each piece of data is of equal value, but rather of a systematic categorization. The underlying theory that an individual collector brings to this work will be the basis of categorization. In that framework, some data may be very significant and most of it will likely be of little interest. However, each item of data will be attended to as a focal point of the collector's value judgment.

The evaluator's approach to the data is different. The evaluator's task is to evaluate programs, projects, or materials. In doing so, the evaluator must first decide which data to attend to. The folk collector, however, who enters a more clearly defined world of folklore does not have the problem of which data to select, but collects everything of interest in a less complex environment. Unlike the folk collector, the evaluator's primary interest is not the data per se or in categorizing it, but instead in a holistic evaluation of the merit or worth of the program. It is to facilitate this judgment that the evaluator collects data.

In evaluation field work, teachers and students who are the frequent sources of data, often perceive the evaluator as a threat. This is true in both positivistic and naturalistic approaches to evaluation. The real source of the threat is that the evaluator is perceived as a person who ultimately judges another's performance. The success of Jackson's (1968) sensitive approach to the classroom hinged on his establishing rapport over a period of time with the teachers and students who were the object of his study. In contrast, the singers or storytellers who provide the folk collector's data are more likely to establish instant rapport with someone who has travelled especially to hear them.

My name is Tom Munnelly. I'm from the Department of Education and I'm in the area collecting old songs and I was told that you were a man who had a few. "I have a mil'n," said the old man [Carroll, 1974, p. 7].

The evaluator must report his findings to an audience that includes the informants who are the likely subjects of either implicit or explicit judgments. The collector's findings, however, do not involve evaluative judgments and are shared with only a limited but appreciative audience of other folk enthusiasts. The folk collector's world generates its own sense of reward but audience and political considerations are not immediate. One's audience is posterity.

"Your immortality is assured," wrote Samuel Bronson to Tom Munnelly upon the inclusion of another of Tom's finds in Bronson's Tunes of the Child Ballads. Tom's comment: "I still can't afford a copy of the damn thing!" [Carroll, 1974, p. 6].

Differences in Degrees of Freedom

Further differences between the evaluator and the folk collector are reflected in the contractual nature of the evaluator's work and the contrasting freedom of the folk collector. Thus, Munnelly's successful trip to the North Kerry region arose from a "very scientific" rationale; in his own words: "The pin stuck in Castleisland" (Carroll, 1974, p. 6). The evaluator is bound geographically by terms of a contract.

While evaluators must carefully plan and schedule workdays in a team effort within the conditions usually of a proposal, the folk collectors may choose their own sites and, depending on circumstances, will adjust their schedule in the interest of fruitful field research. The informality of the work and the attendant hazards of the lifestyle are in sharp contrast to the organized approach of evaluators. The freedom of the folk collector has to be viewed against the background of separation from family, of willingness to forego good meals or to meet the social bind of endless drinks, the patience in what is often dull work, until the search proves fruitful. Most evaluators' orientation is usually otherwise.

Field Techniques

Folksong collecting and naturalistic evaluations both involve techniques of field research. The techniques developed in folksong collecting can, therefore, be usefully considered by the evaluator. In this section we shall outline the steps, procedures, and techniques of the folksong collector that we feel may help the evaluator attempting a naturalistic evaluation of an educational program. We are limited in the detail we can go into in describing procedures and techniques from folksong collecting by considerations of length. The reader who wishes to pursue further any of the points outlined below, is referred to Bartok (1976), Goldstein (1964), and Karpeles and Bake (1951).

Before beginning our outline, it should be pointed out that an evaluator who wishes to conduct naturalistic inquiries needs a multitude of skills and personal characteristics that are quite different from those of the more traditional evaluator. While we have addressed above the personality factors associated with the collector to set a context for the discussion of skills, Nettl's perception of the personal characteristics of a field worker merits quotation:

> Field work is a rather arduous and specialized task . . . it calls for a great deal of patience, understanding and an ability to relate to other people, resembling a combination of public relations and psychic intuition. Maturity is needed on the part of the researcher, who must often spend many long months away from his own culture, immersed in a foreign one [Nettl, 1976, p. 139].

The interdisciplinary skills needed for naturalistic inquiry were recognized decades ago by Bela Bartok (1976) who pointed out that "the ideal folklorist possesses an erudition that is virtually encyclopedic" (p. 10). He lists among the skills needed by the collector: knowledge of phonetics and linguistics, choreography, knowledge of folklore, sociological preparation, knowledge of history, and ability as an observer musician with a good ear. Having described this paragon, Bartok admits that "there has never been, and perhaps never will be, a collector embodying all those qualities, understandings, or experiences. It follows, therefore, that folkmusic research work cannot be carried out by one person at a level which would satisfy scientific requirements" (pp. 10-11). He goes on to urge team work in collecting, but then admits that financial and other considerations make this difficult if not impossible. It should be noted that the famous collectors have worked pretty much alone.

The skills that the naturalistic evaluator needs, like those of the collector, also cut across many disciplines: sociology, ethnography, anthropology, philosophy, history, not to mention the more traditional skills from educational research and testing. Like folksong collecting, naturalistic evaluations might be better served by a team approach, but here again, financial considerations can mitigate against this possibility.

The implications of the need for these multidisciplined skills for training naturalistic evaluators are interesting. For the naturalistic evaluator, who constitutionally prefers the artistic "maybe" of medicine to the "yes-no" aspect of engineering, the traditional courses and skills with a heavy emphasis on testing, research design statistics, computers, and the like are not enough. Instead, the would-be naturalistic evaluator needs training that is truly multidisciplined; and this has important implications for the design of programs aimed at preparing naturalistic evaluators and for the selection of students for such programs. Before turning to the steps, skills, and techniques from collecting, one additional caveat is in order.

Research in folkmusic is one aspect of research in ethnomusicology and both involve two very different types of activities—field work and laboratory work (Nettl, 1976). In what follows, we concentrate on the field work, or collecting, aspect of folkmusic research. We shall consider those steps and techniques from folksong collecting that we feel may be of benefit to the naturalistic evaluator. We shall discuss pre-field preparations, time considerations, the establishment and the maintenance of rapport, observation-collecting methods, and interview-collecting methods.

Pre-Field Preparations

The first step in folksong collecting is preparation for the field trip. In this pre-active stage, the collector first undertakes a thorough review of material collected to date, just as an evaluator, after first deciding whether or not to do the evaluation, might begin by reviewing other evaluations of similar programs. Such a review avoids duplication and gives the field worker some knowledge of existing material and what has already been done (Karpeles & Bake, 1951; Goldstein, 1964; Bartok, 1976).

Next, the field worker should study the history of the area and also learn as much as possible about local conditions. Goldstein (1964) suggests that the field worker begin this task by preparing a working bibliography of sources that may help shed light on the community to be visited. He suggests that the bibliography include any published data on collecting in that area, general studies of the area, travel guides, government publications (e.g., health, census, and economic reports), histories, newspapers, published diaries, novels or biographies based on local life, dialect dictionaries, and popular magazines. Many of these items will be available only on site, but this should not deter the field worker from preparing such a bibliography beforehand and obtaining as many items as possible to read before the field trip (Goldstein, 1964).

Next, the field worker should make preliminary contact with leading personalities in the community to help establish a relationship with key people there (Karpeles & Bake, 1951). The evaluator would have most likely already done this in deciding whether or not to contract for the evaluation in the first place.

Finally, collector-evaluators should equip themselves with notebooks, a diary, two tape recorders (in case one breaks down), tapes, batteries, and a camera. Some field workers may also need a video tape camera for their work (Goldstein, 1964; Karpeles & Bake, 1951).

Time Considerations

One aspect of preplanning the trip is a detailed consideration of the time commitments involved in the upcoming field work. In estimating time, folksong collectors take a number of factors into consideration. First, since collecting involves social interaction between people who initially are strangers, the collector must try and estimate the amount of time necessary to establish sufficient rapport. In collecting, this rapport must be not only at an individual level but also at the level of the entire community. The collector must be accepted within the community (Goldstein, 1964). Second, the field worker must budget time to get away from the community for rest and to digest the material gathered. Third, in trying to calculate the time needed in the field, the experience of the collector is an important variable (Goldstein, 1964).

There are also factors involving the actual field site that can impinge on time. If the community is in a state of flux or in the midst of considerable controversy, or if the population from which interviews are sought is large and/or heterogeneous and spread over a wide area, then a longer stay is indicated (Goldstein, 1964).

In terms of evaluation, these time considerations must be taken into account in determining whether or not to do the evaluation and, if the decision is to go ahead, then in building a budget to accompany the contract.

Establishing and Maintaining Rapport

Perhaps the most essential, yet the most difficult aspect of collecting and of any field-based inquiry, is the establishment and maintenance of rapport. Bartok (1976) found that the "folk" from whom he wished to collect were most suspicious of strangers knocking on their doors. Attempts to explain his reason for collecting were hard for the "folk" to swallow. Most could not understand why a stranger would give up the comforts of home to collect their songs. Bartok, in 1970, was seen as a tax collector and quickly recognized that he could not obtain what he wanted by commanding in the manner of a country squire.

Good advice for the naturalistic evaluator! Evaluations often are perceived by those affected by them as threats, the external evaluator as an outsider, an expert, a snoop in the employ of the superintendent or some external agency. The evaluator's first job then is overcoming this suspicion and obtaining, and maintaining, the trust of those from whom information is to be obtained.

How does one go about establishing the rapport that all agree is absolutely essential to the whole enterprise? Establishment of rapport is, to a very great extent, dependent on the personalities involved, but there are a few general rules (Goldstein, 1964). First, the collector cannot show, or indeed feel, any superiority over the informants:

> To make people sing, one must not act from above as a representative of erudition, but as one who himself enjoys singing simple songs and is delighted to chat about things belonging to the interest of the country people [Karpeles & Bake, 1951, p. 7].

Second, the collector must be a patient person. The collector must adjust the pace to that of the informants. In many cases, the informant must engage the collector in prolonged conversation about matters not germane to the collector. This is often the informant's way of sizing up the collector. Such conversation may be quite time-consuming but in the end may pay handsome dividends (Goldstein, 1964). Further, the collector should:

> guard against impatience and thinking that the informant is dull-witted because he does not respond quickly to . . . interrogation. His mental equipment may be just as good as the collector's but it works differently, and your mode of expression may be strange to him as his is to you [Karpeles & Bake, 1951, p. 7].

Third, the collector must be able to ensure the informants that any information or material they provide will be treated with confidentiality and will not be used in a way that is harmful to the person. Goldstein (1964) comments on this problem:

> While scientific honesty and objectivity demand that he omits no pertinent data, moral courtesy demands that he not identify his

informants with certain data. The collector must solve the dilemma
by means which will satisfy both his scientific objectives and his
humanistic ethics [p. 58].

Fourth, the collector must not overtax the informant. In the spell of
the collection session, the informant may not feel the pressure but may
look on the experience later as exhausting, and therefore be unwilling to
cooperate further with such an inconsiderate collector (Goldstein, 1964).
Naturalistic evaluators must be greater respecters of persons, not only for
personal moral reasons but because the profession itself has a right to
anticipate such sensitivity from individual evaluators.

Fifth, one way of establishing rapport is by helping the informant in
some job, or in the case of the collector, giving the informant a song.
Denny (1978), in his evaluation field work, has done, among other jobs,
voluntary work, baby sitting, automobile repairing, carrying boxes, instal-
ling overhead projector bulbs, assisting at Mass, and editing a term paper.

Sixth, the field worker, by virtue of living in the community, becomes
like the natives, involved in many community activities. The collector
must find housing, transportation, food, fuel, medical services, and so on.
In carrying out all of these daily, often mundane, activities the field
worker can either build and maintain rapport or destroy it. Goldstein
reports on the information he gathered from the milkman, grocer, butcher,
bus collector, doctor. He also reports that his wife and children were
important in building rapport. His wife's socializing with local women
opened a host of social invitations. His children helped arrange meetings
with their friends' parents. Local public entertainment activities, dances,
amateur nights, and theater musicals were also an excellent occasion for
building and maintaining rapport.

Seventh, the collector can use the local media for assistance in spread-
ing the word about the project, easing his acceptance into the community
and letting potential informants know how to get in contact. The collector
can be interviewed by the news and radio/TV reporters; appear on local
radio and TV shows; write an article for the local newspapers, and so on.
Goldstein (1964) warns that this approach will bring many, many inquiries
and the collector must be prepared to answer each and every one. Collectors should exercise great prudence in selecting this option, since they
could easily be inundated with replies, but also such coverage runs risks of
grave distortion of the purposes of the enterprise.

As we noted earlier, such immersion in the community is reactive and
can take a psychic toll on the collector. Goldstein (1964) offers two

factors to keep in mind when determining the degree to which the collector should participate in community activities:

(1) Active participation enables him to assuage suspicion, establish rapport, and enhance the naturalness of his position in the community, and (2) participation opens new avenues to understanding his informants and the community, and should lead to the collection of more and better data to be used in problem solution [p. 76].

The naturalistic evaluator must balance budget considerations against the benefit associated with immersing oneself in the community. However the trade-off is made, the naturalistic evaluator must then solve the problem of establishing and maintaining rapport. This job is not made easier by the fact that a report on the object of the evaluation will eventually be submitted to the contractor. The folksong collector does not have this factor to deal with.

Observation Collecting Methods

Much of the data field workers gather is through their own observation of events. Goldstein (1964) distinguishes between two types of observers: the active participant observer, and the onlooker or inactive participant. The advantage participant observers have is that they are accepted as equals in the situation and therefore can study the situation in as natural and unaffected a state as possible. However, participant observers cannot take notes and must trust to memory what was seen until it can be recorded after the event. In any case, the ability of the collector or the evaluator to be a participant observer is extremely rare (Goldstein, 1964).

The onlooker observer is more often the role of the collector or evaluator. Here the collector must remain on the fringe and take notes or record the event. This role, of course, is reactive and as we noted earlier, can change the performance of the participants. What should the observers look for and note in addition to the actual performance and interaction between participants they are recording? Goldstein (1964) and Karpeles and Bake (1951) recommend that the following items be recorded:

- date, place, time, and duration of the event;
- names of the participants;
- characteristics of the participants (e.g., age, occupation, marital status, relationships, education, general appearance, dress);
- physical setting (e.g., location, size, shape of room, furniture, temperature, unusual sounds, odors, where people sit/stand);

- interaction between participants;
- sentiments expressed both verbally and nonverbally;
- observer's role in the context.

Goldstein (1964) suggests that whenever possible, the collector should record observations on the spot. When this is not possible because it disturbs the situation, then recording of the event should take place immediately after. Goldstein (1964) also cautions the collector—and this piece of advice is also directly pertinent to the evaluator—against confusing observation with interpretation:

> Since a collector is incapable of reporting everything that he has seen, what he actually reports is a selection (consciously or unconsciously made) of the observable phenomena. Selection is, in itself, a factor of interpretation; and when one adds to this the bias which may result from the collector's temperament and outlook, among other unmeasurable factors which may crucially influence selection, one becomes aware of the immense problem in trying to distinguish between interpretation and observation [p. 95].

Goldstein reminds the collector that the very awareness of the problem helps to minimize it, but that the collector must reread first drafts of observation reports with an eye toward separating observation from interpretation.

Interviewing Methods

One of the principal tools of the collector is the interview, which is used to obtain information on the personal history of informants, knowledge of the feeling evoked by materials and the meanings they have for informants, how the material was acquired, and the extent of the informant's repertoire (Goldstein, 1964). Interview techniques are well documented elsewhere and we, therefore, will not outline such techniques here. However, a few pointers from collectors are apropos.

First, the collector must learn not to ask leading or direct questions. Leading questions invite the answer thought to best please the collector; direct questions are an invitation to a distorted answer (Karpeles & Bake, 1951; Goldstein, 1964). Second, the collector is advised to interrupt as little as possible. Third, the collector should not be afraid of long pauses in the conversation, as silence is often a prelude to valuable information (Karpeles & Bake, 1951). Fourth, the collector must be able to hide surprise, conceal boredom, and be able to ask questions conversationally, preferably without the aid of the interview schedule (Goldstein, 1964). Fifth, the interview, while basically verbal, is also an occasion for obtaining information about feelings, attitudes, and the like that cannot be easily verbalized and can only be inferred from observations gained during the interview. Finally, the collector must always be aware that "the evasiveness of an informant or the incompleteness or inaccuracy of his/her information will usually vary inversely with the degree of rapport which has been established" (Goldstein, 1964, p. 116).

Collectors often are concerned about the reliability of the information they have garnered from the interview. Further, collectors are interested in variations in a song from one rendition to another by the same singer, and variations in the song that exist between singers. The interest in variations is more than a matter of reliability in the measurement sense; often the differences are interesting in and of themselves. Differences between informants tell us the features of the material that are significant and meaningful, and those that are not, to the informants (Nettl, 1976). Hence collectors recommend that pieces of information gathered in one interview be checked through interviews with other sources. To check for variants in a song, the collector will often ask the singer to sing the song again after a lapse of several days; the collector might record the song sung by a second or possibly a third singer; the collector might record the song from singers of different ages or sex; finally, the collector may try to record the song after a long time period has elapsed (Bartok, 1976).

A final piece of advice from the collector: As soon as possible after the interview, transcribe the material; the greater the time delay between sessions and the transcription, the greater the loss of memory. Once the material is transcribed safely, copies should be made of all recordings, notes, and interviews made in the field (Goldstein, 1964).

Conclusion

Only a moribund tradition is *dominated* by the past; a living tradition is constantly sprouting new leaves on old wood and sometimes quite suddenly the bush is ablaze with blossoms of a novel shade.

Let us not be deceived by that vegetable metaphor. New songs do not just arise inevitably in the natural course of events; they are a product of work, of the imaginative efforts of individuals, farmhands, factory-hands, sensitive to the ways and conditions of the life they share with their neighbours [Lloyd, 1967, p. 68].

In less than two decades, the field of educational evaluation has grown enormously in sophistication. The body of literature that has emerged is symbolic of this growth. In the last few years, evaluators have been seen to offer new perspectives on the evaluation enterprise. As part of a movement of exploring metaphors offered by other disciplines, we have examined the heuristic possibilities that one old naturalistic discipline—folksong collecting—offers as a metaphor for evaluation. In this effort we found that there were four ways in which the metaphor seemed to work: first, in illuminating the school of naturalistic evaluation; second, in spotlighting some of the tensions between the positivistic and phenomenological schools within the field; third, in describing aspects of the field as a whole; and finally, in suggesting practical techniques for use in field work.

Rich as the evaluation field may be, there is a present danger of polarization between the positivistic and naturalistic practitioners. Perhaps it is a surprise to learn that in a field as purely naturalistic as is folksong collecting, there were Kelvinites and schools of thought inflexible and unreceptive to others. In both fields, the roots of the differences are not methodological but ideological. Deeply held beliefs are not easily compromised.

In the positivistic evaluator's approach there is a danger of ignoring important realities that simply cannot be quantified just as there is a danger in the naturalistic evaluator's approach of drifting into ritualism, codifying the story, and settling on inadequate ways of understanding a situation. In both cases, evaluators, if not careful, could become a priest class that gives warning and advice, but does not take it; a class that preaches on the one hand in the name of science and on the other through charismatic personality.

A song that has passed into the oral tradition of the American labor movement may provide us with an appropriate slogan in integrating the diversity of concerns in program evaluation. The song, "Bread and Roses" emerged from the great Lawrence mill strikes of 1912, when, in response to a Massachusetts law reducing working hours of women and children from 56 to 54 hours a week, the mill owners cut wages and speeded up the machines. The workers struck. In the bitter climate that followed, women were seen carrying signs that read "We want bread—and roses too." Inspired by this sign, James Oppenheim wrote a poem, later set to music by Martha Coleman, in which he wrote: "Hearts starve as well as bodies; Give us bread, but give us roses" (Sing Out, 1976, p. 9). As evaluation has developed as a field, the quantitative dimension assumes the essential characteristic of the bread; the qualitative approach speaks more of the rose. We want bread—and roses too.

Always in a young discipline like evaluation, there is a danger of attending only to the experiences and technologies of its short history. Loren Eiseley (1970) warns of the danger of being isolated in the present:

> The owl, Minerva's symbol of wisdom, is able to turn its head through an angle of one hundred and eighty degrees. It can be not visually anticipatory alone, it can look directly backward. Perhaps it is the lack of this ability that gives modern man and his children a slightly inhuman case of countenance [p. 85].

Looking behind, it is open to the treasury of the past. Looking ahead, the owl is able to envision the future and the implications both of the present for that future and of an envisioned future for the present. In exploring folksong collecting as a metaphor for evaluation, we have looked behind into the treasury of human endeavor. In urging a concern for unity across the diversity that marks the field, we look ahead.

References

Bartok, B. *Essays* (Suchoff, Ed.). London: Faber & Faber, 1976.

Bread and roses: Heritage U.S.A. *Sing Out! The Folksong Magazine,* 1976, 25 (1) 8-9.

Breathnch, B. *Folk music and dances of Ireland.* Dublin: Browne & Nolan, 1971.

Carroll, P. 200 feet of posterity. *Folk Review,* 1974, 4(2), 6-8.

Cooper, B. *A song for every season.* London: Heineman, 1971.

Demeny, J. (Ed.). *Bela Bartok letters.* New York: St. Martins, 1971.

Denny, T. Story telling and educational understanding. Occasional Paper No. 12. Western Michigan University Evaluation Center, Kalamazoo, Michigan, 1978.

Douglas, N. *London street games.* Privately printed, 1916.

Eiseley, L. *The invisible pyramid.* New York: Scribner, 1970.

Eisner, E. W. *The design and evaluation of educational programs.* New York: Macmillan, in press.

Goldstein, K. S. *A guide for field workers in folklore.* Preface by Hamish Henderson. Hatboro, PA: Folklore Associates for the American Folklore Society, 1964.

Green, A. E. Foreword. In F. Kidson, *Traditional tunes.* Yorkshire, England: S. R. Publishers, 1970.

Guba, E. G. Toward a methodology of naturalistic inquiry in educational evaluation. *CSE Monograph Series in Evaluation,* 1978, 8.

Henderson, H. Preface. In K. S. Goldstein, *A guide for field workers in folklore.* Hatboro, Pa: Folklore Associates for the American Folklore Society, 1964.

Hugill, S. *Shanties and sailors' songs.* New York: Praeger, 1969.

Jackson, P. W. *Life in classrooms.* New York: Holt, Rinehart, & Winston, 1968.

Karpeles, M. *An introduction to English folksong.* New York: Oxford University Press, 1973.

Karpeles, M., & Bake, A. *Manual for folk music collectors.* London: International Folk Music Council, 1951.

Kennedy, P. (Ed.). *Folksongs of Britain and Ireland.* London: Cassell, 1974.

Kidson, F. (Ed.). *Traditional tunes: A collection of ballad airs.* Yorkshire, England: S. R. Publishers, 1970.

Lloyd, A. L. *Folk song in England.* Great Britain: Lawrence & Wishart, 1967.

Morton, R. (Collator). *Come day, go day, God send Sunday.* London: Routledge & Kegan Paul, 1973.

Nettl, B. *Folk music in the United States* (3rd ed.). Detroit: Wayne State University Press, 1976.

Opie, I., & Opie, P. *The lore and language of school children.* New York: Oxford University Press, 1959.

Stake, R. E. Program evaluation, particularly responsive evaluation. Occasional Paper No. 5. Western Michigan University Evaluation Center, Kalamazoo, Michigan, 1975.

Thomas, L. *The medusa and the snail: More notes of a biology watcher.* New York: Bantam, 1979.

Tyler, R. W. *Syllabus for education 360.* Chicago: University of Chicago Press, 1960.

Wightman, R. Foreword. In B. Copper, *A song for every season.* London: Heinemann, 1971.

Wilgus, D. K. *Anglo-American folksong scholarship since 1898.* New Brunswick, NJ: Rutgers University Press, 1959.

Williams, U. V. Words. *Folk Review,* 1974, 3(3), 19.

EDWARD L. WACHTMAN
Harold Russell Associates

CHAPTER **3**

Storytelling

The Narrative Structure of Evaluation

Edward L. Wachtman is Director of Evaluation and Senior Associate with Harold Russell Associates. He is currently on extended leave working with Arthur Andersen and Company as a training consultant in instructional design and evaluation. Mr. Wachtman has a Master's degree in religion and did his doctoral work in educational evaluation at Syracuse University.

EVALUATORS ARE STORYTELLERS. This statement might cause grave consternation to those who perceive stories as fictitious, mere fabrications to the storyteller. Yet, the idea of story and storytelling as only fiction is erroneous and rather limited. There is an extensive intellectual tradition beginning with Plato and continuing with the writings of the Church Fathers; the songs of the medieval balladiers and Minnesanger; the insights of Vico and Dilthey; the investigations of the German hermeneuticists, Heidegger and Godamer, that views story in a more didactic light. In fact, the two disciplines of history and literature both share a common and fundamental characteristic—narrative. Through narrative they can trace their beginnings to a common ancestor, the epic story.

The intent of this chapter is to take a closer look at history and literature and to note their similarities and differences especially in their use of narrative to tell their respective stories. I will show that evaluators perform similar activities, and are greatly influenced by both the possibilities and constraints of narrative. In order to do this, I want to first offer a simple analogy: Evaluating a program is like telling a story about that program. This analogy will be the key to understanding this chapter as well as understanding the relationship of narrative and story to evaluation. It is assumed throughout this chapter that it is the evaluator's responsibility to create a believable and coherent story from the myriad events and activities that take place in the program setting during a specified period of time. I will demonstrate that the creation of a story of a program occurs not only at the end of the evaluation inquiry when the evaluation report is written, although both Denny (1978) and House (1979) have published excellent papers emphasizing the evaluation report cum storytelling relationship. I will argue that the evaluator is engaged in creating a story from the first moments of the evaluation effort, that the emphasizing of particular facts and events represents a fundamental structuring of information that is basic to storytelling. This structure is narrative. It is an underlying force that shapes the way we perceive our lives, the lives of others, our past, our present, and the possibility of our future. Narrative is the fundamental framework on which our histories and fictions are built and our stories told, and upon which evaluation activities must also rest. It is narrative that eliminates the apparent contradictions between history and fiction and which enables us to look at the possibility of comparing evaluating and storytelling.

It is by investigating some of the activities of evaluating—especially those of choosing, emphasizing, and ordering relevant information to meet the purpose of the evaluation—that we shall seek the evidence to support the claim that evaluators are essentially storytellers. It is while conducting these activities that the evaluator explores the many and countless actions and happenings that take place in an educational setting. It is during this time, in the earliest stages of the evaluation when the evaluator begins to ask the basic questions: What information should be included; how should it be collected; who should supply it; where should this information be sought; and so on, that the evaluator begins to structure the inquiry and begins to create a story, one of any number of stories, that will be expressed in the product of the evaluation—the report.

This chapter will focus on the phenomenological and structural characteristics of narrative and evaluation; it is from this dual perspective that I will attempt to explore the meaning and relationship of storytelling to evaluating.

For clarity, I have developed the arguments of this chapter in several distinct sections. The first section addresses the issue of narrative from a phenomenological perspective, with emphasis placed on the work of historians, theologians, novelists, and philosophers. The second and third sections focus on the similar structural properties and components that characterize both narrative and evaluation. The fourth section will examine the traditional differences between history and literature and show how evaluation fits both categories. I will end with some reflections on what the contents of this chapter might mean to the future of evaluation inquiry.

The Narrative Quality of Experience

We exist narratively. To be human is to have language. It is also to have a story. Because of this constant familiarity with stories and their underlying narrative structure, it is often difficult to examine them, let alone to explicate them. Like the ring on my finger, the watch on my wrist, the air that I breathe, stories are routinely accepted as part of life and are taken for granted. But should I lose my ring, break my watch, or should the air turn foul with smoke, I would readily rediscover the importance of these things to me. The same is true of story. Should I lose my capacity for creating, telling, and listening to stories, then I would rediscover the importance they have in shaping my life and making it uniquely mine.

The Jewish novelist, Elie Wiesel (1972) wrote "God created man because he loves stories" (p. 10). We all love stories. In both literate and preliterate societies the storyteller is held in high esteem. Why? I believe the answer to this question lies in what theologian Stephen Crites (1971) calls "the narrative quality of experience." He argues "that the formal quality of experience through time is inherently narrative." And since humankind is distinguished from the beasts by its incessant preoccupation with the passing of time, it would follow from Crites' argument that narrative is an important, maybe even essential, component of our lives. If this is so, how then can we discern its importance? Crites suggests that it is at the interface of action and time that narrative takes on its importance. He offers as an example, the image of a dancer leaping across a stage. Even if this dancer, through superb training and strength, were able to cross the stage in a single bound, that leap would still involve a steady and perceivable change of the dancer's position relative to the stage (action) and it would take place over a discernable period of time. In addition, the dancer would exhibit a certain style, graceful maybe, clumsy perhaps, and this style would be apparent *only* in the movement of the dancer. If I were to take a still photograph of this leaping dancer, at a shutter speed fast enough to "stop the action," I would be able to capture only an incomplete sense of the dancer's movement and no sense of the dancer's style. The reason for this incomplete sense of movement lies in the fact that action is apparent only in relation to time. A photograph that "stopped the action" would also freeze that action in time. There could be no sense of style because both action and time are necessary components of style.

Style is each person's unique way of behaving, or it is at least a way others perceive how that person acts. I have a particular style of walking across a room. My friends can distinguish my walk from the way their other friends walk. Style is important because it enables each one of us to be perceived differently by others. In some way, style gives each of us a sense of self, as well as a sense of other. Style is a unified and composite way, if not a totally conscious way, of perceiving ourselves and those around us.

Style somehow captures a wholeness, a sense of unity about a person's actions. A person's life is composed of literally millions of discrete behaviors that can transpire over seventy or eighty years. Yet, when we picture a person in our minds, or describe that person to another, we tend to combine those countless behaviors together into a "composite picture"—a sense of style. Narrative as exhibited by the simultaneous presence of a story and a story teller performs a similar function. According to Michael Novak (1971), "A 'story' ties a person's actions together in a sequence. It unites past and future. It supplies patterns, themes, motifs, by which a person recognizes (or someone else recognizes) the unity of his or her life" (p. 60).

In order to delve deeper into the intricate relationship between narrative, action, temporality, style, and story, Crites (1971) has generated the following analogy: "Narrative quality is to experience as musical style is to action" (p. 291). Music is pure style. It exists in time alone. In order to appreciate the fullness and magnificence of a Bach cantata it is necessary to listen to the performance as a whole. The cantata is composed of successive notes, melodies, and rhythms that are inherently temporal. We do not experience the rhythmic melodies, the singers' voices, the individual notes of the instruments all at one time; that would be cacophony at its most dramatic. Rather, we experience the entire cantata as an organic and coherent unity. It is not by the individual musical notes that we distinguish the style of Bach from that of Beethoven, Handel, or even John Coltrane. It is by the unified and coherent style of the total work that we are able to discriminate the style of one composer from that of another. It is only through time that we are able to experience music in general and to differentiate divergent musical styles in particular.

Narrative is like music, according to Crites, because it is necessarily bound to action and time. Like music, narrative is capable of joining discrete and independent events, like the notes in a musical score, into a coherent and meaningful whole. We traditionally call these stories. By "meaningful whole," I am echoing Aristotle's dictum that every story has a beginning, a middle, and an end. This is nothing more than creating patterns, sequential relationships, from those countless events that make up our daily lives. It is essentially the same activity that the composer engages in when writing a musical score. Crites' explication of narrative, action, temporality, and story is an in-depth reiteration of the statement made by the great German novelist, Thomas Mann (1969) in *The Magic Mountain:* "For time is the medium of narration as it is the medium of life. Both are inextricably bound up with it, as inextricably as bodies are in space" (p. 541). Narrative and time are intimately bound together, because it is by structuring the experience of our actions in time—by the stories that we tell about ourselves (and to ourselves) and about others—that we are able to create a sense of unity and wholeness from the innumerable, discrete events that make up our individual and collective lives. To exist temporally is to exist narratively; it is to have a story. We intuitively accept Aristotle's observation about all stories having beginnings, middles, and ends because we perceive our own lives and experience our own actions in a very similar way. We are born, we grow older, and we inevitably die. The *content* of our lives, our individual stories, will vary from person to person—we may be rich or poor, healthy or sick, but the *form*, the narrative quality of the experience of our lives, is universal. Just as we cannot appreciate the unity or form of a Bach cantata by paying attention only to the individual notes of the singers and the instruments, neither can we imagine our lives as an unrelated series of isolated events. A life imagined in such a way would have no meaning, it would contradict our temporal experience of the world. We would experience our lives without unity or wholeness. Our lives experienced in this manner would lack a beginning, middle, and end. We would have no story, no sense of where we came from, who we are, nor would we have a sense of future possibilities. Style would be lacking and without style there could be no differentiation of behavior and therefore, no uniqueness of person. In the words of theologian Charles Windquest (1978): "Without a story we are bound to the immediacy of the moment" (p. 103). Narrative is the means by which we create our stories and make comprehensible the millions of individual moments in our lives. Because of narrative we are able to have individual life stories (autobiographies), as well as collective social stories (histories, myths, legends), and with these stories the security of a past and the possibility of a future.

Crites, Novak, Mann, and Windquest have all spoken to the inherent narrative quality of human experience. They have approached narrative from the distinct points of views of their respective disciplines and have argued well and strongly for a phenomenological understanding of narrative and story—that is, we perceive and order our world from a point of view that is essentially narrative. The importance of this phenomenological point of view to the evaluator lies in the need to structure and order the events and activities that are investigated and documented during an evaluation so that together they will create a unified and coherent story about the program being evaluated. This story will illuminate the style of the program—those actions and happenings that distinguish it from other programs. This story, through the temporal nature of narrative, will delineate and order those events and activities in such a way that the dynamic characteristics of the program are apparent to the evaluator. Most importantly, this story, by defining a beginning, a middle, and an end, will itself assist the evaluator in perceiving the diverse and various aspects of the program as related parts of a coherent and unified whole.

There is yet another argument that stresses the importance of story and its narrative structure. Louis Mink (1978) makes an even stronger claim than Crites, Novak, Windquest, or Mann. He asserts, "Narrative is a primary cognitive instrument—an instrument rivaled, if fact, only by theory and metaphor as irreducible ways of making the flux of experience comprehensible" (p. 132). To support his claim, Mink uses the historical existence of a watch as an example. I will paraphrase his explanation.

Mink believes any event or object, in this case a watch, can be described in two ways: (1) generally, that is, in a theoretical sense according to general laws and principles; and (2) particularly in a narrative or historical sense. Theory makes it possible to explain any particular object or event—in this case a spring driven watch—by describing it in such a way that it is directly related to a set of systematic laws or general principles. For example, a spring driven watch can be adequately described in terms of the general principles of mechanics; i.e., spring driven watches "run down," a descriptive term appropriate to all objects that are governed by the principles of mechanics. Knowledge of the principles of mechanics will help our understanding of the operation of all spring driven watches, as well as of other objects governed by the same principles, i.e., spinning tops, planets in motion, and mill wheels. Each of these examples, like the spring driven watch, can be described by the principles of mechanics. But these descriptions are limited to watches, spinning tops, and mill wheels in general. They can not inform us about differences that may exist between two different watches or among mill wheels on different rivers.

What about a particular watch, the watch on my wrist for example? It can be described more specifically by the particular descriptions that were appropriate to it at certain times in its history. This watch on my wrist was manufactured, shipped, sold, bought, broken, fixed, lost, found, slow, fast, and so on. Because it exists in time it can be appropriately described differently at various points in its existence, thereby distinguishing it from spring driven watches in general (as well as from mill wheels and tops) and from other watches in particular. At each moment of its existence this watch on my wrist (an appropriate description in its own right) intersects in some manner with other objects or events; at these moments of intersection the watch becomes subject to a particular description that is appropriate only because of this intersection. A *new* watch, a *broken* watch, a *pawned* watch, *my* watch, are each an example of a particular description. These particular descriptions are functions of the watch's movement through time; they describe the watch at certain moments of its history. Any one of these descriptions may appropriately describe the watch. Which particular description (or descriptions—a watch can be *broken* and *pawned* simultaneously) is used depends upon the story that is being told about the watch. The only constraint on the use of a particular description is that it maintain an internal consistency within the larger context of the story. By internal consistency I mean that a particular description must "fit" into the overall unity of the story in the same manner as the notes, rhythms, and melodies of a musical score add to and are part of unified whole. Simply stated, mere descriptions of events do not by themselves, create stories. Rather, narrative, because it must create a sequence that is internally consistent, determines which particular descriptions are appropriate for a given story and where in the structure of the story they should appear. It violates the internal consistency of the story for me to describe my watch as being both old and new at the same time. In this case the unifying characteristic of the story dictates that one of these two particular descriptions of the watch be omitted, or that a new event be introduced to explain the apparent inconsistency. For example, I may be buying a "new" watch at a pawn shop only to discover to my surprise that it is actually my "old" watch which I pawned years ago when

I was unemployed. Roland Barthes (1975) addresses this subordination of described events to narrative:

> The function of narrative is not to 'represent,' it is to put together a scene . . . but (the scene) does not belong to the mimetic order in any way. The 'reality' of the sequence does not lie in the 'natural' order of actions that make it up, but in the logic that is unfolded, exposed, and finally confirmed in the midst of the sequence [p. 271].

The unfolding logic of the narrative gives these two apparently contradictory descriptions—an "old" and a "new" watch—meaning and the unity and coherence of the story is maintained.

I might have chosen to tell a totally different story about my watch, a story in which my watch is not a primary object being particularly described but only a secondary object. In this story the presence of my watch becomes a minor event within the context of a larger story. The story might tell of how, because my watch was slow, I missed the 5:00 flight from Washington to Boston and decided to wait for the next flight in the airport lounge. While drinking a beer and watching the news, I met, by sheer luck, an old dear friend from college, and so on. . . . In this case the particular descriptions of the watch are "my" and "slow"; all other potential particular descriptions do not fit into the story. To talk about old, new, or pawned watches in this very short vignette would violate the internal consistency of the story. These additional descriptions would detract from the story's wholeness and unity. Having chosen to tell the story of a missed plane and a chance encounter with an old friend, I have no choice but to disregard all those other events and actions in my life (even my seeming preoccupation with watches!) that cannot be appropriately described within the story's structure without violating the internal consistency of the story.

The cognitive function of narrative, in the opinion of Mink (1978), is not merely the enumerating of a series of different or even successive events, but the embodiment of those events as interrelationships of many different kinds into a single whole. Those events that do not add to these interrelationships must be omitted. Narrative is a way of knowing because through it we isolate particular events, describe them in a particular manner, and place them into structured and ordered relationships with one another. Through narrative we make comprehensible the countless interrelationships that comprise our lives. These interrelationships form the unified patterns, themes, and motifs that tie independent actions and events together in a sequence that we call a story.

Narrative orders all events and objects within the context of time. Describing an event or an object at a particular point in time enables us to differentiate it from others. Narrative differentiates between the theoretical generality of "*a* watch" and those successive and appropriate descriptions that distinguish "*my* watch" from all other watches. Narrative enables us to describe an object, like my watch, in such a way that it can be particularized and known. This is why Mink believes that narrative is an irreducible form of understanding and knowing.

We love stories for many reasons. Through narrative, stories structure our perception of our experience in life so that we are secure in our past, alive in our present, and hopeful of a future. They allow us to differentiate the theoretical ("a watch") from the particular ("my watch"). They help us give coherent meaning to the multitude of events and objects that pass through, and intersect with, our daily lives by offering an internal logic on which to construct sequential relationships. We love stories because we must love them. Stories have to be told because they are an integral part of how we experience our lives and recollect our life activities. The narrative structure of story is but a reflection on our own experience in life and time.

Evaluators are storytellers, not because they fabricate their findings, but because they, like all people, rely on narrative to construct ordered and sequential relationships. When evaluators talk about a specific program, they are capable of doing so only by differentiating it from all other programs and also from a general or theoretical idea of "program." This differentiation is achieved by placing the program within the context of time and space—in other words, structuring it narratively and telling a story about it: "Peg's classroom was in a building that is similar to other school buildings of the 50s" (Kelly, Wachtman, Reeves, Cashell, McKee, & Hutcheson, 1977, p. 3). The structure of the story, the need for the parts to yield a unified whole, forces me to focus on Peg's classroom. This is where the story begins. All the events that are included in the evaluation must be described in such a way that they somehow add to a unified and coherent whole (e.g., they must refer to Peg, her students, her school). That is the responsibility of the evaluator as story teller.

The Components of Narrative

The French have coined the work *narratologie* to define the analytic study of narrative. Narratologie, or poetics, to use a broader term preferred by English and American theorists, is a discipline that asks: What are the basic components of narrative? In the previous section we have seen that there are strong arguments supporting the claim that we experi-

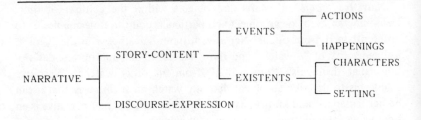

Figure 3.1

ence our lives narratively and that we organize our understanding and knowledge of the world according to a fundamental narrative structure. If this is correct, then it will be beneficial to explore further the components of narrative.

Seymour Chatman (1978) argues from a structuralist perspective that every narrative has two parts: story and discourse. Story is composed of content or chains of *events* (actions and happenings) plus what may be called *existents* (characters and settings). Discourse is the expression, the means by which the content or events of the story is communicated. The story is *what* in a narrative is portrayed; discourse is *how* it is portrayed. See Figure 3.1 for Chatman's diagram of the components of narrative.

Structure is identified by the characteristic properties of wholeness, self-regulation, and transformation. Chatman (1978, pp. 21-23) examines narrative in light of these three essential properties.

Narrative is whole because it is made up of elements, the events and existents, which, although single and discrete, form a sequential composite. In a narrative, the events and existents tend to form relationships that are manifested in a discernible unity—the story. Narrative also requires self-regulation and transformation, two characteristic properties that exist in a complimentary manner within the narrative system. Self-regulation implies that the narrative system maintains and closes itself—it must admit only the description of those events and objects that will ensure internal consistency. Because of self-regulation, narrative is able to maintain order and consistency in the relationship of events and existents to one another. Transformation is the process by which a narrative event or existent is expressed. Self-regulation limits the transformation of events to a limited number of posibilities. These possibilities in turn, reflect the self-regulatory properties of the narrative system. In other words, for narratives to be considered from a structural perspective, the components of the narratives—the events and existents—must be so expressed that they add to the unity of the narrative structure. This means that individual events and existents of the narrative must not violate these relationships that create a sense of wholeness. Chatman indicates in his argument that narrative fulfills this warrant.

For the purpose of this chapter I will attempt to address the structural nature of narrative by focusing almost exclusively on story and its components, discussing the nature and function of discourse only when it explicates story and the narrative events and existents that comprise it. The purpose of this focus is to investigate the narrative process by which a story is constructed, rather than how it is finally expressed.

The events of a story are composed of happenings and actions. Happenings are events, the results of natural or humanly manipulated actions; both happenings and actions represent changes of state. The events of a story constitute a plot.

Chatman (1978, p. 43) defines plot functionally, by how the story teller uses narrative to structure the content of the story: "to emphasize certain story events, to interpret some and to leave others to inference, to show or to tell, to comment or remain silent, to focus on this or that aspect of an event or character." The storyteller can include or omit, emphasize or deemphasize, organize the events in any number of ways; and each arrangement produces a different plot. However, once a plot is developed, once certain events begin to be included or omitted, emphasized or deemphasized, then the plot because it is the structure of the content (and requires that all components of structure remain faithful to its characteristic properties—wholeness, self-regulation, and transformation) dictates what types of relational events may follow to maintain internal consistency. Aristotle's classic view of stories having beginnings, middles, and ends requires that narrative events of a story somehow be related and chained together.

Plot can be viewed as a degree of explication—leaving less to the imagination of the reader as the plot unfolds. As the story moves from its beginning to its end, the descriptions of the events described in the plot form relationships that become more rigid as the story reaches its end. Paul Goodman (1954) addresses this phenomenon: "In the beginning anything is possible; in the middle things become probable, in the ending everything is necessary" (p. 14). Chatman (1978) concurs: "The working out of plot (or at least some plots) is a process of declining or narrowing possibility. The choices become more and more limited and the final choice seems not a choice at all" (p. 46). By including one event to develop a plot at the beginning of a story, I am forced by the characteristic properties of narrative structure to include only those events that relate to the original event in an internally consistent way. My choices of events decrease from a universe of all possible events to only those that enhance the unity and coherence of the story. I will call this the principle of limiting choice; it will be restated in terms of evaluation activities in the following section. The arguments of Goodman and Chatman reinforce Mink's (1978) claim concerning the cognitive function of narrative: "Events are not the raw materials out of which narratives are constructed; rather an event is an abstraction from a narrative. An event may take five seconds or five months, but in either case whether it is one event or many depends not on the definition of 'event' but a particular narrative construction which generates the event's appropriate description" (p. 147). This particular narrative construction is plot.

Obviously, not all the events and existents that comprise a plot are of equal importance. The events in a narrative are not only temporally ordered, they also constitute a logical hierarchy. There are major and minor events. These major events have been called "kernels" and the minor events "satellites." Each major narrative event, or kernel, is a necessary part of the plot. Kernels force the action of the story in one direction and therefore, influence the entire plot; in Camus's *The Stranger,* it is Meursault's inappropriate mourning of his mother's death; in Kazantzakis's *Zorba the Greek,* it is the narrator's chance meeting and hiring of Alexis Zorba. Chatman (1978) states that kernels are so necessary to the plot that "they cannot be deleted without destroying the narrative logic" (p. 53). Satellites are minor events. They are not as crucial to the logic of the plot as the kernels; a satellite could be omitted without disturbing the logic of the plot. Again, using Camus's *The Stranger,* Meursault's affair with Marie is a satellite event, it adds a touch of humanism to Meursault and pathos to the story, but it is not a major narrative event; the plot would not be seriously altered without its presence. In the brief story summary, presented as an example in the previous section, I told how, upon missing a plane, I met a friend in an airport lounge. Missing the plane was a kernel event; not having missed the plane I could never have been in the bar in the first place. The "slow" watch is only a satellite narrative event, it explains why I might have missed the plane; but I could have missed the plane for any number of reasons, for example, the cab was late getting to the airport, my tickets were not in order, and so forth.

Kernels and satellites are important concepts in understanding the hierarchical structure of plot because they help us to determine which narrative events are essential to the story and which are unnecessary. They help us to understand that by including a kernel event at the outset we are already determining the structure of the story. And this structure, in a sense, predetermines which kernels and satellites will follow. In essence, the development of a plot is very much like a decision tree in systems research; each kernel event moves the action in a specific direction, which in turn eliminates some possibilities while opening up new ones. Chatman (1978) states this well: "Proper interpretation of events at any given point is a function of the ability to follow these ongoing selections, to see later kernels as consequences of earlier (ones)" (p. 53).

The existents of a story, as they are defined by the structure of the narrative, are settings and character. Existents, like events, help to determine the boundaries of the story; they are also (especially character) capable of being included in the plot and can take on various degrees of importance much like the kernel and satellite events do.

Setting is basically the environment in which events of the story take place; it has been likened to a background against which a character's actions merge and take on meaning. The importance of setting varies from story to story. *Wuthering Heights* must take place in Yorkshire country— the violent weather, the remoteness, the desolation are as crucial to the plot as Heathcliff and Cathy (McCauley & Lanning, 1964). On the other hand, Camus's *The Plague* could take place anywhere. The North African city of Oran is but a silent backdrop for character and plot development. The virulent disease could have struck anywhere, and Camus could still have told his story.

Characters are the persons, or in some cases, fantastic or inanimate objects, who inhabit a story. Characters are often so interwoven into the plot that it is difficult to separate them from their actions. Stories can revolve around a particular character who can maintain the wholeness and coherence of the story, even when setting and narrative events seem to be dissolving. Vonnegut's Billy Pilgrim (his name is a mode of characterization itself) in *Slaughter House Five,* is such a character; he time travels, space travels, sometimes he's a middle-aged man, sometimes a World War II prisoner of war, other times an oddity in a zoo on the planet Trafalmador. The action and happenings "bounce" through time, but Billy Pilgrim remains the continual focus, if not the theme of this story. It is interesting to point out here that although Billy Pilgrim appears throughout the story, the story is not about him. He is but a vehicle used by the story teller to tell the story. Characters can personify the theme of a story thereby becoming a major factor in the plot. Kazantzakis's *Zorba The Greek* is an example of this. The plot unfolds around the wild and seemingly impulsive Alexis Zorba and his relationship to the unnamed narrator—"boss." But this is but a very clever vehicle for Kazantzakis to explore the age-old dichotomy of light and darkness, emotion and restrained reason. It is a classic confrontation between Dionysus and Apollo, and the plot must unfold in such a way that this confrontation is explicated and the action adequately portrayed.

Action, happenings, setting, and character are the critical elements—the events and existents that comprise a story. It is the structural properties of narrative, wholeness, self-regulation, and transformation, that bring the events and existents together in a fashion such that their relationship to each other within the story reflects a recognizable unity. But how is a knowledge of the structural components of narrative going to help an evaluator conduct better evaluations? The answer lies in the presupposition stated at the beginning of this chapter: Evaluating a program is like telling a story about that program. A phenomenological investigation into narrative and story illuminates the analogy even more—we experience the countless and independent events of our lives not randomly, but in Michael Novak's (1971) words, as stories providing "patterns, themes, motifs." In addition, there is the argument offered by Mink (1978) that narrative allows us to distinguish one event from another, as well as to discriminate particulars from generalities, therefore performing an important cognitive function. If the phenomological view has any validity, and story telling and evaluating are somehow similar, the preceding section, which briefly analyzed the components of narrative, might help evaluators understand the narrative quality and structure of evaluation.

The Narrative Quality and Structure of Evaluation

Consider the evaluation of educational programs. No one would argue that education is not a dynamic process, that it does not take place over time. Nor would I expect an argument when I say that evaluating educational activities takes place over time and is also a process. Stake (1967) implied this dynamic nature of education evaluation in his Countenance model when he urged evaluators to examine not only educational outcomes but also the antecedents and transactions that exist prior to and affect these outcomes. Stake's model is in perfect symmetry with Aristotle's belief that a good story must have a beginning, a middle, and an end. Even at this level of superficial comparison it is apparent that evaluating and story telling have at least gross structural similarities. House (1979), in a recent article, would agree that "story is the basic underlying structure of evaluation." I suspect that the similarities between evaluation and story are based on a mutual interest in time, and the organizing and structuring of temporal events into internally consistent relationships. Both evaluation and story have an inherently narrative structure.

Because of the dynamic nature of education, time and the organization of specific educational events over time are necessary components of evaluating the educational process. Evaluators must be interested in events and actions that take place over time. Again, it is Robert Stake (1978) who addresses this important issue when he quotes the nineteenth-century German philosopher, Wilhelm Dilthey: "Only from his actions, his fixed utterings, his effects upon others, can man learn about himself . . . what we once were, how we developed and became what we are, we learn from the way we acted" (p. 5).

We learn from the way we acted, by our experience of life and time. We learn from the near infinite number of experiences that comprise our individual and collective lives. As Crites, Novak, Mann, and Windquest have all argued, we experience our lives in time, narratively, and recollect the innumerable individual events of our lives by grouping some of those events together to form stories. Their thoughts are more important in light of Dilthey's words because to understand "what we once were, how we developed, and became what we are" requires a major assumption: that there is some order, some structural relationship between "what we once were" and "what we are." That structural relationship and order is narrative and is exhibited in the stories we tell. It is by our use of story—and its underlying narrative structure and temporal dimension—that we are able to bring together and order the wide range and diverse "actions," "fixed utterings," and "effects" that form the continuum between "what we once were" and "what we are."

In a previous article (Wachtman, 1978) I briefly suggested that some of the activities engaged in by preliterate story tellers, modern novelists, historians, and evaluators had a common foundation: the ordering and structuring of events into a unified and "understandable body of knowledge" (p. 7). Camus (1956) in a discussion of the novelist's craft wrote, "There is not one human being who, above a certain elementary level of consciousness does not exhaust himself in trying to find formulas or attitudes that will give his existence the unity it lacks" (p. 262). Evaluators, too, are commonly called upon to perform similar tasks to bring unity to a disparate array of data, to delineate, obtain, and provide useful information for decision-making (Stufflebeam et al., 1971). "Delineate," "useful," and "information" are the key words here. And it is these words paired with Dilthey's "from his actions, his fixed utterings, his effects upon others" that suggests the dilemma facing the evaluator in delineating useful information.

What actions? Which utterings? What effects upon others? In the course of a lifetime, an individual will perform countless acts, mutter ceaseless utterings, and affect thousands of others in thousands of ways. Which of these actions, utterings, and effects does the evaluator choose from? Obviously, not all of them are of equal value or utility. If they are not of equal value or utility, what criteria does the evaluator use to delineate useful information and distinguish it from useless information? How does the evaluator decide what information to use, how to use it, and how to judge its importance against other types of information? In some evaluation efforts these questions are answered. In these cases the client has specific, or at least preconceived notions of what information is needed and perceives the evaluator more as a technical expert—hired to ensure that the information is collected properly according to the warrants of established procedures. But in many cases it is the evaluator's role to assist the client in determining what information will be useful. To do this well, the evaluator might benefit from a conceptual framework from which to view the entire inquiry, to give it a structure and a sense of unity, so that the decision maker can gain a sense of the usefulness of the information and see that the individual bits of information sum to a meaningful whole. The evaluator has such a framework. It is the narrative quality and structure of evaluation.

To be considered in a structural sense, evaluations must have the same characteristic properties as other structures: wholeness, self-regulation, and transformation. Evaluations can be considered whole because they are composed of many independent and discrete events, arranged in such a fashion as to form relationships that are observable as being unified.

Evaluations can be considered to possess the properties of self-regulation and transformation in the same manner as narratives. Self-regulation requires that the evaluation remain true to the wholeness of the inquiry insofar as the events described relate to each other and add to the unifying nature of the evaluation. This ensures that the evaluation maintains its unity by requiring that all the events included in the inquiry have an internally consistent relationship to each other. Events are not included in evaluations simply because they are measurable or accessible; self-regulation requires that all events add to the coherence of the evaluation. In other words, self-regulation requires that events included in an evaluation "make sense" not only individually, but in the composite. The process by which an event is expressed is called transformation. The expression of the event is limited by the property of self-regulation; the ordering and describing events in a manner that does not obscure or destroy the relationship of the events to each other and to the whole. House (1979, pp. 8-9) alludes to these three properties that structurally inform the evaluation: "It is not too surprising that the 'story' of evaluation is more basic than the aesthetic rendering, since the story line relates events to each other in specific ways, such as cause and effect relationships [self-regulation]. The events of the story may be presented in different dramatic forms, [transformation] but both the story and the aesthetic elements contribute to the overall coherence [wholeness]." Narrative and evaluation both possess the properties of structure that allow us to overlay one model upon the other to see if an understanding of the components of narrative can assist the evaluator in ordering and choosing those "countless actions, utterings, and effects" which will tell us "how we developed and became what we are."

Using Chatman's structure as a "template" we can examine the components of narrative in relation to a particular evaluation model—in this case Stake's (1967) "Countenance of Educational Evaluation." This will illustrate any similarities between narrative and evaluation at a theoretical level. Because there are many diverse models of evaluation, the arguments presented to this point, would not be sufficiently tested solely by the comparison of Chatman's model of narrative to Stake's Countenance model. To further illustrate the structural similarities between narrative and evaluation I will show how an actual evaluation was planned and conducted using Chatman's structural components of narrative as its framework.

Chatman has identified events—actions and happenings—and existents—characters and setting—as components of story. The educational events that are represented in an evaluation are all the activities of teaching and learning. Stake (1967) calls these "transactions" and defines them as "the countless encounters of students with teachers, students with students, author with reader, and parent with counselor—the succession of engagements which comprise the process of education" (p. 48). Educational events are also composed of happenings corresponding generally to what Stake (1967) terms "outcomes." "Outcomes are the consequences of education" (p. 48). Educational outcomes are some indicator of what happened during the educational process.

The educational existents that may be identified as important sources of information are character and setting. Characters are the people who participate in the many possible educational events that comprise a program. These people might include teachers, students, administrators, counselors, parents, bus drivers, cafeteria staff, school board members, and the like. Stake (1967) alludes to the need to identify characters who will supply useful information for an evaluator when he addresses the issue of judgment: "Evaluators will seek and record the opinions of persons of special qualification" (p. 47). What specially qualifies a person is the congruence between the information that the evaluator needs, the information that a particular person has, and the story that the evaluator chooses to tell. A study of student behavior on school buses would undoubtedly identify bus drivers as "persons of special qualifications."

The setting of an educational event is where the characters participate in the educational process. The setting of an evaluation can also be where the investigation of a particular program or educational event takes place. Education can and does take place in many places and in diverse settings; the classroom is only one of hundreds of settings that the evaluator should explore. As in the case of literature, sometimes settings are secondary—a mere backdrop to the plot and the actions and happenings that comprise it. In other cases, the setting is itself a critical component of the program being evaluated.

In the preceding paragraphs I have attempted to demonstrate that narrative and evaluation share the same structural properties—wholeness, self-regulation, and transformation—and the same structural components—actions, happenings, characters, and setting. Assuming this shared structure, we can extend Chatman's diagram to the evaluation process (Figure 3.2). The concept of evaluation as story should not be surprising because structurally, the components comprising a story, be it a fictional story, a history, or an evaluation, are essentially the same. Any differences lie not in the structure, but rather in the specific purpose for which any of these narratives are created. It is the purpose for which the story is being told that will give us the final clue as to what "actions," "utterings," and "effects" are to be included in an evaluation, how they are to be ordered, and which ones will be emphasized.

The plot of any story is directly related to its purpose. What events and existents the storyteller allows into the plot depends on the purpose of the story being told. Different genres have different plots; epic plots

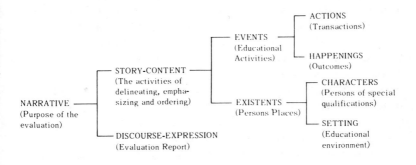

Figure 3.2

SOURCE: Reprinted from Seymour Chatman, **Story and Discourse: Narrative Structure in Fiction and Film.** Copyright © 1978 by Cornell University. Used by permission of the publisher, Cornell University Press.

NOTE: Parentheses distinguish evaluation structure from narrative structure.

appear to differ from romantic plots, which in turn tend to differ from comic plots. These differences do not detract from the structural nature of plots; they are rather differences in the degree of structure. Some plots are very loose, others are intricate and tight; some focus on the lives and deeds of a specific person, others on the activities of large groups of people. How tight or how loose the plot may be is a function of the storyteller's intent, the purpose of the story. It is the purpose that sets the first limits as to the degree of structure required by the plot. For example, plots of local folktales or legends can vary from region to region and fluctuate in detail over time, but the basic purpose, usually entertainment or enthrallment, with a touch of allegory, remains the same. Conversely, sacred stories, those with vital impact on the mythical life of the community, are often so rigidly guarded that not only do the events and existents remain unchanged from generation to generation, but the intonation of every word is specified. The function of plot is to determine which events and existents might be included in the story to fulfill the necessary requirements of structure.

The importance of story's purpose to the plot and ultimately to the individual elements of the story is obvious. For the evaluator, this means that before the evaluation can be structured—"emplotted" to use the term of historian Hayden White (1978, p. 47)—the purpose or the intent of conducting the evaluation must be fully understood. Different evaluation purposes or intents will require different plots, which will then, by the looseness or tightness of their structure, tend to "emphasize or deemphasize" certain events or existents. Purposes that reflect the evaluator's role in assisting decision makers (Stufflebeam, 1968) may require plots different from those required to persuade a given group of policy makers to make a particular action (House, 1977) or from those that attempt to portray the broad workings of a program (Stake, 1972). In each of these cases the differing intents and purposes will require looser or tighter plot structures. Tighter plot structure will be more deterministic as to which specific events and existents will comprise the evaluation; pretest-posttest experimental and quasi-experimental designs reflect this tighter structure. Looser structures allow the evaluator more freedom to decide which events and existents will be included in the evaluation; case studies, portrayal type evaluation, and some ethnographic studies fit this category. In any case, the evaluator, through the process of determining the purpose of the evaluation, and developing a plot to include the events and existents that will be most appropriate to further the purpose, is engaged in what I, in an earlier section of this chapter, called the principle of limiting choice. According to this principle, the evaluator's choice of what actions, utterings, and so forth to include becomes increasingly more limited as the evaluation becomes more structured. The evaluator's universe of choices diminishes at each successive level, beginning with the determination of a purpose, continuing with the emphasizing, ordering, and highlighting of general events and existents which are manifested in the plot development, and moving into specific actions ("transactions") happenings ("outcomes"), characters ("persons of special qualifications"), and setting. The principle of limiting choice is a manifestation of the need for all the components of the evaluation to relate to each other and to the overall unity of the evaluation. It is the ordering and structuring of certain events and existents, into a coherent and unified whole; it is choosing a few from the many for the purpose of creating an understandable body of knowledge.

To further illustrate the structural similarities between narrative and evaluation and their role in structuring and ordering events and existents into a unified whole, I would like to briefly show how an actual evaluation was planned and conducted using the structural components described previously as a framework.

In the fall of 1979 Harold Russell Associates, of Waltham, Massachusetts was awarded a contract by the Office for Civil Rights to demonstrate exemplary practice in the implementation of Section 504 of P.L.

93-112.[1] This demonstration was to take place in a large, urban school system. One of the stated goals of this contract was to provide written guidance to other large urban school systems as to the achievement of cost-effective compliance within the requirements of this federal mandate.

In order to accurately document and meaningfully portray the implementation of this exemplary practice, the evaluation team chose to conduct an ongoing case study of the project throughout the course of its 18-month duration. However, before any other evaluation decision could be made, a structure had to be put in place that would enable the evaluators to choose what information should be collected, how it should be collected, and from whom it should be collected. The complexities involved in this kind of study of a large urban school system are staggering. There are multiple layers of administrative and organizational hierarchies; there are political issues to deal with; there are thousands of teachers with a multitude of roles and responsibilities; there are programs scattered throughout the system—some apparently similar to others, but having a distinct programmatic flavor of their own. Faced with the myriad possibilities and problems associated with an evaluation of this magnitude, we decided that our best alternative was to create a story about this city's school system ponderous movement toward compliance with Section 504. We chose this alternative after close comparison of Chatman's components of Narrative and Stake's Countenance model of evaluation, because we were convinced that by following these schemes we would be able to come to grips with the very real issue of choosing what information to include, what information to emphasize, what information to downplay, and where and from whom this information should be collected.

Because of the structural relationship of purpose to plot and of plot to the choosing of relevant events and existents, we first grappled with the question of purpose. Why were we telling this story? To what end would this story be used? The answer to this question was that, essentially, we wanted to teach, to inform administrators in other large, urban school systems how they, based on our demonstrated successes and failures, could themselves begin the compliance process. By deciding that information dissemination was the general purpose for which our evaluation/story was being told, we quickly came to the next level of questioning—information about what. The dual answer to this question, cost-effectiveness and compliance to Section 504, provided the clue for the development of the evaluation/story's plot, a plot that was to act as the underlying framework on which the other components of the evaluation/story—actions, happenings, settings, and characters—would take shape.

With the dual purpose of the evaluation/story in mind, we began to identify those essential components, the major events and existents, that were necessary for the development of the plot. Chatman has called these necessary components *kernels.* Compliance to any federal mandate such as Section 504 is guided by a Regulation that states in various degrees of detail what is deemed necessary to meet the intent of the Act. It was very obvious that the direction that our evaluation/story would take was related to the Section 504 Regulation; without following the Regulation, compliance is nearly impossible. We analyzed the Regulation and identified 17 subparts within it that were critical to any school system's compliance efforts. We reviewed these 17 subparts, keeping in mind the dual purpose of the evaluation/story we were creating. Our review supported our original belief concerning these subparts; we would not be able to tell the story we wanted to tell, if we did *not* include these sections of the Regulation in our evaluation/story. These 17 subparts of the Section 504 Regulation were indeed kernels in the plot. Any event or existent that was directly related to these subparts would have to be included in our evaluation/story.

With the identification of the 17 subparts, kernels of the plot, if you will, we had a structural framework on which to judge the value of including or omitting specific educational actions, happenings, settings, and characters. Each educational event that we included had to somehow relate to the 17 subparts, and to ensure internal consistency, each had to "fit" into a unified and coherent whole—the evaluation/story of a large urban school system's compliance to major federal legislation. Because of what I termed earlier as the principle of limited choice, the identification of the 17 subparts marked the beginning of an ever-decreasing universe of choices concerning *what* events and existents were to be included in the evaluation/story. For example, where the evaluation was to take place (what Chatman calls the setting) was now identifiable as the three community districts within the school system where exemplary Section 504 compliance practice was being implemented. This obviously sharpened the focus of the evaluation effort. Within these three community districts we were able to determine where specific programs and educational activities (what Chatman terms "events"; Stake calls them "educational activities") that might be important to the further plot development of our evaluation existed. This further sharpened the focus of our investigation because the evaluation team was now able to think in terms of specific schools and neighborhoods. And this increasing focus, of both setting and activities, based on the principal of limiting choices, assisted us in identifying specific teachers and administrators (Chatman's "characters"; Stake's "persons of special qualifications") who might inform us how the programs were being implemented (Chatman's "actions"; Stake's "transactions") and how they effected the school system's compliance to the Section 504 Regulation (Chatman's "happenings"; Stake's "outcomes").

By conceptualizing our evaluation effort using the structural quality of narrative, we were able to grossly identify and choose what information to include and what to omit. We were able to focus our investigation even more sharply by relating all of the events and existents that were investigated during the conduct of our evaluation/story to each other and to the overall purpose of the inquiry, so that we could monitor if they "made sense" in relationship to each other and added to the unity and coherence of the investigation as a whole. For example, in an investigation of physical accessibility, an important "kernel" event of the plot, we realized that in the three community districts where the demonstration of Section 504 exemplary practice was taking place, we had to include information not only about the findings concerning building accessibility, but also about what needed to be done to improve building accessibility; how to do this in the most cost-effective way; how to train engineering and design personnel; what to look for and how to document it; how to choose which buildings to remodel for accommodations; how to make realistic cost estimates for renovation; and so forth. Each of these activities was crucial to the purpose of the evaluation/story as we had begun to define it through the development of the plot. This part of our investigation remained true to the structural characteristic of wholeness because each of the activities related to each other, that is, they possessed an internal consistency, and did in fact add to the unifying nature the evaluation/story. We believed that this section of the evaluation/story met the structural characteristics of self-regulation because the activities "made sense," on the whole, as a composite picture. The characteristic of transformation was met by omitting those bits and pieces of information that did not relate the individual events to each other and to the overall evaluation/story. In this case, concerning physical accessibility, we included *what* was needed to make a building safe and accessible (e.g., the addition of ramps, elevators, visual-cue fire alarms). This information was included because it directly related to other issues concerning accessibility and added to the coherence and unity of the evaluation/story. Without the inclusion of *what* is necessary, the dual purpose of demonstrating cost-effective compliance to other large urban school systems could not be met. Conversely, the issue of *how* to install any of these necessary accommodations was intentionally omitted; this information would differ from location to location, and be dependent on any number of different variables (e.g., age of building, site location). In addition, including this information would not add to the unity of the evaluation/story, and in fact, it might detract from this unity by obscuring the relationships between those events and activities that are necessary for cost-effective compliance and which therefore, directly relate to the plot and the purpose of the evaluation/story.

I do not wish to imply that the events and existents included in an evaluation are totally predetermined and that it is the evaluator's burden to discover what exactly happened in the program being evaluated. Rather, it is the evaluator's responsibility to create a story of what happened, one of many possible stories that might have been created about that program. There is no one universal truth that evaluators will discover in evaluating educational programs. There are, however, multiple truths that reflect a multitude of education events, some important, some trivial, but all predicated on events that came before them. It is the evaluator's task to make sense of these many events, to order them, structure them, and give them meaning. Evaluators do this by creating stories. We recognize stories by their unifying structure, by the way their actions are connected in a sequence, and by the patterns and themes formed out of apparently patternless events.

In this section I have attempted to show, by using model-to-model and model-to-practice examples, that structurally, evaluations and narratives are governed by the same properties and that they share the same components. If evaluators are to be good storytellers, if they are to choose, order, and structure events into meaningful patterns, they might benefit from knowing these similarities. They should be able to understand the differences between kernel and satellite narrative events and see that these concepts can help them in the choice and delineation of useful evaluation information. They should understand that character and setting are concepts that can be easily adapted to evaluation efforts—that sometimes "character" would be the focus of an evaluation as in the attempt to evaluate faculty performance for instructional improvement, tenure, or promotion, and that other times "character" would be only "persons of special qualifications" from whom to collect judgments. Evaluators must be aware that it is narrative that allows them to form patterns and choose and order events, and if they violate the requirements that govern this structure—wholeness, self-regulation, and transformation—the patterns and order of the story will disappear along with coherence and unity.

Evaluators are storytellers in the manner of historians; they try to "learn from the way we acted." Like historians, they often look back at events that have already occurred and attempt to order those events and establish patterns of meaning. The following section will investigate this "backward glance" of historians and evaluators and see how it might affect a "forward view."

History, Poetry, and Evaluating

Denny (1978) suggests that evaluation is a "kind of journalistic documentation"; he adds, "A story documents a given millieu in an attempt to communicate the general spirit of things" (p. 2). I agree that stories communicate a general spirit of things, but I take cautious exception to his use of the word "document." At one level, storytellers and the stories they tell do document, they do address what has happened. The preceding section of this chapter dealt with such historical issues. But at another equally valid level, they transcend what has actually happened and deal with what might possibly be.

Over two millenia ago, in the *Poetics,* Aristotle contrasted history and poetry. He stated that while history must faithfully adhere to what has actually taken place, poetry is free to explore the possibility of what might be, as well as what has happened. Poetry was superior to history, according to Aristotle, because it represented universal truth and not merely the accuracy of specific facts. The poet is capable of looking both backward and forward, from what is to what might be, and with this dual vision can compare the reality of actual occurrences with the ideal of what ought to be.

From early times, narrative has been perceived in two major and antithetical modes—the emprical mode and the fictional mode. The emprical mode is composed of the historical and mimetic form. The historical form owed allegiance to that truth of fact and observed reality, emphasizing the happenings of the actual past rather than a mythical or traditional past. Mimetic form stressed observation of the present—a here-and-now slice of life—over the factual investigation of the past (Scholes & Kellogg, 1966.)

The fictional mode, like its empirical counterpart, has two narrative forms, the romantic form and the didactic form. The romantic form presents a world that has been idealized and emotionally sensitized to the concepts of justice, beauty, and the good. The didactic form is moralistic and intellectual in character. It serves a normative and prescriptive purpose by stating how humanity ought to behave.

The empirical mode freed the storyteller from the constraints of tradition and myth, emphasizing instead a focus on observed events. It was an early experiment in empiricism. The fictional mode, on the other hand, freed the story teller from the constraints of empiricism. The empirical mode stressed historical and psychological fact and was grounded in experience. The fictional mode placed emphasis on the ideal—what ought to be.

Based on this brief summary, it is apparent that evaluators—by employing the empirical mode of narrative—can and should be storytellers. But is it possible that evaluators create and tell stories not only like historians, but like poets as well, freed in some way from investigating what actually occurred and with the possibility of at least touching upon the ideal? To explore this possibility, it would be useful to review Stake's Countenance model again.

Stake (1967) makes the claim: "To be fully understood, the educational program must be fully described and fully judged" (p. 45). In describing an educational program, the evaluator is focusing on truth of fact based on observed reality. The evaluator is performing the role that Aristotle assigned to historians. It is the judging component of the evaluation inquiry that offers the potential for crossing the barely discernible that which separates the realm of factual occurrence (history) from the realm of universal possibility (poetry).

Judging, in the way Stake uses it in his article, is a value-laden activity.[2] When evaluators, or "persons of special qualifications," make judgments about an educational program they are doing so with at least a tacit sense of what ought to be. According to Stake (1967), "There are two bases of judging the characteristics of a program" (p. 56). Judgments based on relative standards are essentially comparative in nature; the program being described is compared to the descriptions of other, existing programs of similar nature. Judgments based on absolute standards are made between the descriptions of the program being evaluated and some idealized sense of what the program under description ought to be, how it ought to function, what its intended outcomes should be, and so forth. Prior to making judgments about the descriptions of an actual program based on absolute standards, the standards themselves have to be determined. It is at this point, the selection of absolute standards, that the evaluator moves from reliance on the empirical mode of narrative, with its strict adherence to factual happenings, to the more idealistic, romantic, and didactic forms of the fictional mode. Here, the evaluator throws off the cloak of the historian and puts on the mantle of the poet. When choosing absolute standards against which to compare the descriptive data of the program being evaluated, the evaluator must relinquish the constraints of historicism and focus on the myriad possibilities of how the program might be. Of course, these absolute standards must be realistic in terms of stated program goals, fiscal constraints, and common-sense practicality. But these issues do not detract from the fact that setting absolute standards and judging a program accordingly reflects Aristotle's view of the poet's function: "He has to decide what can happen, that is, what is possible because it is either likely or necessary" (Bambrough, 1963, p. 419). That is precisely the role of the evaluator in establishing absolute standards.

In the preceding paragraphs I have tried to show, by comparing Stake's (1967) Countenance model with the major modes of narrative, that in describing an educational program the evaluator takes the role that Aristotle would ascribe to the historian, and that in judging according to established absolute standards, the evaluator performs the role of the poet. Evaluators seem to tell stories in many different ways and from different perspectives. A loose translation of the classical Greek word for poet is "creator, or one who makes." I would like to think of evaluators not only as technicians, but as makers of program possibilities based on the historical perspective of "what we once were," and the poetic potentiality of "what we ought to be."

Epilogue: Reflections on Evaluation as Story

Evaluators are storytellers. I have stated this belief many times and in many ways throughout this discussion. What does it mean to say that evaluators are storytellers? What real differences do story and storytelling make for the field of educational evaluation? Will it help evaluators produce better evaluations and subsequently improve education in general? I have thought a great deal about these questions during the preparation of this chapter. In conclusion, I would like to share my thoughts.

What *does* it really mean to say that evaluators are storytellers? This question must be addressed at several levels. At one level, the most basic, it is simply a restatement of what philosophers and historians have known since the early eighteenth century. We live in the world linguistically. Language is the foundation of our conception of the world, or in Heidegger's formula, "Language is the House of Being."[3] By naming, by telling stories, we bring meaning to our lives. The implication for evaluation can be stated similarly: We create our programs by the stories we tell about them, that is, the evaluations we conduct of them. The argument against national standardized testing is based on the belief that declining writing ability is predicated on the willingness of the educational community to teach skills that will be tested at the expense of other, valuable skills (Wheeler, 1979).

At another level, the statement that evaluators are storytellers reflects the fact that programs and program evaluation are essentially complex human activities. Any valid understanding of the operations of a program requires evidence of both the "humanness" and "complexity" of the program. The eighteenth-century historian, Giambattista Vico, doubted that mathematical and scientific knowledge could adequately portray the complicated interactions of human qualities such as values, goals, friendships, and the like (cited in Stevenson, 1969, p. 53). Contemporary perspectives on evaluation reflect Vico's concern. Elizabeth Vallance, (1975, abstract) alluding to the work of John Mann, asserts, "A curriculum, regardless of its objectives, and outcomes has a unique 'lived in quality' which is immediate, experiential, and essentially aesthetic." Vallance is arguing for the use of what Stephen Crites (1975) calls first-order language: "When we speak to or of what is immediately real to us, we tell stories and fragments of stories" (p. 31). In contrast, second-order language is philosophical, abstract, and analytical. We use it when we wish to explain phenomena that we have experienced through first-order language. Stories are told in first-order language because "In stories we meet what is concrete in experience, in the most concrete language we have" (Crites, 1975, p. 32). If evaluators become good storytellers they might better do what Stake (1973) encouraged them to do—convey a total, holistic impression, the mood and the mystery of the program. If evaluators were good storytellers they might avoid what House (1973) warned as the oversimplification of scientism: "The empirical delusion that confuses behavior with humanity, appearances with reality" (p. 24). If evaluators were good storytellers, our educational programs might be evaluated for providing students with such attributes as "virtue" and "talent," which to Thomas Jefferson were the most desirable of educational outcomes.

The final and most detailed level at which evaluators may be said to be storytellers is the structural level. In the activity of deciding which educational events to include, which to emphasize and which to downplay, how to order them, and so forth, the evaluator is following a narrative structure similar to one used by historians and fiction writers. For evaluators, this means that there is a model with specific components and rules of order that can serve as a possible template to guide their activities. Evaluations take place in specific and identifiable settings, and are peopled by characters who engage in actions that make things happen. These actions and happenings are governed by the requirement that each individual action or event relate to the others and combine to form a coherent, unified whole that is presented in a credible product—the evaluation report. An understanding of the components of this structure that are common to narrative and evaluation and the need for these components to form unified patterns and motifs might assist evaluators in the conceptualization and conduct of their evaluations.

In the early years of this century when Werner Heisenberg was a young graduate student, he asked the great Niels Bohr why classical Newtonian theory was not appropriate to explain quantum physics and why no new theory had been generated to explain this "new physics";

> "These models," Bohr replied, "have been deduced, or if you prefer, guessed, from experiments, not from theoretical calculations. I hope that they describe the structure of the atoms as well, but *only* as well as is possible in the descriptive language of classical physics. We must be clear that, when it comes to atoms, language can be used only as in poetry. The poet, too, is not nearly so concerned with describing facts as with creating images and establishing mental connections" [Heisenberg, 1972].

Evaluators are engaged in both endeavors—describing facts and creating images and mental connections. They do these by creating stories about the programs that they evaluate. This is not such an outlandish idea, even for a discipline that has borrowed heavily from the quantitative methods of agronomy and psychometrics. Evaluation is a young discipline. There is room for exploration of new modes of thought, new ways to conceptualize problems, and innovative strategies and methods. Evaluating as storytelling is one of many possible ways that evaluators can conceptualize what in fact they do, so that we might first be able to understand and then, maybe, explain the complexities of our social processes.

Notes

[1] Section 504 guarantees that no qualified person . . . shall, on the basis of handicap, be excluded from participation in, be denied the benefits of, or otherwise

be subjected to discrimination under any program or activity which receives or benefits from federal financial assistance.

2Paul Taylor has addressed the complex issues surrounding valuing, judging, and setting standards in his excellent book *Normative Discourse.* Englewood Cliffs, NJ: Prentice Hall, 1961.

3Heidegger is referring to the episode in Genesis 2:19 "So out of the ground the Lord God formed every beast of the field and every bird of the air; and brought them to the man to see what he would call them; and whatever the man called every living creature that was its name."

References

Bambrough, R. (Ed.). *The philosophy of Aristotle.* New York: New American Library, 1963.

Barthes, R. An introduction to the structural analysis of narrative. *New Literary History,* 1975, (6), 237-272.

Camus, A. *The rebel.* New York: Vintage, 1956.

Chatman, S. *Story and discourse: Narrative structure in fiction and film.* Ithaca, NY: Cornell University Press, 1978.

Crites, S. The narrative quality of experience. *Journal of American Academy of Religion,* 1971, 39(3).

Crites, S. Angels we have heard. In J. B. Wiggins (Ed.), *Religion as story.* New York: Harper & Row, 1975.

Denny, T. Story telling and educational understanding. Occasional Paper Series No. 12. Western Michigan University Evaluation Center, Kalamazoo, Michigan, 1978.

Goodman, P. *The structure of literature.* Chicago: University of Chicago Press, 1954.

Heisenberg, W. *Physics and beyond.* New York: Harper Torchbooks, 1971.

House, E. Technology and evaluation. *Educational Technology,* 1973, 20-26.

House, E. The logic of evaluative argument. In E. Baker (Ed.), *CSE Monograph Series.* Los Angeles: Center for the Study of Evaluation, University of California, 1977.

House, E. Coherence and credibility. *Educational Evaluation and Policy Analysis,* 1979, 5-17.

Kelly, E. F., Wachtman, E. L., Reeves, T., Cashell, J., McKee, B., & Hutcheson, S. *A story of ESSENCE: The portrayal of a science curriculum.* Syracuse, NY: Center for Instructional Development, 1977.

McCauley, R., & Lanning, G. *Technique in fiction.* New York: Harper & Row, 1964.

Mann, J. Curriculum criticism. *Teachers College Record,* 1969, 71(1).

Mann, T. *The magic mountain* (H. T. Porter, trans.). New York: Vintage Books, 1969. Chapter 7.

Mink, L. Narrative form as a cognitive instrument. In R. H. Canary & H. Koziki (Eds.), *The writing of history.* Madison: University of Wisconsin Press, 1978.

Novak, M. *Ascent of the mountain, flight of the dove.* New York: Harper & Row, 1971.

Scholes, R., & Kellogg, R. *The nature of narrative.* New York: Oxford University Press, 1966.

Stake, R. E. The countenance of educational evaluation. *Teachers College Record,* 1967, 68, 523-540.

Stake, R. E. An approach to the evaluation of instructional programs. Paper presented at the Annual Meeting of the American Educational Research Association, Chicago, April 1972.

Stake, R. E. To evaluate an arts program. *The Journal of Aesthetic Education,* 1973, Fall.

Stake, R. E. The case study method in social inquiry. *Educational Researcher,* 1978, 7(2), 5-8.

Stevenson, W. T. *History as myth: The import for contemporary theology.* New York: Seabury, 1969.

Stufflebeam, D. Evaluation as enlightenment for decision making. In *Improving Educational Assessment.* Washington, DC: Association For Supervision and Curriculum Development, 1969.

Stufflebeam, D., Foley, W. J., Gephart, W. J. Guba, E. G., Hammond, R. L. Hammond, H. O., & Provus, M. M. *Educational evaluation and decision making.* Itasca, IL: Peacock, 1971.

Vallance, E. *Aesthetic criticism and curriculum description.* Unpublished doctoral dissertation, Stanford University School of Education, 1975.

Wachtman, E. L. Evaluation as story: The narrative quality of educational evaluation. Paper presented at the Annual Meeting of the American Educational Research Association, Toronto, Ontario, April 1978.

Wellek, R., & Warren, A. *Theory of literature.* New York: Harcourt, Brace, Jovanovich, 1942.

Wheeler, T. C. *The great American writing block.* New York: Viking, 1979.

White, H. The historical text as literary artifact. In R. H. Canary & H. Koziki (Eds.), *The writing of history.* Madison: University of Wisconsin Press, 1978.

Weisel, E. *The gates of the forest.* New York: Avon Books, 1972.

Windquest, C. The act of storytelling and the self's homecoming. *Journal of the American Academy of Religion,* 1978, September.

PATRICIA A. TEMPLIN
ROLM Corporation

CHAPTER **4**

Still Photography in Evaluation

Patricia A. Templin, formerly Assistant Professor at the University of Wisconsin—Milwaukee, is presently a planner at ROLM Corporation, Santa Clara, California. An outgrowth of her primary interest in multiple methods for evaluation is the development of a methodology for evaluating programs using photography. Her photographic evaluations explore classroom environments, a conference, and a computer literacy program.

USING STILL CAMERAS to gather information about the subjects of a study is scarcely a new technique in the social sciences. Anthropologists in particular have been packing cameras along with their notebooks virtually since it first became possible to carry a camera into the field. And, as Stasz (1979) has shown, the early volumes of the *American Journal of Sociology* often carried articles either illustrated by or based partly upon photographs. The still camera is, in one respect, simply one of many technological devices used by the social scientist to collect data in the field, preserve it, and take it back "home" for study at leisure. In this sense, still cameras are no different from disc recorders, wire recorders, tape recorders, movie cameras, video recorders, or, for that matter, notebooks and pencils. All such recording devices are essential compensations for the fallibility of human memory and the difficulty of analyzing fleeting stimuli.

121

Limitations

Why do evaluators routinely enter the study situation equipped with notebooks, pencils, and tape recorders, yet hesitate to use—or show positive resistance to—still photography as a means of gathering information about what they are studying? There appear to be several reasons for this resistance. For one thing, most investigators seem to sense, almost intuitively, that there are profound differences in the methodologies and interpretational schemata that are appropriate to visual as opposed to verbal data. Then too, photography does not come to the hands of the social scientist as a pure technique; there is no use denying that the *practice* (as opposed to the merely technical resources) of photography that is most closely fitted to the needs of social science is that of documentary photography. The history of documentary photography is largely a history of the creation of audience effects through the photographic image: One picture of elementary school children waiting in line to have a teacher check self-paced workbooks is worth a thousand pictures of them working placidly at their seats. At times, the creation of audience effects is in the service of a Zolaesque naturalism, while in other instances it is based on a romantic expressive aesthetic and may even culminate in the creation of private mythologies. No such situation is conducive to the application of rigorous methodologies, either of collection or analysis. Finally, most investigators fear that the addition of still photography to their repertoire of data collection techniques will create whole new realms of logistical problems for them. Will I be able to do the photography myself, and if so, at what cost to my other activities in the field? Will a photographer working with me have to be specifically trained and constantly supervised? Will the presence of the camera complicate my access problems? Any of these considerations may make still photography a research technique that gets deferred "until the next study."

In this chapter I have attempted to address both the methodological and practice-related questions surrounding the use of still photography as a data-gathering technique in evaluation studies. The theoretical considerations underlying the social science uses of photography are quite complex— necessarily so because we are all still struggling with the concept of visual literacy and the differences in the way meaning is conveyed by visual and verbal means. Thus, I have chosen to approach this area by means of a literature review, interspersed with interpretational material relating the existing theoretical approaches to the specific methodological problems of evaluation studies. Next, I have embodied the results of this theoretical consideration in a discussion of the application of still photography to evaluation studies. Here I have tried to address some of the philosophical, ethical, logistical, and purely technical problems facing the investigator who utilizes photography as a primary component of evaluation. Finally, in the concluding section I discuss the actual use of still photographs as part of the "results" of an evaluation study, an essential consideration because still photographs have a way of being both the "data" and the "results" of a study in which they are involved.

The scholarly debts that I owe will largely be evident from my citations in the text. However, I would like to acknowledge a more general debt to Howard Becker and Rob Walker, who provided thorough criticism of a draft of the methodological section. In August, 1979, at the time I was first developing my views of the methodological and practical problems involved, I was a participant in a week-long seminar presented by Howard Becker at the Visual Studies Workshop in Rochester, New York. I benefited greatly from many of the ideas Becker presented, although generally in ways that cannot be specifically cited. Frank Anderson, Conrad Katzenmayer, and Diane Rinehart also contributed helpful comments during the formation of the methodological section. Finally, Adrianne Bank and Michael Sawdey suggested some of the areas of concern I have addressed in the practice-related sections of this monograph.

Visual Communication

> Photography has achieved an unprecedented mirroring of things of our culture. We have pictured so many aspects and objects of our environment in the form of photographs that the composite of these representations has assumed the proportions and identity of an actual environment. Within this environmental context the giving of a pictured significance to ordinary objects through photography has contributed greatly to a shifting graphic vocabulary of the twentieth century [Lyons, 1967, p. 1].

We live in a media culture in which we may consider that photography is the primary technology of visual communication. The power of photographic images with respect to our sense of reality raises possibilities of social change being replaced by changes in images (Sontag, 1977). As a corollary to this possibility, we may note that the synthesizing and representational power of photographic images represents an important resource for the practice of the social sciences in the twentieth century— somewhat as the invention of optical instruments and the extension of mathematical techniques provided powerful tools for the natural sciences of the seventeenth century.

Still photography has been used as a medium of social documentary inquiry by sociologists, anthropologists, and psychologists (Becker, 1974; Templin, 1979a). It is a major educational influence in our lives, continuously informing and changing our images of what is worth attending to and what we shall observe (Sontag, 1977). As a form of representation it conveys information. This implies that photographic images have the ability to represent ideas in ideographic terms, as well as to provide illustrations for words (Lyons, 1967; Searle, 1979), and thus further understanding.

While photographic images have become commonplace in the visual landscape, they are often regarded as too subjective to be taken seriously as a form of evidence. Unlike audio and videotape, they have had little impact on the technology of evaluation. This chapter explores the potential of photography as a nondiscursive form of representation alternative to other symbolic forms of data represented in the statistical tables, graphs, and figures that are so widely used in the traditional approaches that dominate evaluation.

What can photography add that present evaluation methods do not already tell us? Still photography may be considered useful in any model of evaluation because it constitutes a form of visual communication that provides relevant nonverbal information and basic imagery not available by other means. Photographs convey a nondiscursive kind of visual knowledge that cannot be distinguished in discursive language (Langer, 1953). Sontag (1977) claims that photography provides visual images by which we learn to attend and respond. By their nature, photographic images have the power to evoke stories. As a pervasive form of visual communication, photography is continuously educating us and actually changing our process and limits of perception: In many important ways, we now see the way we do because of what we have learned to observe through photographs.

The assumptions of the evaluation model and the audience requirements may of course determine the various kinds of information required in a given evaluation study. Photography can add visual description that helps develop insights and improve understandings in appraising the context and interactions in a program.

Overview

Photographic methods and techniques have been used for inquiry purposes in various social, behavioral, and natural sciences, from which evaluation has also borrowed. Among the disciplines most akin to evaluation, photography has perhaps been used longest by psychologists, ethnographers, and sociologists (Stasz, 1979). They have photographed their subjects, the physical environment, various aspects of their travels, and the groups under study. As an evaluation methodology, however, photography is in a fledgling stage of development. Still photographs have been generally regarded as mildly interesting but peripheral to the issue of seriously improving the quality of explanation or understanding in evaluation studies. Yet there are several examples of studies where evaluators have made it their business to use photographic methods as a serious contribution. Two case studies in the Case Studies in Science Education curriculum evaluation report for the National Science Foundation (Stake & Easley et al., 1978) incorporated photographic material. Serrano's (1978) photographs illustrated his finding that the persistence of racially segregated peer groups was discrepant with the perceptions of school personnel about the effects of integration in racially balanced schools. Walker's (1978a) photographs of Pine City depicted the community context, which he concluded was a primary influence on the school curriculum.

Bernadine Stake's (1973) photographic evaluation of a children's visual arts program focused on the materials and processes of making art, using color slides without written text. Walker's (1978b) collection of photographs of the school headmaster tended to dispel some central myths about rational decision-making and agenda-setting in school administration. Wachtman (1978) provided photographic documentation of the activities and effects of an outside observer in the innovative Essence Science Curriculum evaluation. Anderson's (1975) Artists-in-Schools dance evaluation report began with pages of photographs capturing unique qualities of the program context. Walker's and Adelman's (1979) and Walker's and Wiedel's (1979) photographs of interactions between teachers and students that they used for photo-interviewing also appeared as sequential statements in the evaluation reports.

In the Teacher Corps 10th Cycle evaluation, Tabachnic and Fox (1975) used photographs to illustrate the report, and presented a 20-page photo essay of one aspect of the teacher training program. In a study of university housing patterns, Peterson and Brown (1979) compared the application of three models of evaluation using predominantly photographic data.

In most cases, these evaluations represent initial attempts at a variety of photographic approaches. A more widespread adoption of photography in evaluation requires that we have a greater knowledge of methodological problems and issues of photographic inquiry in social explorations. Thus it seems useful to examine current developments in other disciplines, particularly areas using the documentary genre.

This chapter looks to general photography, sociology, and anthropology for this methodological knowledge. The theoretical perspectives and methods explored and the examples cited are all from those disciplines, although they are not by any means comprehensive. In each field I have relied particularly on one author whose work represents an outstanding effort among others' to address the issues in using photography for documentary purposes. The contributions of these authors seem to help sustain the argument that photography may be adaptable to evaluation, although it is clear that there is still much room for ongoing refinement of the methodology of photography-assisted evaluation studies.

The term photography as used in this paper refers generally to black-and-white stills, although occasionally one might substitute color slides or prints. While focusing on possible adoptions from still photography, I am excluding some other potentially fruitful media forms that might also apply—film and videotape, historical photographs, and the photographic work of children or other actors in a setting.

There are both methodological and technical reasons for my concentration on black-and-white still photography. I had scarcely stepped in the door of the first site where I constructed a photo-assisted evaluation when I was confronted by a professional bystander who wanted to know: "Why black-and-white stills? Why not, say, color video?" It is a valid question, and one to which there are some sound answers.

First, one must consider the use to which photographic images are put in the study. They may be examined closely and reflected upon, arranged in sequential order, then used in tentative theoretical constructs that may, in turn, guide further picture-taking. These uses are perhaps better fulfilled by black-and-white still photography than by any other image medium. The images can be handled, examined, and sorted (in the form of enlargements) without the intervention of special equipment. Costs are low, so many pictures can be made; processing in the field is simple and rapid, permitting continuous feedback to guide further picture-taking; finally, the images yield much detail for examination (the resolving power of even a badly made photograph is at least 10 times that of a video image, for example). Conversely, of course, there are some types of information that a black-and-white still photograph does not convey, or conveys imperfectly: complex and rapid sequences of motion, and some (but not all) color information. As with any data-gathering tool, both the strengths and limitations of black-and-white still photography must be observed.

Documentary Visual Inquiry

We may treat the camera as a pen and accept documentary photography as a method of social inquiry that can help evaluators make evaluative statements rather than as a mere data collection instrument. By documentary photography I refer to a representational form that is intended to contribute visual information to a critical understanding of the social world under study (Sekula, 1978a). Many questions arise: What can evaluators learn from looking at pictures? What is represented by speaking in visual as opposed to verbal terms? What is the connection between pictures and discursive text? What is the impact of social conditions on the visual message, and what are the effects, in turn, on audiences? What is the quality of photographic evidence? How is the meaning of the visual record to be interpreted? Some of these questions are considered here in this chapter before a methodology for visual representation in naturalistic inquiry is described and practical problems in photo-evaluation are examined.

In addressing these questions, I am taking a view that is constructivist and perspectival. The form of representation that elucidates our visual sense is dialogic, constructivist, and stylistic. It is dialogic because that is the nature of communication between the subjects photographed, the photographer, and the viewer, given that certain procedures are followed that reduce threats to validity. On the assumption that people, not cameras, take pictures (Byers, 1966), photographs may be seen as constructions of social reality. Photography is constructivist as a function of the choices the photographer makes about what to photograph, in terms of time, place, light, frame, and angle. It is stylistic in that the photographer seeks to discover and portray patterns in the events and instances under study in an evaluation. It is perspectival in that multiple perspectives represented may contribute to the "thick description" of a situation (Geertz, 1973). As inquiry data, photographs embody various levels of interpretation—the value perspectives of the photographer, the constituents in a situation, and the viewers. By representation of reality, then, I mean presentation of reality.

Sontag (1977) argues that to photograph is to appropriate, that it means putting oneself into a certain relationship to the world that feels like knowledge and therefore like power. Images provide most of the knowledge people have about the past and the reach of the present, she claims. While what is written is frankly an interpretation, photographic images do not seem to be statements about the world so much as pieces of it. They are information. Such power has the capacity to distort as well as represent and, therefore, evaluators must look closely at the validity of such information.

Consideration of the validity of photographs in evaluation is very much tied to the historical development of photography as a medium of reportage. One cannot simply dismiss as irrelevant the fact that photography has had many other uses besides data-gathering in the social sciences. The techniques and technical resources of each branch of photography are borrowed and derived from others. Likewise, our "ways of seeing" with respect to one type of photography are never pure: They are formed, modified, and informed by what we have experienced in other visual situations. In other words, our visual literacy is learned globally, and we must understand its manifold origins before we can shape it to the purpose of interpreting photographic data in a specific social science context, such as the evaluation study. In the next sections, then, I will review the history and types of photographic practice from the perspective of what these antecedents can tell us about the application of photography to evaluation uses.

General Photography

Some would identify four general kinds of photography: news, advertising, fine arts, and science. Goffman (1976) defined private and public photos, with the latter subdivided into commercial, news, instructional, human interest, aesthetic, and publicity pictures. Photographs are popularly believed to be art or science, but not both. They are at once considered direct representations of objective truth and reality or entirely subjective expressions (Eisner, 1980). A brief look at general photography will help establish a conceptual orientation for a later discussion of the documentary genre, including such issues as validity, bias, and objectivity that evaluators would likely be concerned about.

Antecedents: the photo essay. From its beginnings photography has been used as a tool for exploration of society, and photographers have taken that as one of their tasks (Becker, 1974). Early photographers used the camera to record far-off societies, and later to expose the evils of urban industrial society. Lewis Hine and others published articles with photographs in the early issues of the *American Journal of Sociology* (Stasz, 1979). Photographs were also used to report the news and to record important events, e.g., Matthew Brody's extensive coverage of the Civil War.

The development of the illustrated weekly in Europe in the 1920s produced a group of photographers, including Alfred Einsenstaedt and Erich Salomon, who used the photo essay as an instrument of social analysis. Later, the *Picture Post* in England and *Time, Life,* and *Fortune* in the United States provided outlets for photo journalists employing the photo essay form, including Margaret Bourke-White, Walker Evans, W. Eugene Smith, and Robert Capa.

During the 1930s, photographers such as Dorothea Lange, Walker Evans, Russell Lee, and Arthur Rothstein, assembled by Roy Stryker and sponsored by the Farm Security Administration, recorded the conditions of Depression poverty, operating on the basis of various kinds of social science theory (Becker, 1974). More recently, political and social movements such as the civil rights movement have brought socially conscious photographers and social scientists with cameras to exploring a range of varied topics about communities, occupations, institutions, and organizations.

These photo essays combine a journalistic and ethnographic style with a self-conscious and deliberate artistic purpose (Becker, 1974). According to Becker, art and social exploration, whether ethnographic or sociological, describe two ways of working, not two separate kinds of photographers. The distinction between kinds of photographic work has melded to some extent on a common ground—documentary photography. Social scientists and socially concerned photographers often do work that is personally expressive and aesthetically interesting, apart from the social meaning of its subject matter, as in Robert Frank's *The Americans* and Larry Clark's *Tulsa.*

Meaning in documentary photography. On the other hand, Sekula (1975) suggested a different perspective on the question of photographic meaning and its relationship to documentary work:

> The meaning of a photograph, like that of any other entity, is inevitably subject to cultural definition. The task here is to define

and engage critically something we might call "photographic discourse." A discourse can be defined as an arena of information exchange, that is, a system of relations between parties engaged in communicative activity. In a very important sense, the notion of discourse is a notion of limits. That is, overall discourse relations could be regarded as a limiting function, one that established a bounded arena of shared expectations as to meaning [p. 37].

Sekula argued three points to support this view of photography as discourse. The first qualified the notion of the exchange of visual information by claiming that all messages are manifestations of interest. Second, photography as an embodiment of a message is an incomplete utterance whose meaning depends on external conditions. Third, because photographs communicate by means of associations with some implicit text, the meaning of a photographic message is context-determined. It follows that photographic literacy—reading messages—is learned. Sekula proposed that understanding the conventional nature of photographic communication depends on understanding both the emergence of photographic sign systems constructed in pictures, and the context in which photographs are made and interpreted.

Using this conceptualization of photographic discourse in considering the question of whether photographs are art or science, Sekula outlined two dominant perspectives in photographic history that persist to the present. I want to suggest that these are important to evaluators because these two photographic traditions are germane to our understanding of what documentary photography is and what possibilities it offers us.

One school, epitomized by the early work of Alfred Stieglitz and his journal *Camera Work* (1903-1917), attempted to develop photography as art—the movement was mannerist and expressive; it considered photographs as precious art objects, emphasized formalism, and elevated the importance of single photographic prints. The other school was exemplified by the early work of Louis Hine, a sociologist working in the same time period, whose collections of photographs of child labor and other workers' conditions helped define the documentary character of photographic discourse as a force for social reform. In the former school, photographic meaning was assumed to derive from the affective domain, based on the intrinsic value of the photograph as an art object. In the latter school, photographs were intended as information, with meaning tied to a political context that assigned them the status of documents representing reality in the sense of direct evidence. Even so, because of his reformist bent, Hine tended toward expressionism or "mystical realism" and, through his own empathy, tended to portray his subjects as victims. Sekula found both these views of photographic discourse inadequate for a documentary genre since they were both expressionist. He defined a continuum on which photographs range from metaphor to report, within an expressionist context:

> All photographic communication seems to take place within the conditions of a kind of binary folklore. That is, there is a "symbolist" folk-myth and a "realist" folk-myth. The misleading but popular form of this opposition is "art photography" vs. "documentary photography." Every photograph tends, at any given moment of reading in any given context, toward one of these two poles of meaning. The oppositions between these two poles are as follows: photographer as seer vs. photographer as witness; photography as expression vs. photography as reportage; theories of imagination (and inner truth) vs. theories of empirical truth; affective value vs. informative value; and finally, metaphoric signification vs. metonymic signification [Sekula, 1975, p. 45].

The reformist view, through expressionist intent, empathy, and nostalgia, limited the social context and the informational value of photography as well as the resultant discourse.

Characteristics of the ideal documentary. Sekula (1978a) defined a third form of photography that deals with the social ordering of people's lives. He conceptualized the documentary as a strategy against making photography a high art, resulting, rather, in a representational art in which form, mannerism, and empirical truth were not ends in themselves. Its purpose is to put photography to documentary use in contributing to a critical understanding of the social world. Such work, Sekula argued, addresses the question of how people invent a limited range of possibilities, and how their lives are invented for them by those in power. He recognized a small but growing number of contemporary photographers doing social documentary studies on subjects ranging from social realities to personal space. Such social exploration is expected to provide logical, coherent accounts of power structures and of cause and effect in social situations, framing the discourse and the context.

Sekula described various characteristics of the documentary genre. It supplies information from unexpected sources because at every level of society photographs are treated not as privileged objects but as common cultural artifacts. It functions to elicit dialogue with the people photographed rather than affirming the photographer's own point of view. It assumes that the photographer's close relationship to the subjects performs a referential function to the quality of information in a discourse. It uses the evidence of terrain and language of context as a socially mediated construction. The inherent language of the situation under study may openly bracket the collection of photographs, using texts in some fashion to anchor, contradict, reinforce, subvert, complement, particularize, or go beyond the meanings of images themselves (Sekula, 1978a).

The expectation that single photographs can tell a story alone is rejected in favor of using a large collection of photographs, especially close-ups rich in information. In reports, pictures are sometimes located within an extended narrative text, as in the Smiths' *Minamata* (1975), a study of the fishing industry's response to the effects of mercury pollution on a Japanese fishing village. Other reports rely primarily on photographs captioned briefly with descriptions, or with simple headings and no text, as in Cancian's *Another Place: Photographs of a Mayan Community* (1974).

In actuality, good documentary studies are mixtures of expressionism from a social point of view and mannerism in the sense of good technical form. The emphasis is placed on the photographer's social construction of reality for purposes of developing a critical understanding of a social situation. For purposes of evaluation, general photography tells us that photographs can be used for interpretation or reportage. As a socially mediated representation of reality, documentary photography is limited not by the nature of photography but by the intention of the photographer.

Anthropology and Photography

Anthropologists share many of the concerns of documentary photographers about reporting and interpreting cultural situations with photographs. While they may agree that in such visual portrayal meanings are context-bound, anthropologists differ from general photographers in their application of social science methods and theories to interpreting cultural situations and events. The camera has been used by ethnographers, physical anthropologists, and archaeologists. Photographic material is regarded as visual evidence. Like other forms of evidence collected in the field, photographs may be taken as analyzable data or as evidence to support an anthropological idea. This section addresses some problems of photographic inquiry that concern anthropologists.

Photographic data. Ruby (1976) defined an anthropological photograph as a photograph taken by or under the direction of a professional anthropologist in order to convey an anthropological statement pictorially. Mead (1972) recalled that in the early days a camera was an essential piece of field equipment along with the note pads and pencils that were taken into the field even before ethnographers had developed a firmly conceptualized field methodology.

Ruby (1973) hypothesized that anthropologists take photographs in the field and subsequently use them at home not primarily as a means of generating analyzable data or even as illustrative evidence to support their ideas, but rather as a means of establishing and maintaining a social role and identification with the anthropological community. Picture-taking is a way of being an anthropologist, but rarely a means of doing anthropology. Ruby claimed that anthropologists have for years produced snapshots of their travels, but no one seriously regards these pictures as professional scientific products. Occasionally, pictures taken in the study of nonverbal communication are used for the purpose of generating photographic types of data that are used analytically, on such topics as body language, proxemics, gesture, and the like.

In rare cases pictures are published as partial evidence to support or illustrate a research finding. Such an example is Bateson's and Mead's (1942) Balinese study, where the analysis of photographically generated data is the focus of the research and of the subsequent published report. Photographs were used to cross-check data gathered by observation and interview, and were published as eloquent statements about Balinese customs, comprising over half the material in the report.

Problems of inference. A model of communication proposed by Worth and Gross (1974) suggests that human beings interpret and assign meaning to objects, persons, and events by utilizing two basic strategies: attribution and inference. To make an attribution one makes an assumption that a particular sign-event is natural and existential. Meaning is assigned by attributing characteristics to the signs photographed, not to the photograph. On the other hand, to make an inference about a photograph, one begins by making an assumption of intent—that someone created the sign-event, and that it was organized, structured, and put together purposefully. Meaning is then assigned on the basis of various sociocultural conventions assumed by the viewer of a photograph to apply to the particular structures recognized in the photograph. Inferences are made about the whole photograph as a created symbolic articulation.

Ruby (1976) pointed out that photographs are assumed to be the most accurate representations of reality that are possible. This assumption is based on our cultural notion that photographic sign-events are made of iconic signs that bear a strong resemblance or correspondence to their referent. As did Sekula in critiquing Hine's work, Ruby distinguished this view of photographic data corresponding to or capturing external reality from the view of the construction of a more holistic documentary photographic statement about an anthropological idea. In photographically generated data, viewers are asked to interpret the behavior represented in the photograph as they would had they experienced it first hand. In the case of a photographic statement, Ruby contends that the viewer is asked to infer concepts from a collection of photographs, that is, to assume that an anthropological photographer constructed the image utilizing a socially shared symbol system because that photographer wanted the viewer to know something about anthropology.

The range of inferential and attributional paradigms currently employed in our culture to assign meaning to photographs appears to be limited. Sekula (1975) argued that there were two basic folk models used in photographic communication within the binary folklore he outlined. These are a symbolist myth and a realist myth. The popular form of this dichotomy is "art photography" vs. "documentary photography." That is, we treat photographs as either art or depictions of reality, but seldom as organized photographic statements employing inferences and about which further inferences can be made by a viewer.

Similarly, the uses of photography in anthropology involve two limited interpretive strategies: making inferences about photographs as art and aesthetic objects; and making attributions about photographs as records of reality that lead to limited judgments about the contents. Ruby contended that both strategies are at odds with the fundamental purposes of anthropological communication—to make more scientific inferences about culture. Ruby argued that the use of inferences employing attributions is based on a theory of perception that is counter to the basic anthropological idea that culture organizes perception, and that making attributions leads to subjective judgments. The misguided assumption that a photograph is an unmediated record of the real world is a consequence of two related concepts: that cameras, not people, take pictures (Byers, 1966), and the idea that the world is as it appears to be. By contrast, assuming that *people* take pictures and that reality is *constructed* reveals photography to be a mediated representation of the world.

From the perspective of cultural relativism, culture is viewed as a systematic means of ordering experience (Sapir, 1949). This view in turn suggests that visual perception is a creative, constructive act—one that causes the individual to construct a reality out of socially shared experiences. Thus the camera in the hands of the photographer should be regarded as a means of creating a photographic reality that reflects the cultural reality of the anthropologist; it is not a device that reliably transcends the cultural limitations of the picture taker. On the other hand, anthropologists aim to present the world as the investigated see it. But seeing the world the way the actors do is not the sole interpretive aim of anthropology. Geertz (1973) asserted that the purpose of anthropology is to interpret culture from the viewpoint of the anthropologist. This implies that we cannot capture reality on film, but that we can construct a set of images that is consistent with our view of it. In photographic ethnographic research of a constructivist persuasion, the result would be at best a combination of the two perspectives—an honest translation by the investigator of how the investigated see their world.

Ruby suggested some approaches that might lead toward more fruitful use of photography in the communication of anthropology. He outlined two tasks. One is to explore ways of creating and displaying photographs that instruct viewers to regard these images as constructed pictorial statements and not as mere records of the world. Anthropologists should remind the viewers of presentations that they are seeing the world of the subjects through the eyes of the anthropologist.

A second task is to explore ways of establishing pictorial systems of inferences that are based upon more scientific anthropological paradigms. Worth and Gross (1974) suggested that the meaning of any photographic message is not inherent within the sign itself but, rather, within the social context. Sekula (1975) regarded the photograph as an incomplete utterance, a message that depends on some external matrix of conditions and presuppositions for its readability. There are two contexts that yield meanings inferred about photographs. One is the context in which photographs are made; the other is the context in which they are viewed. Photographs taken by anthropologists generally appear in four formats: as illustrations in books, articles, and monographs; as slides used to illustrate lectures; in galleries and museum displays; and in published photographic essays. Ruby (1976) argued that in order to increase our understanding of the current place of pictorial statements within anthropology and to open up the possibility of developing and expanding the place of this visual mode in the communication of anthropology, it is necessary to explore the ways in which these formats cause viewers to derive significance and meaning about contexts and events photographed.

Establishing pictorial systems of inference would include developing a scientific anthropological pictorial code. This depends upon broadening our understanding of the gap between visual statements and implied texts and of the processes of photographic communication in general. If photographs continue to be regarded as either aesthetic objects or records of reality then they serve a limited function in anthropology. Ruby asserted that what we need is both to understand the role of pictorial statements in culture, and to provide anthropologists with a more rigorous pictorial medium of communication.

This discussion of photography in anthropology has several implications for evaluators. One is the view that reality is not a set of conditions waiting to be captured on film. Making photographic inquiry more systematic and rigorous means viewing photographs not as either art or an unmediated record of reality, but rather as a set of images consistent with the photographer's perspective of the situation. Second, inference occurs at two levels of context; the context in which photographs are made and the context in which photographs are viewed. Interpretation is limited not by the nature of photographic evidence but by the rigor of the strategies employed to make inferences rather than attributions. Improving the rigor of these strategies depends upon developing pictorial systems of inference for visual communication so that viewers understand what the photographer wanted them to know about the anthropology of the situation.

Sociology and Photography

Like anthropologists, sociologists who espouse the use of photography to explore society have been critical of the field for not developing more widely accepted, rigorous methods of photographic inquiry. This section attempts to describe some theoretical and methodological issues in social documentary photography as it applies to sociological research. The section is organized around the place of theory in improving rigor, and a method of grounded theory field work.

Becker (1974, 1981) asserted that sociologists and photographers alike have always wanted to understand how society worked, to map its dimensions and then look into big sectors and little crannies so mapped. Among them have been a few who have attempted to describe what has not yet been described, in the style of the ethnographer; to tell the big news, in the style of the journalist; and to combine these (more or less) with the desire for rigor and general theory.[1]

Closer study of the results of this type of social documentary photography reveals that much of it is intellectually thin, based on reiterating simple themes or hinging on a few compelling images. Those who are responsive to the tradition of ethnographic field work would want photographic explorations to provide results as rich and interesting as verbal descriptions. Becker argued that the answer lies in the role of theory in making photographs of social phenomena.

Improving rigor. The photographer exerts some control over the medium—the final image, the information, and the message it contains. The way the photographer controls it depends on two primary influences. First, the professional traditions, technical expertise, and conditions of work are all relevant to the kind of photograph the photographer has come to value as a pictorial medium of communication. Second, the theory the photographer subscribes to influences what that photographer is looking at and the understanding of what is being investigated. Within limits, skilled photographic investigators can make the images look like they want them to.

But photographs have the power to distort and surprise with unanticipated images (Sontag, 1977). To some extent this power compromises the photographer's control. Photographers are not usually required to make their practice square with their theory. Like all artists, they use whatever comes to hand and to some extent whatever will get the job done, endeavoring at the same time to control the medium. In social documentary photography, there is a need to have prior theory to pose questions and direct the study and to have some assurance about the photographic practice that follows it. Yet perhaps the greatest threat to validity is not the danger of being guided by an unfruitful line of theorizing, but, rather, having to account for photographic data that "just happened" and that cannot be shown to have arisen from the rules of sampling or data collection. This serendipitous quality of photography has powerful influence over the place of theory in the interpretive process taking place, and requires continuous searching for new information that may contest or modify the interpretation.

Becker (1974) contended that photographers should be aware of the social content of their photographs and their relevance to current ideas and theories, and be able to talk at length about them. He claimed that when photographers' work gives a satisfyingly complex understanding of a subject it is because they have acquired a sufficiently elaborate theory to alert them to the visual manifestations of that complexity. He proposed that making photographic explorations of society more systematic means knowing society better by knowing sociology or ethnography better through their theories, concepts, and methods.

According to Becker, sociological theory, whether large-scale abstract theory or a specific theory about some empirical phenomenon, is a set of ideas with which investigators make sense of a situation while they photograph it. The theory tells when an image contains information of value—when it communicates something worth communicating. It furnishes the criteria by which worthwhile data and statements can be separated from those containing nothing of value—those that do not increase our knowledge of society.

However, it is apparent that because the photographs may at any time contribute something new beyond the theory, the photographer spends part of the interpretive effort ameliorating and adapting the theory, so that new information is accommodated in new theoretical notions. Were this not the case, the discovery of new information in photographs would be neglected in generating explicit ideas during the appraisal of a situation, and photography would be relegated to mere illustration of some prior theory.

Explicit theories may be put to work guiding the photographer's thinking, the visual organization of the study, and the methods. Such theories need not be elaborate, grand, or middle-range theories but, rather, tentative hypotheses and concepts used in a metaphorical sense to answer questions in the field. In the theorizing process, progression occurs from the particular to the general, from images to theory. Micro-ethnographic or emergent theories emanating from the ground up are defined here as a set of informed conjectures close to the specific situation that suggest questions of interest. Investigators may not know the questions until they have seen observable data.

Such theories help focus the topic and guide the investigative process until the final interpretations and presentation. The aim in photographic investigation is to discover meanings in daily behavior by connecting ideas with visual counterparts, working from specific images to somewhat larger ideas.

Grounded theory model. One research model that is appropriate and directly transferrable to photographic documentary investigation comes from the participant observation tradition of sociological and ethnographic field work (Denzin, 1970; Hill, 1976; Lofland, 1970; Schatzman &

Strauss, 1973; Smith & Geoffrey, 1968; Smith & Pohland, 1974, 1976; Stake and Easley, 1978). Sociological and ethnographic ideas can be used in photographic explorations of society in the manner of the discovery of grounded theory procedures of sequential analysis (Glaser & Strauss, 1967). Such a naturalistic approach allows the investigator to make use of what is learned one day in the next day's data collection. As field workers write up their notes of verbatim descriptions from observations and interviews, they simultaneously make preliminary analyses or interpretations of the information by raising questions:

> What is there in what they have recorded that they don't understand? How can they find out more about it? What ideas does it suggest about the organization they are studying and people's experience in it? What patterns of interaction, of cause and effect, of interrelationships are suggested by what they now know? If the rest of what they observe is like this, what generalizations will they be able to make? Where should they look to find evidence that these preliminary ideas are wrong (or right) [Becker, 1974, p. 12]?

As they conduct the study, field workers develop tentative hypotheses, specific theories grounded closely in the data, set in the context studied, but shaped by relevant theoretical formulations that emerge and orient the next day's observations and interviews along the lines suggested by the analysis (Becker, 1974). Analysis is continuous and simultaneous with the
As they conduct the study, field workers develop tentative hypotheses, specific theories grounded closely in the data, set in the context studied, but shaped by relevant theoretical formulations that emerge and orient the next day's observations and interviews along the lines suggested by the analysis (Becker, 1974). Analysis is continuous and simultaneous with the data-gathering; it is simply a way of interpreting sequentially what is learned as data accumulate and the study is constructed. Photographers intending to conduct documentary social inquiry may do much the same thing.

To summarize briefly, Sekula, Ruby, and Becker have all argued that a more rigorous approach to documentary photography is needed. While Sekula separated symbolist (art) from realist (documentary) photography, Ruby and Becker contended that some amalgamation of the two persists in most contemporary investigative photography. All three asserted that the improvement of social photographic exploration hinges on upgrading theoretical knowledge and borrowing methodological rigor from the qualitative social sciences. They advocated more systematic application of ethnographic procedures in transferring conventional grounded theory research methods to photographic inquiry.

If photographic discourse is an arena of information exchange, then it has the potential to bring evaluators information about the problems under study. For purposes of evaluation, the objective of using rigorous photographic methods would be not to test or build theories but to discover theoretical interpretations that could enhance our understanding of the issues in a situation.

Photographic Methods of Inquiry

The elements of a method of photographic inquiry that evaluators could regard as credible and promising must include the following:

- sampling
- reactivity
- procedures for data collection
- validity
- interpretation

The reason these five elements are necessary and sufficient for a method of photographic inquiry is that this list covers, from beginning to end, all aspects of photographic data collection and interpretation that are needed in order for the method to meet the usual standards of methodological rigor that are applied in the qualitative areas of the social sciences, from which evaluation borrows. Sampling selects what to photograph and helps delimit the collection of photos on which to base interpretation. Reactivity accounts for the obtrusiveness of the camera and the relationships that develop between the photographer and those photographed. Procedures for data collection assure that the photographer makes a rigorous attempt to take photographs that fairly represent the situation. Validity contributes methods for minimizing threats to the validity of inferences made. Interpretation provides sense-making procedures for grounding systematic efforts at making inferences and assertions about photographs. Validity is a key element, since there are several conditions that may render photographs useless as data and these threats will be of major concern to the evaluator who is attempting to establish a rigorous method.

A methodology that distinguishes documentary photography from other kinds of photography has been developed in anthropology and sociology. In particular, the work of Becker (1974, 1979) and Collier (1967) offer one systematic approach to using the camera as a research tool. This method of inquiry seems compatible with the tasks of evaluators.

Sampling

While composition may imply what is important in a single picture, sampling implies what is important in a collection of documentary photographs. Collier (1967) claimed that sampling in photography connotes authenticity. The model of sampling applied in this photographic method is Glaser's and Strauss's (1967) notion of theoretical sampling for purposes of generating theory. Units of observation (categories of information) are chosen because some theory, in particular an emergent theory, suggests they are strategic for understanding the data.

Social scientists in general deal with threats to the validity of assertions and inferences by applying various conventional sampling techniques that show their photographs in a way that implies generalizability, that what they say applies to a wider population. Some sampling techniques pertinent to photography include time-sampling, checking up on people at regular intervals (minutes, hours, days, weeks, seasons), or sampling across actual time to get a full range of times and activities represented. Another sampling technique entails shadowing or following one person through an entire daily or other routine. A third approach is snowball sampling, asking each subject who else and what else the investigator should talk to, and photograph, letting one subject lead to another. Other variants of these sampling methods will be proposed in a later section of this monograph.

Photographers may translate these sampling conventions into their practice, depending on what they are observing. Photographers may expose a roll of film every hour. They may photograph certain activities or places on a schedule that counters the tendency to photograph only what appears personally interesting. Using theory as a sampling device may direct the photographers' attention to things toward which the bias of their interest or intuition might not otherwise lead them, things that indicate what might constitute more full description of the situation under study. Techniques of the randomization and theoretically informed sampling might indicate that the photographer do something different to gather evidence—shooting from low, high, or varied angles, from behind the subjects, over the shoulder, from the torso with preset exposure and distance. Whatever sampling devices are used, photographers need to identify the photographs by date, time, film roll and frame, and place, in addition to specifying the overall sampling strategy.

Reactivity

The problems of reactivity with respect to the influence of the observer's presence raise the question of whether that which is observed and recorded by the photographer is an accurate reflection of ordinary behavior or a result of the photographer's presence. The camera is considered by Becker (1974, 1978) and Collier (1967) to help reduce reactivity. They argue that carrying a camera validates the investigator's right to be there. People generally want their pictures taken, whether the photographer is a tourist, a member of the group, or a media representative. Under many circumstances, observing and photographing is commonplace, expected, and accepted. At least people know specifically what kind of data an observer is collecting with a camera, even though the presence of the camera may produce some anxiety at first.

Becker (1974, 1978), Collier (1967), and Walker and Wiedel (1979) claim that camera facilitates the photographer's access and helps in developing trust relationships between the subjects and the investigator. The kind of relationships developed are related to the kind of conceptualizations that are possible in a study. This seems particularly true when photographs are shown to subjects for purposes of interviewing them about what has been depicted. Whenever and wherever investigators put themselves in relationship to the subjects, the trust that has been established is revealed. The social and physical distance between subjects and photographer, and the position from which photographs are taken, indicate whether the photographer has taken the role of observer or participant.

The presence of the photographer does not in the long run change anyone's behavior since observing and photographing become part of the scene. In many situations, people being observed are engaged in ordinary activities that are important to them. They cannot change what they are doing for an observer even if they want to. Also, reactivity is itself part of the data. How people react indicates how they view and feel about the situation in which they are involved. Some photographers encourage reactivity in the hope of making the reaction a basis of their exploration of people and events. In this case, the photographs become a record of their relationships with the people they photograph.

Reactivity often reflects apprehension and fear about what will be done with the information being gathered and photographed. The observer must give evidence that subjects will not be put in jeopardy.

Procedures for Data Collection

Ethnographic documentary photography as described by Becker and Collier represents a form of participant observation in which the most obtrusive element—the camera—goes into the situation first. The camera immediately facilitates the observer's access by requiring engagement with the subjects to explain its presence. The process of data collection has several continuous parts. It entails taking many pictures, theorizing continuously about them, developing inferences about the situation that help guide the next round of photographing, supplementing photos with verbatim data from interviewing and observing, staying in the situation as long as possible, and repeating the process. All the while, the investigator is attempting to confirm or disconfirm the inferences and assertions made until the collection of new data appears not to be adding substantially to understandings already developed.

Taking many pictures. The investigator begins by shooting a number of pictures in the situation under study—photos of almost anything that seems interesting or potentially meaningful. This may be done initially in an unstructured way, covering a sufficient variety of situations or events to satisfy the notion that a broad range of features and activities has been represented. Close-ups contain more information, but some long, mapping photos also are useful in developing a side-angle view of the scene under study. Initial photographing may also be done in a structured way, if the study has been so designed, using a specific time or spatial sampling plan—for example, positioning the camera at particular places, such as the four corners of comparable classrooms at comparable times (Addis, 1979). It is vital at this stage that a quantity of photos be taken for studying.

Focusing on the topic. Film is developed daily if possible. The initial results are likely to be a large collection of relatively incoherent prints. Once a number of first prints are available for scanning, it is possible to decide more specifically what the topic of the photographic study is. The investigator studies contact sheets and working prints and hypothesizes tentatively about them, returning continuously to the site to take more pictures on the basis of the interpretation that is developing. This saturation approach performs several simultaneous functions. It allows the researcher room to change the topic or the theoretical orientation of the topic. It allows the researcher to learn early about the lighting and spatial conditions in the situation, simultaneous with developing access to the subjects being chosen. It allows the researcher to learn and raise questions about what is happening, who the people are, what they are doing, and why they may be doing it that way. In making inferences about such information, it is important to pay careful attention to details, including those that do not immediately make sense, or those that seem distinctive or discrepant.

Gathering verbatim data. In the next phase of photographic documentation, the investigator begins interviewing and observing, keeping verbatim field notes, while continuing the photographic pursuit of questions that are emerging. Analytic categories serve as developing themes in the situation. Establishing close purposeful relationships with people in the situation from the beginning helps build trust and assure access to as much data as possible. Staying in the situation as long as possible is important. Once the investigator is accepted, people are likely not only to offer their own perspectives more freely in interviews, but they may also help point out things that warrant being photographed and allow more close-up shots to be taken.

Photo-interviewing. Additional information may be gathered by photo-interviewing, defined as the technique of showing the subjects the pictures to gather their perspectives and meanings. Photos are read in the context from which they were taken. The chief advantage of this photo-interviewing technique is that it may elicit more data (Collier, 1967). Another is that when subjects see photographs of themselves they may be reassured about potential jeopardy or incrimination from photographic information. The photo-interviewing procedure places emphasis on the investigator continuously returning to the site with photographic material, to compare the investigator's interpretations with the subjects' interpretations so that both perspectives are represented.

Confirming, disconfirming, and the theorizing process. Woven throughout the photographing process are attempts to develop an interpretation of information in the pictures. Each day's pictures will bring some tentative answers to questions. These questions and answers help distill and winnow analytic categories, spot recurring regularities, and develop themes. Subsequent photographing may confirm or disconfirm these interpretations. The investigator stays alert to new information that calls for changing and reformulating theories about what is happening.

As work progresses, the photographer looks for visual embodiments of ideas, for images that contain and communicate the understanding being developed. While it is important to go into a situation with some theory about what one may expect to find there, reconceptualizing what is happening frequently may change the interpretation. If the photographer remains skeptical and is willing to give up or modify concepts during the theorizing process, then the study may be over when it appears that new data are no longer disconfirming or adding to the interpretation. As Becker observes:

> The theories will inform (the photographer's) vision and influence what he finds interesting and worth taking pictures of. His theories will help him to photograph what he might otherwise have ignored. Simultaneously he will let what he finds in his photographs direct his theory building, the pictures and ideas becoming closer and closer approximations of one another [Becker 1974, p. 14].

The photographer arranges the visual materials into patterns and sequences that are the visual analog of inferences and assertions made during the study. As discussed later, the final report may take one of several forms.

Validity of Photographs as Evidence

If we are going to use photographs as evidence for social assertions, we need to know whether they can be trusted as evidence, whether and how they "tell the truth" (Becker, 1978). Photographs are taken as representations of reality that convey a sense of truth. Sontag (1977) argued that despite the presumption of veracity that gives photographs their authority, seductivity, and interest, they have high potential for distorting and misrepresenting reality. When we look at a photograph we may take it as evidence of incontrovertible reality or as a piece of art (Templin, 1978). A photographer may present photographs in a way that conveys some essential or important truth about the topic, perhaps a personal or artistic statement. If a picture is an incomplete statement in a discourse, then we are dealing with both the interpretation of the photographer and the interpretation of the viewer (Arnheim, 1975; Byers, 1966; Goffman, 1976). Evaluators will want to know if photographs are reliable evidence and whether they are relevant, fair, and accurate representations of the phenomena under study.

For evaluators, the question becomes not only whether photographers are telling the truth, but what the photographs are telling the truth about. Becker (1978) maintained that the first step in deciding what truth photographs assert is seeing what answers can be extracted from material in the photographs to specific questions that either we or the photos have suggested. He qualified four points about the validity of such assertions:

- The truth need not be a whole truth. It is irrelevant to criticize the assertion we have extracted from a picture because there is some other assertion it will also support, unless the two assertions are contradictory. Since pictures often contain a wealth of information it is not surprising that more than one true thing can be said on the basis of a single image.

- The truth will ordinarily not be verified by a single photographic image and usually not by any number of photographic images taken by themselves. We generally decide important questions on the basis of all kinds of evidence, balancing all the fragments of fact assembled to arrive at the best judgment we can make about a proposition. Those fragments will ordinarily include other photographs . . . and a variety of textual materials: documents, interviews, and so forth.

- We can never be absolutely sure of the truth of an assertion. Our knowledge is always partial and therefore fallible . . . new information can shift our ideas about the validity of an assertion and thus the degree to which those ideas rest on more than the internal evidence deducible from one photograph.

- No single standard of proof is acceptable for all social groups and all purposes . . . we demand a higher standard of proof if we are going to base some important action on our conclusion [Becker, 1978, p. 11].

On the basis of these qualifications, Becker proposed several threats to the validity of propositions based on photographic evidence, analogous to Campbell's and Stanley's (1966) threats to validity in experimental and quasi-experimental designs. In conceptualizing these threats, Becker (1978) identified four general problems and offered corollary solutions to them. These threats appear useful in reducing doubts about conclusions drawn from photographic evidence.

Altered photographs. The most obvious threat to the validity of a conclusion based on photographic evidence is the suspicion that the photograph was faked or doctored in some way. These practices would include retouching, composite negatives, using models, arranging or staging the scene, and the like. The "truth" of information depends in part on the inferences drawn from it, that is, the extent to which conclusions about photographs may be generalized. For example, Owens' (1973) photographic study *Suburbia* conveys a great deal of information about how suburban families live in one particular location. Should we wish to generalize conclusions to suburban life in other places, we need to be satisfied that the photos present a naturalistic, unaltered portrayal. On the other hand, obviously altered photographs, such as in Dawne Ade's *Photo-*

montage, would suggest to viewers that generalizable inferences were not appropriate, but rather that the photographs stand instead as symbolic artistic statements in themselves. Altering photographs would not appear to be much of a problem in most photographic evidence collected for evaluation, because of the rigorous methods that are generally applied.

Artistic intent. The desire to make "art" may lead photographers to suppress details that interfere with their artistic conceptions, conceptions that might be perfectly valid in their own right but that render the photographs unsuitable for use as evidence for certain kinds of conclusions. These threats depend on what artistic conventions and fashions were current when the photograph was made. We can look for those kinds of sampling and presentational omissions, or for biases that might be associated with those artistic conventions. Validity would rest on the internal coherence and documentary style of photographic approaches designed to increase informational value, rather than on exclusion or distortion of information for artistic purposes—practices such as using cropped photos, out of focus prints, extreme lighting, selective distortions, or whatever constitutes artistic convention. However, there are also some less obvious types of distortion. For example, Diane Arbus did not do anything obvious to her photos, but her selection and presentation apparently constituted an artistic statement and obviously slanted reality.

Inadequate sampling. We may suspect that the photographer has inadequately sampled the events that might have been photographed, failing to see all the things relevant to the questions and answers of interest, or, having seen them, failed to photograph them. One of the major problems limiting adequate sampling is the photographer's access. Another is the terms accepted to negotiate that access. Does the photographer have full access to a range of relevant activities and on what terms was that access negotiated? Access and terms either determine or limit to some extent what information is available to the photographer. The concept of adequate sampling includes information about the photographer's relationship with and distance from the subjects, whether that be intimate, friendly, hostile, or voyeuristic. This pertains to how much time the photographer spent at the site and what was available or restricted from photographing. The sample is considered more trustworthy the longer the time period the photographer spent there.

Another problem of sampling, related to artistic intent as well, has to do with the photographer's theory. Photographers tend to make pictures only of what is interesting or meaningful to them. What has meaning or interest is a function of the theory being put to work during an investigation. Theories may restrict or inhibit what is photographed, or on the other hand may alert the photographer to an increased range of elements in a setting. The importance of theoretical orientation is illustrated by the contrast between Paul Strand's (1971) posed formal portraits of peasants in other countries around the world showing them as noble, and Frank Cancian's (1974) collection of candid pictures of Mayan Indians in their natural home and work settings. All these sampling problems are topics about which the photographer should supply information to diminish threats to the validity of inferences or assertions.

Censorship. Some form of censorship may have prevented viewers from seeing all the pictures that they could possibly have seen, and the ones that have been withheld might have substantially changed the interpretations or altered the conclusions. Censorship may be imposed by the state, by a general cultural atmosphere, or by the photographer's own personal or political convictions; or by compromises the photographer may have agreed to in negotiating access to the site of the study. Censorship from any of these sources could make some photographs unfavorable or distasteful. One way to reduce the photographer's selection bias is by presenting a number of prints in the study, and by including proof sheets for independent checking. Another way is to include appended textual material, especially that from interviews with the subjects in the photographs. Such texts vary, ranging from information on a variety of topics depicted, to the values, hopes, aspirations, and dreams of people. For example, in Owens' *Suburbia* study, the photographs are elaborated and interpreted with information gathered from the subjects. In Banish's (1976) study *City Families,* which contrasts families in London and Chicago, formal portraits are accompanied by edited interviews with the subjects that deal largely with aspirations and hopes.

With respect to inferences, conclusions, and what questions can be answered plausibly by photographic materials, viewers must take into account what they know or suspect about the degree to which censorship or some kind of bias, misrepresentation, or distortion occurred. In presenting photographic evidence, photographers would want to avoid such biases or explain their presence.

Interpretation

The interpretation of photographic evidence suggested here implies that generalizability is a matter of logical inference that is plausible and validated against experience, rather than causal explanations validated with empirical proofs. The logic of inference depends in part on the kinds of questions asked. The questions emanate from ideas about what the investigator anticipates finding, is finding, and is theorizing about in the situation under study. A theory—that is, a set of ideas—can help tell the investigator that an observation is interesting (Becker, 1979). However, "theory" may well be implicit in the viewer: We may start to examine photographic data on one theoretical basis, but the photos may excite interest by validating or supporting or otherwise recalling another theoretical construct that we also hold, but that might not otherwise have been applied to the present situation. Such a view seems consistent with the notion of the structure of ideas in the concept of grounded theory. Such telling theories direct the investigation to whole classes of information. The kinds of questions asked of the data allow the photographer to develop certain interpretations.

Becker (1974) transposed basic sociological theory of a functionalist persuasion into a list of questions that can be answered photographically in the field. He cautioned that answers do not come all at once, but through a process of progressive refinement and constant testing against new information that contains visual counterparts.

(1) What are the different kinds of people in the situation? They may or may not look different; they will certainly be called by different names.
(2) What expectations does each kind of person—members of each status group—have about how members of other groups ought to behave? What are the recurring situations around which such expectations group?
(3) What are the typical breaches of these expectations? What kinds of gripes and complaints do people have? (A complaint is a sign of a violated expectation: "He's supposed to do X and he hasn't.")
(4) What happens when expectations are violated? Is there a standard way of settling those conflicts [Becker, 1974, p. 14]?

Becker contended that these questions put in a common-sense way ideas that are integral to much sociological analysis. Question 1 refers to the cast of characters and status groups; question 2 refers to norms, rules, or common understandings; question 3 refers to deviance or rule violations; and question 4 refers to sanctions and conflict resolution (Becker, 1974). Seeing an instance of one of these concepts alerts the photographer to look for other visual counterparts of elements that embody the theory.

An example of such a telling sociological theory that may be useful in directing our attention to the small-scale details available for interpretation is Goffman's frame analysis (1974, 1976). He defined social situations as a unit of social organization and contended that social situations are arenas of mutual monitoring. In them, ritual, behavior displays, and ceremonies function to affirm basic social arrangements. He hypothesized that in social situations individuals can communicate in the fullest terms; most of the world's work gets done in social situations, and as such they are rich settings for investigation.

The interpretative task comes down to a procedure of classification and sorting of photographic evidence. Interpretation is based on attempting to answer the kinds of questions previously cited here, interwoven with further photographing in a process of simultaneous data-gathering, analyzing, and reconceptualizing. The photographer looks for alternative interpretations to reformulate the theoretical position, meanings that may emerge suggested by the data about what is happening.

Collier (1967) contended there are two levels of sorting involved in the inferential process. The first level of sorting is merely a descriptive account of material elements and cultural/social arrangements. The second level of sorting is an interpretive account, identifying and evaluating the overall patterns of the subgroup culture or situation under study based on available research data. This correlation is made not by counting or measuring but by the photographer's making judgments that can qualify the visual evidence of personality, behaviors, and the character of the situation. Developing and confirming the validity of such judgments is accomplished through photo-interviewing subjects, using the provocative quality of pictures as the interpretive key to situations; and then through the photographer's calling on personal judgments to express inferences and assertions that have been informed and stimulated by the multiple evidence that has been gathered.

The basic idea is to clarify how the photographer thinks things really are, and to present photographs that use imagery as evidence for inferences and assertions that have developed. Three interesting examples that illustrate how photographic evidence may be interpreted are found in Goffman (1976), Levine (1975), and Sekula (1978b). Goffman analyzed gender displays depicted in advertising photographs, using small-scale categories that he regarded as repeating themes in social situations. He presented a number of photographs supporting each category. Levine did an elaborate analysis of the social and political implications of the many fine details in a *Life* photo of President Nixon in China. Sekula analyzed a series of photographs of a husband and wife taken over time in different settings, in terms of their life stages.

Conclusion

This section has described important elements of a method of photographic inquiry. What it tells evaluators is that incorporating photographic methods creates minimal threat, and does not require wholesale revision of the process of evaluation. Rather, to add photography would require only an expansion of existing evaluation methods.

More weight appears to have been given to problems of various threats to validity. This does not mean that other elements are not important considerations. The attention given in these pages reflects the attention given to validity matters in the literature. Other methodological elements need to be developed more by evaluators using photographic methods. The fact that we can discuss such elements in photographic investigation attests to its compatibility with evaluation.

Implications for Evaluation

There are several kinds of implications with respect to adopting photography in evaluation. Of particular concern are problems of the limitations of photographic methods. Another has to do with the status of particular evaluation models under which photography would be appropriate. A third delineates some communication functions that might prevail. This section is organized around these classes of complications.

Limitations of Photographic Exploration in Evaluation

It is the responsibility of the photographer to help the viewer see what is presented as the photographer intends, whether the photographer is an insider or outsider, a member of the program staff, or an external evaluator. Recently, the persistant call in evaluation circles for more descriptions of things as they are in programs has raised questions about the rigor of naturalistic description. Microscopic studies are believed capable of bringing an improved understanding of a program.

In documentary photography, the rigor of description depends to some extent on the adequacy of the representation of elements in the situation. This problem of the selection and bias of the photographer is inherent in the procedures followed by investigators, requiring that they consult their own informed judgment for purposes of selecting and analyzing prints. The photographer/evaluator also works systematically toward engaging in closer relationships with the subjects in order to have greater access to data.

One of the major limitations in adapting photographic exploration to evaluation study is that such procedures would be considered subjective under the assumptions of the predominant scientific tradition, in spite of the fact that there have long been calls (Hastings, 1969) for evaluation to go to other disciplines besides the natural sciences for its models and methodologies. Yet, the quantified studies considered more objective by many evaluators and assumed to embody the concept of academic disinterest still involve subjective elements in the choice of theories, sampling strategies, instrumentation, and other procedural matters. In photographic inquiry, the principal checks on the problems of subjectivity lie in multiple methods and data sources, and in the checks on validity enumerated above. Taken together, these checks constitute a method of triangulation (Denzin, 1970; Stake, 1975b); that is, cross-checking photographic data from three sources focusing on the same issues and themes—documentary photography, art, and prose. The technology of social documentary photography is sufficiently rigorous that evaluators could be trained in its methods, as are some sociologists and anthropologists.

Evaluation Models

Documentary photographers have studied a great variety of topics, settings, groups, institutions, organizations, and communities. It would follow that few programs being evaluated would be exempt from study, since interesting visual materials abound in them. While not all models or settings would be appropriate, evaluation creates some situations that may be best handled photographically.

In terms of evaluation models, those based upon methods of testing and measurement of student outcome would be least compatible with photographic methods except perhaps in skill areas offering visible results, such as physical education and the arts. Models whose purview would most likely be compatible with photography include those emphasizing attention to naturalistic observations, context, multiple methods, portrayal, hearings, and goal-free approaches.

Certain kinds of photographic materials may be more pertinent to particular evaluation models. With respect to the fit between photographic evidence and models, the quality of evidence may determine the appropriateness of the model chosen by an evaluator. The kinds of evidence—what is photographed—best captured photographically are: interactions between people; processes of teaching, learning, administration, policy-making, and the like; and terrain—physical facilities, materials, and the contextual backdrop of classrooms, schools, offices, hospitals, and communities.

Communication Functions

The chief communication functions photography could offer to evaluation appraisals fall generally into three categories. Photography functions to make pictorial statements, contextual statements, and visual discourse. All of these are pertinent to the concept of evaluation as appraisal of the merits in situations, programs, and curricula. What distinguishes appraisal from other evaluation purviews is that the valuings made are embedded in part in the evaluation process rather than reserved exclusively for a set of recommendations in the conclusions.

Photography provides pictorial statements, illustrations that communicate fast visual translations of complex data to an audience—the legislators, the school board, the teachers, the parents, or other constituents and policy makers. While this chapter has focused almost entirely on developing a method of documentary inquiry in which photographs are the primary data, the illustration function of photography in evaluation reports should not be undervalued. It may make reports more palatable to some by correcting impressions arising from other data and by acting as an illustrative cross check. It could help target the project during the formative stage of an evaluation, and summarize an immense amount of data by the specificity of detail associated with summary statements. Under current accountability pressures, photography might help evaluators get the attention of legislators and of newspapers about their findings. For other audiences, photography would be useful in tracking problems as they are developing and in contributing some pictorial understandings to their solution.

As for contextual statements, photographs may convey a strong sense of the physical facilities and the use of learning materials. Many evaluation studies attempt to deal with the context of a program, whether it be the racial mix of participants, the neighborhood that influences the program, or the bureaucratic atmosphere that hinders innovation. It is believed by photographers that visual codes may communicate some of these contextual features more efficiently and succinctly than narrative descriptions.

Visual discourse constitutes its own form of information, but there is little to assure us that some well defined visual code is universally understood. The problem has to do with the gap between visual codes and implicit texts. A code of iconic elements that are mutually understood by many depends on communication well beyond locally defined groups. But everyone has had experience with, for example, schooling, and this experience has made particular visual images of education powerfully familiar to us. Where the time element is longest, photographic inquiry may take advantage of these icons and yield accounts of the visual images that inform people's discourse about educational problems. Applying the concepts of social documentary study could probably bring a closer critical understanding of educational problems than merely illustrating with pictorial statements.

Applications of Still Photography to Evaluation

Given that a methodological base for photo-assisted evaluation does exist, what are the practical considerations involved in developing and carrying out a research plan that embodies the methodological elements we have described? This is the overall question that will be addressed in this section. As in the case of the theoretical discussion, I will approach this aspect of the problem by addressing what I consider to be the five necessary elements of a sound method of photographic inquiry: sampling, reactivity, procedures for data collection, validity, and interpretation. This discussion will, however, be prefaced by consideration of two matters that may be antecedent to implementing a study: the question of personnel and the role of telling theory at the outset of a study. Then, after covering the necessary elements of the study itself, I will conclude by discussing some of the uses to which photographs may be put when they are considered as results rather than data, that is, with the problems of display, presentation, and inclusion of photographic results in evaluation reports.

Technical and Personnel Considerations

While it is beyond the scope of this monograph to provide detailed information on the technical aspects of photography as applied to evaluation, it is appropriate here to discuss the extent of technical involvement required, review relevant techniques in general, and consider the matter of personnel.

Equipment and processes. The vast majority of photography in evaluation is rapid, unobtrusive, available light work, involving the taking of a large number of pictures. The nature of this work more or less dictates that it must be done with 35-mm equipment, most often with the ubiquitous single-lens reflex. These cameras are relatively noisy, and some people have difficulty focusing them in dim light, but they are generally satisfactory for the purpose, especially since their normal lenses are readily interchanged for telephoto, wide-angle, or close-up ("macro") lenses. Compact 35-mm rangefinder cameras are also suitable. Few of these cameras have interchangeable lenses, and their normal lenses are usually slightly wide-angle. However, they are inexpensive, easy to operate, focus well in dim light, and are very quiet. Whatever camera is used, it will need to have a lens with an aperture of at least f 2.8 to permit available light photography in average office and classroom lighting.

It is not usually necessary to use ultra-high-speed films for evaluation photography. A film with an ASA speed of 400 (such as Kodak Tri-X or Ilford HP-4) is sufficiently fast for photography in ordinary room light, but will still provide fine-grained photos that will enlarge well. Likewise, there is no need to use exotic developers in the darkroom. Standard developers (such as Kodak D-76 or Agfa Rodinol) are inexpensive and provide plenty of speed and contrast for the purposes of evaluation photography.

In evaluation photography it is usually necessary to develop and print pictures daily, as detailed later in this section. This is not as difficult as it sounds. Film can be loaded into developing tanks in room light by using a changing bag. A darkroom for printing can be set up in almost any bathroom that can be more or less darkened. A compact enlarger can be carried in a suitcase, plastic chemical trays lined up in the bathtub, and prints made on resin coated paper that requires no special equipment for drying.

Personnel. In many cases, the evaluator may also wish to serve as photographer on a study, but in other instances it may make more sense to hire (and possibly retrain) a photographer. Should evaluators wish to employ photographers to work for them, it seems useful to suggest a few caveats. Some interviewing could be conducted around the following considerations.

First, what is the level and extent of the individual's technical competence? Competence in using the camera is not the only criterion for selecting a photographer. Competence in darkroom techniques is also essential. Of particular importance in these areas are speed, high standards of quality, and efficiency. Humor under tension is singularly related to technical competence. A good balance between technical and aesthetic knowledge is preferable.

Next, what is the photographer's philosophy about photography? Social documentary photography requires that the photographer understand that collections of photographs make social statements. The viewpoint that a single photograph is a work of high art is inappropriate under these circumstances. The documentary philosophy of inquiry coupled with a keen ability to observe and make connections between factors in a social situation are vital. Looking upon the camera as a research tool also means that the photographer distinguishes between research and evaluation problems and methods.

Finally, is the photographer socially competent? It is necessary in documentary work to engage with the participants in a program. Social competence under these circumstances determines to some extent the trust established. This implies that the photographer is able not only to gather higher quality data but to relate to people in some fashion with reassurance, empathy, and humor in addition to understanding something about evaluation.

Getting Started: The Role of Telling Theory

A telling theory is a concept or set of concepts that helps tell what to photograph by raising questions about a setting. Telling theories need not be elaborate but, rather, are relatively straightforward ideas that are close to the situation. They are useful for getting ready for the evaluation by anticipating some explicit problems and issues that may arise in making judgments about the mechanics and operations of a program. Such a theory helps direct evaluators to the issues in a program by expanding their scope and drawing attention to priority questions and ways of spending their time (Stake, 1978). This use of theory helps focus the topic, organize the evaluation process, and guide the interpretation of the pictures. Such theories provide some tentative prior understanding of what to expect by offering a point of view to adopt or rule out, and also by suggesting some specific events to photograph. Using telling theory provides an initial orientation for discovering what is going on in the evaluation situation so that photographers do not go into it unprepared. Telling theories are held lightly; the photographer has to be willing to give them up or change them the moment that photographic information reveals something new that does not fit the interpretation. Otherwise, one may wind up with a large set of disorganized pictures that are hard to make sense of. Worse yet, holding rigidly to prior theory may lead the photographer to excessive coverage of items that turn out to be situationally unimportant, at the expense of adequately reporting items that are important.

Selecting telling theories. Photographers have to know roughly what to take pictures of before they begin, and what to photograph next. There are too many things to photograph to be able to enter the evaluation situation without some preconceptions. When photographing for evaluation purposes, there may be a tendency in the beginning to photograph everything, including nonparticipants. This seems to be inevitable, and, in the interest of providing some margin for error, is not usually a cause for concern. Some things go by fast, take place simultaneously, or will never happen again. In other situations some things will be more stable. In any case, telling theories should provide the initial guidance needed to begin taking pictures, without blinding the photographer to the unanticipated elements that emerge as photographing proceeds.

The selection of telling theories for photo-assisted evaluation is not markedly different than in the case of studies utilizing other data collection techniques. It is necessary, however, that the questions asked by the telling theory be ones that can be satisfactorily answered by photographic data. Such questions must commonly involve the interaction of persons with each other and with the environment, on both spatial and temporal dimensions.

Initially, the selection of telling theories arises from consideration of two types of information: existing data about the situation to be evaluated, and existing literature that provides theoretical constructs of potential descriptive utility. Existing information about the situation (e.g., outreach literature, written program products, management plans, floor plans, activity schedules) can provide a sense of what the planners and participants see in the situation, and what they expect to happen. Likewise, existing theoretical constructs can provide an initial sense of what is likely to happen in the situation, and what occurrences may have significance. The questions one then asks—and attempts to answer with photographic evidence—may thus constitute attempts to either confirm or disconfirm aspects of the theoretically predicted structure of the situation. First in its tentative and then in its modified form, telling theory helps shape the procedures for sampling, data collection, and interpretation.

Sampling

Depending on the kinds of questions being asked by the initial telling theory, the evaluator may decide upon any of several general types of photographic sampling—or on a combination of sampling methods. The five types of sampling I will consider here are time-based sampling, shadow sampling, blanket sampling, event-based sampling, and dimensionally based sampling.

Time-based sampling. In this type of sampling, the viewpoint and spatial coverage of the camera vary from one frame per second to one frame per minute. One method of collecting data with this method is to use a 16-mm movie camera fitted with an extreme wide-angle lens (often covering a whole room), and in intervalometer. Alternatively, a 35-mm still camera can be used, fitted with a bulk film magazine, motor drive, extreme wide-angle lens, and intervalometer. The advantage of the movie camera is that the resulting film can be projected as a time-lapse movie, thus showing motion patterns and changes in the spatial distribution of persons in the environment. On the other hand, time-based photo sequences taken with the 35-mm still camera can be examined minutely for such details as eye contact, and prints can be measured to quantify the proximities of subjects.

An advantage of time-based sampling is that it accurately reveals shifting patterns of persons in space over time. As such, it can be extremely useful in studies of the use of space and also can provide information on the changing relations between groups and between members of groups. A disadvantage of this method is suggested by Goffman's (1976) observation that human interaction is largely ceremonial, being concentrated in liminal events: Collecting data on a constant time base may tend to exaggerate the importance of the large proportion of "inactive" time that tends to separate such liminal events.

Shadow sampling. This method involves following a single subject through the program, recording the experiences and interactions of that individual. An advantage of this method is that the photographic data collected will all share a common independent variable: the individual being shadowed. This is of course also a disadvantage in that the individual chosen for shadowing may introduce systematic bias into the data through the types of interactions and situations in which that individual typically and habitually engages (or does not engage). Taking this viewpoint, shadow sampling may result in collecting data about the individual, rather than about the program. This problem can be overcome to some extent by shadowing several subjects, either simultaneously or consecutively. However, simultaneous shadowing generally requires multiple photographers, which is likely to be very obtrusive, while consecutively shadowing several subjects through a program of any length may require unrealistic amounts of contact time.

Blanket sampling. This method does not constrain the photographer to follow a given session or event through to completion. Rather, the photographer attempts to cover as much of the entire span of events and sessions as possible by moving about freely, and fairly constantly, from location to location. When this method is followed, it seems likely that the photographer will gather a rather large proportion of liminal events, generally at the expense of sequences showing development of action, changes of groups, shifts in proximities, and so forth. Basically, this is the methodology of traditional photo journalism, and the fact that it tends to gather only liminal events probably accounts for both the strong impact and the uncontrolled biases of most photographic documentaries.

Event-based sampling. Sometimes the research question posed for a study is not concerned with the program or system as a whole, but with a particular type of action, interaction, sequence, or event within the overall context. In such cases, the photographer may be assigned to sample as many events as possible within a certain category. Such categories may be relatively broad ("question-and-answer periods," "mealtime groupings"), or very specific ("handshakes between persons of the opposite sex after the presentation"). Whatever the category, event-based sampling is generally only appropriate in response to specific research questions. It should probably be accompanied by some more global technique (e.g., blanketing the event area, having another person take field notes, tape recording) in order to provide contextual information for interpreting the category of specific events.

Dimensionally based sampling. This approach would appear to be most useful where the initial aim of the study is descriptive appraisal, but the constraints of time, space, and work force make it impossible to cover all events in the program. Any information available about the program (field notes, previous reports, informants' reports, printed programs, informational brochures, and the like) is examined to determine a set of apparent dimensions for classifying the events and components of the program. Events are then selected for photographing to represent the largest possible range of dimensions and combinations of dimensions. Other constraints, such as photographing a whole event, or spending a predetermined amount of time at each event, may also be imposed.

The advantage of this sampling procedure is that it offers some guarantee of representativeness in the description of the program. It should be noted, however, that, in a photographic study of any length, this method will usually need to be progressively modified during the course of the study to reflect the specific research questions that arise as a result of analysis of the photographic data. Once it has been established that the data collected are truly representative of the program, then it may be appropriate to initiate more specific event-based sampling to study apparently significant or pivotal aspects of the program in greater depth.

Sampling protocols. Whatever sampling procedure is chosen, the evaluator will need to prepare some form of protocol for photographing. This may involve time-and-space charts of what should be photographed, checklists of events, or specifications for camera placement and frequency of sampling. As a result of examining photographs, debriefing photographers, and collating other types of data, the protocols will be subject to constant revision. Taken together with field notes and successive revisions of the telling theories, such protocols can become an important part of the records of the study.

It is important to bear in mind that photographic protocols must generally be kept fairly simple: They must be designed so that they can be assimilated beforehand, since it is nearly impossible to refer to detailed instructions while actually engaged in photographing.

Reactivity: Strategies for Entering the Situation

The camera is an obtrusive instrument. It is not easily ignored, and, even if they do not do so deliberately, people do react to its presence. This may be true of any observer, of course, and the fact that reactivity occurs in response to a photographer is not a very unusual or difficult problem. The camera may actually help an observer gain access to the situation since the presence of a person using a camera is largely self-explanatory in our society. Yet, it forces immediate explanation, and interaction with subjects. In general, people photographing for evaluation studies should have a prepared explanation for their presence: It should be brief and matter-of-fact, much like the sort of prepared statement a survey interviewer uses to preface an interview.

The actual act of photographing need not to be highly obtrusive. With modern films and equipment there is no need to use flash under the lighting conditions found in most offices, buildings, and classrooms. If there is much activity going on, the noise of the camera will usually not be very noticeable and photographers, like any other type of observer, can learn to move about in the situation without calling undue attention to their presence. (In fact, unobtrusiveness and an ability to enter a social situation gracefully without disrupting it are qualities that most documentary photographers must develop in order to carry out their work successfully—just as evaluation observers must.)

Finally, it is important to bear in mind that reactivity itself is often a significant form of data. The reaction of a subject to the intrusion of an observer tells us much about the subject's relationship to the situation. Different types of reactions to observation may indicate that the subject is or is not under stress, is or is not comfortable with the situation, and so forth. In the case of photographic observation, the very action that produces reactivity (taking pictures) may also record information about the reaction for later analysis.

Procedures for Sequential Data Collection

Data collection strategies are designed to assure that photographers make a rigorous attempt to take pictures that fairly represent the activities and persons in a situation. Ideally, the procedures form a continuous sequence of levels of data collection, as follows:

- taking many pictures
- classifying the photographs, focusing the topic, selecting the most relevant
- gathering verbatim data by interviewing and observing
- photo-interviewing or showing photographs to the subjects for their interpretations
- going back frequently to confirm or disconfirm the data, staying in the study site as long as possible
- repeating the process
- selecting and interpreting photographs and arranging a final report

To some extent, this process is self-explanatory to those who are familiar with participant observation techniques. However, there are some special circumstances that arise from the nature of photographic observation, and these will be discussed here.

Taking many pictures. Black-and-white film is extremely inexpensive relative to the time of the professional personnel involved in evaluation. The quantity of film on hand should be sufficient to prevent the photographer from feeling any real constraints as to the number of pictures that may be shot. This is important in the initial stages of the study if one is to have a hope of answering the questions of a telling theory. And as the study progresses, one must have the opportunity to refine and test the emerging picture of the situation as many times as necessary.

Classification, focusing, and selection. It is almost essential to have facilities for rapidly developing and printing pictures. This generally needs to be done each day, so that the results can be examined and the next day's shooting planned. This is not as much of a problem as it may appear, since, as we have already noted, black-and-white processing can be carried out readily almost anywhere.

Initially, the pictures need only be printed up on contact sheets so they can be examined with a magnifier. From such examination it is possible to start forming categories, noting sequences of action, repeated themes, and isolated occurrences that may be worth further investigation. At this stage it will also be possible to begin selecting pictures to be enlarged for closer study.

Gathering other data. Simultaneously with the photographing process, the evaluator needs to gather other types of data that will aid in the interpretation of the photographic evidence. Depending upon the overall methodology of the study, this auxiliary data may be in the form of taped interviews, field notes, survey data, and so forth. This information can provide new insights into what is seen in the photographs.

Photo-interviewing. When enlargements of key photographs are available, they can be used to interview subjects and thereby obtain their interpretations of the situation. This is a procedure long used by ethnographers, and it would seem to be particularly appropriate in evaluation because it can help elicit the participant's interpretations of the situation. Another important outcome of photo-interviewing may be that the participants will be able to provide suggestions for other things that should be photographed. This information can be used to expand and refine the sampling protocols.

Confirming, disconfirming, repeating. With film being processed and examined each day, and several days set aside for photographing at the site, it is possible to go through several stages of refining the description of the situation. Within the limits of time on the site—and time to examine and interpret the results tentatively—this process should be repeated as many times as possible, or until further repetitions yield no new, significant data.

Final selection and interpretation. This step ordinarily takes place in the (relative) leisure time after the completion of the field observations. Carrying out this process is heavily dependent on having all the collected data arranged in orderly fashion, so that photographs can be viewed in sequence, grouped by categories, cross-referenced to the various aspects of an emerging theory, and collated with all other types of data collected.

Record keeping for photographic data presents no great problems, but procedures must be clearly established and consistently applied. During the photographing, each roll of film should be assigned a number. The photographer can simply carry a pad of paper, write down the roll number, date, time, subject, and so on, and photograph the sheet. The roll numbers and other information can then be recorded later from the film. The individual frames of a roll of 35-mm film are identified by numbers exposed along the edge of the film at the factory. Thus, each exposure can be completely identified by reference to roll number and frame number. Contact prints, enlargements, and slides made from the negatives should all be identified by these numbers. Field notes and photo-interview results should also be keyed to roll and frame numbers, so that the data can be collated later.

Validity. Establishing the validity of photographic data is accomplished in much the same way as for other types of data—by specifying the conditions of data collection and adhering to the procedures thus established. Completely specifying these conditions in the final report should be a standard part of any photo-assisted evaluation.

The reader of such a report needs to be reassured on several points:

- That the photographs have not been altered. That is, that they have not been retouched, cropped in such a way as to alter important content, and so on.
- That sequences did in fact occur in the order claimed. Providing a copy of the contact sheet can easily confirm this.
- That the methods of photographing did not introduce technological distortions. Some distortions can be readily detected from examining the photographs. For example, consistently high or low angles of view can give a distorted impression of the relation between persons and the fixed features of the environment. Other distortions may be less readily detectable. Use of a wide-angle lens, for instance, tends to give the sense that objects and persons are thinly scattered in the environment, while a telephoto lens tends to have the opposite effect of bunching subjects together. Any technical information of this sort should be fully disclosed, together with sufficient explanation to make the implications of the information clear to readers who may lack knowledge of the technical aspects of photography.
- Disclosure of record-keeping procedures. The reader should be able to determine that all types of data have been reliably collated and, hence, that errors in interpretation have not arisen from faulty record keeping.

Figure 4.1

- That sampling and data collection have been sufficiently extensive. The reader should have adequate indications of the number of exposures made and the time period covered. The report should also make clear any gaps in the photographic coverage.

Interpretation

The act of interpretation is both a tentative and ongoing process during the on-site phase of the study, and a final process of drawing together the various types of data collected and uniting them with the overall system of description that has been developed through successive refinements of the initial telling theory. In the methodological section of this chapter I have collected a number of concerns relative to interpretation. From an applications standpoint the most important element is that the logical inferences made from photographic evidence must be accessible to the reader, in more or less the same way that inferences from quantitative data are presented in a form that allows the reader to be assured of the strength of the inference. In the case of photo-assisted evaluation, this task often requires a clear, narrative explanation of the inferential process, accompanied by the photographs in question and any other data that may have contributed to the strength of the inference. At this point, as when dealing with other types of data, the questions of interpretation and presentation of results begin to merge into a single issue. The following pages from a photographic evaluation of a conference are examples of results of the interpretative process (Templin, 1979b).

Cocoons. At the end of paper sessions, cocoons (Bloland, 1982) form among people sitting next to each other, colleagues, friends, new acquaintances (Figure 4.1). Cocoons are circular in form, and are groups that function to promote discussion and recognition. Colleagues of equal professional status—for example, participants recently out of graduate school—may be joined by a mentor of higher status, and chat as the cocoon enlarges, diminishes, and dissolves (Figures 4.2-4.6). Some cocoons form after a session and go to lunch or dinner (Figures 4.7-4.8).

By contrast, a cul de sac is a cocoon of higher status persons, sometimes associating persons from the same school by doctoral work or faculty membership (Figure 4.9). A cul de sac tends to maintain its impenetrability, even for other high status persons not in the same informal network.

From Datum to Result: What Becomes of the Photograph

The transformation of photographic data into project results is often less clear and dramatic than the transformation that quantitative data undergo. A photograph appearing in the final report is, after all, physically the same as a photograph in the mass of project data. The difference is that the selection of photographs for inclusion in the report is performed as a means of achieving economy of representation, while still providing examples of data that will support the inferences made in the report.

Project reports based wholly or partially on photographic evidence must often differ physically from traditional reports. Ordinarily, project reports are simply the final, typewritten copy of the results, reproduced in as large a quantity as necessary by whatever means available (mimeograph, zerography, spirit copying, offset printing, even carbon paper). The inclusion of photographs immediately limits the processes that can be used, and in any case multiplies the cost of producing a report. The standard format of reports (letter size, or 8½ x 11 inches) is also less than ideal: Larger pages would make it easier to present groups of photographs together (for comparison or sequence), with the narrative interpretational material kept close by, for the reader's convenience. However, any nonstandard format

Figure 4.2

Figure 4.3

Figure 4.4

Figure 4.5

Figure 4.6

Figure 4.7

Figure 4.8

Figure 4.9

will multiply production costs, drive librarians to distraction, and perhaps reduce readership because the report looks unwieldy or unprofessional.

For some purposes, of course, a hard-copy report is unnecessary, in which case the photographic data may need to be incorporated into a presentation. Black-and-white negatives can be converted readily to black-and-white slides by contact printing the strips of negatives onto strips of what is known as positive print film. The process is fast and inexpensive and results in slides that can be mounted for projection in a standard 35-mm slide projector. Properly sequenced and identified, the slides can then be used both to illustrate and support the interpretations in a presentation of the project results.

It would also be possible to combine aspects of the written report and the slide show presentation. The text of the report could be presented in the normal, printed fashion, accompanied by a carousel or other magazine of properly sequenced slides. The written text would contain indications of slide numbers for the reader to project and examine while reading. If only a few copies of the report were to be produced, this format might actually be less expensive than providing a set of original photographic prints in each copy. Some readers may also find it easier to examine the large, projected image than to examine a print, especially if the prints have been kept to modest size to save space and printing costs.

Whatever format is chosen for the final report or presentation, certain criteria need to be met in order to achieve clarity:

(1) Photographs and the narrative relating to them must be kept in very close proximity to each other, preferably on the same page or facing pages. This is standard practice in book design, but it must be observed very closely in photo-assisted studies, because the reader must be able to grasp photographic and verbal interpretation together.

(2) Photographs must be reproduced with sufficient size and sharpness so that the inferences made in the text can be verified by the reader by examining the photographs. If original prints are included in the report, this will usually not be a problem, so long as the prints are not miniscule. However, if the photos are printed as half-tones along with the text, the photographs will usually have to be larger, and it will be necessary to have the printing done on a good grade of paper, using a fine half-tone screen (100 lines per inch or finer).

(3) A figure numbering system must be used so that the photographs can be referred to in the text. If the report also includes extracts

from field notes and photo-interviewing sessions, then the photographs may also have to be identified by roll and frame number, or whatever system was used to identify them during the course of note taking and interviewing.

(4) Narrative text and photographic data may not by themselves be sufficient content for a report. In order to establish the validity of the photographic evidence and complete the description of the research methodology it may be necessary to include additional documentation. Complete contact sheets, tables correlating film exposed by subject and date, sampling plans, photographing protocols, and photo-interviewing protocols may need to be included or described in summary form in order for the reader to validate and accept the interpretations of the photographic evidence.

The final results of photo-assisted evaluations are quite likely to be bulkier than reports generated from other types of data, for two reasons. First, photographs as results do not condense data in the same way that tables, graphs, and statistics can be said to condense their quantitative antecedents. A photograph, however used or in whatever context, remains an extended, nondiscursive representation, in an analog rather than a digital mode, a point from which verbal inferences and descriptions expand rather than toward which numerical ones contract. Thus, although a picture can be said to be "worth a thousand words" for descriptive purposes, it may also serve to generate thousands of words as we tease out inferences from pictorial information and struggle to convert nondiscursive, analog symbol systems into another system of representation—language—which is also symbolic, but discursive and digital in nature.

And this is the second reason that photo-assisted evaluation may appear uneconomical in its results. In the verbal interpretation of visual information we are still in our infancy. In most instances we have no short-hand notation to render our inferences and descriptions verbally compact (one notable exception is Birdwhistell's [1970] notations for kinesics). For the most part, our inferential/descriptive language is a mixed (and not always systematic) borrowing from the vocabularies or art history, aesthetics, literary criticism, philosophy, and, at times, the figurative language of the poetic tradition. From one aspect, it is a bulky system of representation, but from another it may be seen as a means of bringing us closer to the realization of what Stake (1975a, 1975b) has called responsive evaluation—evaluation that provides needed information for all concerned by portraying interactions rather than outcomes, and by achieving a multiple perspective from *within* the scene. In the long run, an evaluation methodology incorporating photography may be one of the richest and most sensitive means of achieving this goal of responsive evaluation.

Appendix A: Bibliography of Photographic Studies

Abbot, Bernice. *New York in the thirties*. New York: Dover, 1973.
Abramson, Michael. *Palante: Young Lord's party*. New York: McGraw-Hill, 1971.
Adelman, Bob. *Down home*. New York: McGraw-Hill, 1972.
Allen, Harold. *Father Ravalli's missions*. Chicago: School of the Art Institute, 1972.
Banish, Roslyn. *City families*. New York: Pantheon, 1976.
Cancian, Frank. *Another place: Photographs of a Mayan community*. San Francisco: Schrimshaw, 1974.
Clark, Larry. *Tulsa*. New York: Lustrum, 1971.
Collier, John. *The awakening valley*. Chicago: University of Chicago Press, 1949.
Evans, Walker. *Many are called*. New York: Houghton Mifflin, 1966.
Evans, Walker. *American photographs*. New York: East River Press, 1975.
Fitch, Steve. *Diesels and dinosaurs*. Berkeley, CA: Long Run Press, 1976.
Freedman, Jill. *Circus days*. New York: Crown, 1975.
Fonyat, Bine. *Carnaval*. 1978.
Fusco, Patricia S., & Fusco, Marina. *Marina and Ruby*. New York: William Morrow, 1977.
Jackson, Bruce. *Killing time*. Ithaca: Cornell University Press, 1977.
Koudelka, Josef. *Gypsies*. New York: Aperture, 1975.
Lesy, Michael. *Wisconsin death trip*. New York: Pantheon, 1973.
Lyon, Danny. *The bikeriders*. New York: Pantheon, 1973.
Lyon, Danny. *Conversations with the dead*. New York: Holt, Rinehart & Winston, 1971.
Meiselas, Susan. *Carnival strippers*. New York: Farrar, Strauss & Girou, 1975.
Museum of Modern Art. *Brassai*. New York: New York Graphic Society, 1968.
Owens, Bill. *Suburbia*. San Francisco: Straight Arrow, 1973.
Slavin, Neal. *Portugal*. New York: Lustrum, 1971.
Smith, Dennis, & Freedman, Jill. *Firehouse*. New York: Doubleday, 1977.
Smith, W. Eugene, & Smith, Aileen M. *Minamata*. New York: Holt, Rinehart & Winston, 1975.
Stock, Dennis. *California trip*. New York: Grossman, 1970.
Strand, Paul. *A retrospective monograph*. New York: Aperture, 1971.
Tice, George A. *Paterson*. New Brunswick, NJ: Rutgers University Press, 1972.
Turner, Alwyn Scott. *Photographs of the Detroit people*. Detroit: by author, 1970.
Winogrand, Garry. *Women are beautiful*. New York: Farrar, Strauss & Girou, 1975.

Note

[1] For a thorough review of the photographic literature in this social documentary genre, see Becker (1974).

References

Addis, W. Unpublished doctoral ...rtation, Teachers College, New York. Cited by Becker, H. S., personal communication, 1979.

Ade, D. *Photomontage.* Unpublished photo essay, San Francisco, 1974.

Anderson, F. E. *The dance component of the artists-in-schools program, year two, Decatur, Illinois: Observations, issues, and realities.* Unpublished manuscript, Center for Instructional Research and Curriculum Evaluation, University of Illinois, 1975.

Arnheim, R. On the nature of photography. *Afterimage,* 1975, 2(10), 10-12.

Banish, R. *City families.* New York: Pantheon, 1976.

Bateson, G., & Mead, M. *Balinese character.* Special Publications of the New York Academy of Sciences, Vol. 2. New York: New York Academy of Sciences, 1942.

Becker, H. S. Photography and sociology. *Studies in the Anthropology of Visual Communication.* 1974, 1(1), 3-26.

Becker, H. S. Do photographs tell the truth? *Afterimage,* 1978, February 9-13.

Becker, H. S. *Exploring society photographically.* Seminar remarks presented at Visual Studies Workshop, University of Rochester, New York, August 1979.

Becker, H. S. Exploring society photographically. Chicago: Block Gallery, Northwestern University, 1981.

Birdwhistell, R. L. *Kinesics and context.* Philadelphia: University of Pennsylvania Press, 1970.

Bloland, H. G. Opportunities, traps, and sanctuaries: A frame analysis of learned societies. *Urban Life,* Spring 1982.

Byers, P. Cameras don't take pictures. *Columbia University Forum,* 1966, 9(1), 27-31.

Campbell, D. T., & Stanley, J. C. *Experimental and quasi-experimental design for research.* Chicago: Rand McNally, 1966.

Cancian, F. *Another place: Photographs of a Mayan community.* San Francisco: Schrimshaw, 1974.

Collier, J., Jr. *Visual anthropology: Photography as a research method.* New York: Holt, Rinehart & Winston, 1967.

Denzin, N. K. *The research act.* Chicago: Aldine, 1970.

Eisner, E. W. On the differences between scientific and artistic approaches to qualitative research. Paper presented at American Educational Research Association Annual Convention, Boston, Massachusetts, April 1, 1980.

Geertz, C. *The interpretation of culture.* New York: Basic Books, 1973.

Glaser, B. G., & Strauss, A. *The discovery of grounded theory.* Chicago: Aldine, 1967.

Goffman, E. *Frame analysis.* New York: Harper & Row, 1974.

Goffman, E. *Gender advertisements.* New York: Harper & Row, 1976.

Hastings, J. T. The kith and kin of educational measurers. *Journal of Educational Measurement,* 1969, 6, 127-130.

Hill, J. B. Event analysis. In J. I. Roberts & S. K. Akinsanya (Eds.), *Educational patterns and cultural configurations.* New York: John Wiley, 1976.

Langer, S. K. *Feeling and form.* New York: Scribner, 1953.

Levine, L. The last book of LIFE. *Triquarterly,* 1975, Winter, (32).

Lofland, J. *Analyzing social settings.* Belmont, CA: Wadsworth, 1970.

Lyons, N. (Ed.). *Toward a social landscape.* New York: Horizon, 1967.

Mead, B. *Blackberry winter: My earliest years.* New York: Morrow, 1972.

Owens, B. *Suburbia.* San Francisco: Straight Arrow, 1973.

Peterson, C., & Brown, R. D. Photographic evaluation from three perspectives: Portrayal, goal-free, judicial. Paper presented at the Annual Meetings of the American Educational Research Association, San Francisco, 1979.

Rist, R. Ethnographic case study methods. Seminar presented at the Annual Meetings of the American Educational Research Association, San Francisco, April 1976.

Ruby, J. Up the Zambesi with notebook and camera or being an anthropologist without doing anthropology . . . with pictures. *SAVICOM Newsletter,* 1973, 4(3), 12-15.

Ruby, J. In a pic's eye: Interpretive strategies for deriving significance and meaning from photographs. *Afterimage,* 1976, 3(9), 5-7.

Sapir, E. In D. Mandlebaum (Ed.), *Culture, language, and personality: Selected writings of Edward Sapir.* Berkeley: University of California Press, 1949.

Schatzman, L., & Strauss, A. L. *Field research: Strategies for a natural sociology.* Englewood Cliffs, NJ: Prentice-Hall, 1973.

Searle, L. Language theory and photographic praxis. *Afterimage,* 1979, 7(1-2), 26-34.

Sekula, A. The invention of photographic meaning. *Artforum,* 1975, 13(5), 35-45.

Sekula, A. Dismantling modernism, reinventing documentary (Notes on the politics of representation). *Massachusetts Review,* 1978, 29(4), 859-83. (a)

Sekula, A. Meditations on a triptych. *Afterimage,* 1978, Summer, 32-33. (b)

Serrano, R. The status of science, math, and social science in Western City USA. In R. E. Stake & J. A. Easley et al. *Case studies in science education* (Vol. 1). Washington, DC: Government Printing Office, 1978.

Smith, L., & Geoffrey, W. *The complexities of an urban classroom.* New York: Holt, Rinehart & Winston, 1968.

Smith, L. M., & Pohland, P. Education, technology, and the rural highlands. AERA Monograph Series on Curriculum Evaluation, 1974, 7.

Smith, L. M., & Pohland, P. Grounded theory and educational ethnography: A methodological analysis and critique. In J. I. Roberts & S. K. Akinsanya (Eds.), *Educational patterns and cultural configurations.* New York: John Wiley, 1976.

Smith, W. E., & Smith, A. *Minamata.* New York: Holt, Rinehart & Winston, 1975.

Sontag, S. *On photography.* New York: Farrar, Strauss & Girou, 1977.

Stake, B. Saturday's children: A photographic essay evaluation. 35-mm Kodachrome slides. University of Illinois, Urbana, Illinois, 1973.

Stake, R. E. Program evaluation, particularly responsive evaluation. Occasional Paper No. 5. Western Michigan University Evaluation Center, Kalamazoo, Michigan, 1975. (a)

Stake, R. E. *Evaluating the arts in education: A responsive approach.* Columbus: Charles E. Merrill, 1975. (b)

Stake, R. E., & Easley, J. A., Denny, T., Hill, J., Hoke, G., Peshkin, A., Serano, R., Smith M. L., Stufflebeam, D., & Sanders, J., Walker, R., & Welch, W., et al. *Case studies in science education* (Vol. 1 and 2). Washington, DC: U.S. Government Printing Office, 1978.

Stasz, C. The early history of visual sociology. In J. Wagner (Ed.), *Images of information,* Beverly Hills, CA: Sage, 1979.

Strand, P. *A retrospective monograph.* New York: Aperture, 1971.

Tabachnick, J., & Fox, G. T., Jr. Using photographs for interpretation. Technical Report No. 4. In *Descriptions and Interpretations.* Contract No. 300-75-0100, Teacher Corps Member Training Institute 10th Cycle Impace Study Interim Report. Unpublished document, University of Wisconsin-Madison, 1975.

Tabachnick, J. Together: A photographic essay. Technical Report No. 4. In *Descriptions and Interpretations.* Contract No. 300-75-0100, Teacher Corps Member Training Institute 10th Cycle Impact Study Interim Report. Unpublished document, University of Wisconsin-Madison, 1975.

Templin, P. A. Still photography: Can it provide program portrayal? Paper presented at the Annual Meetings of the American Educational Research Association, Toronto, March 31, 1978.

Templin, P. A. Photography in evaluation. Monograph No. 23, Research on Evaluation Program, Northwest Regional Education Laboratory, Portland, Oregon, 1979. (a)

Templin, P. A. Photography as an evaluation technique. Monograph No. 32, Research on Evaluation Program, Northwest Regional Educational Laboratory, Portland, Oregon, 1979. (b)

Wachtman, E. L. The camera as an evaluation and research instrument: Snapshots of a science curriculum. Symposium paper presented at the Annual Meetings of the American Educational Research Association, Toronto, 1978.

Walker, R. Pine City. In R. E. Stake and J. A. Easley et al. *Case studies in science education* (Vol. 1). Washington, DC: Government Printing Office, 1978. (a)

Walker, R. Personal communication, 1978. (b)

Walker, R., & Adelman, C. *A guide to classroom observation* (Photographs by Janine Wiedel). New York: Methuen, 1979.

Walker, R., & Wiedel, J. Using photographs in a discipline of words. Mimeograph. Center for Applied Research in Education, University of East Anglia, Norwich, England, 1979.

Worth, S., & Gross, L. Symbolic strategies. *Journal of Communication,* 1974, 24(4), 27-39.

ALTERNATIVE WAYS TO COMMUNICATE EVALUATION FINDINGS

If evaluators are to improve their communication of evaluative information, they need not only to deepen their understanding of the ways in which forms of representation influence our understanding of reality (as suggested in Part I), but they also need clear procedural alternatives for use in their daily work. Part II contains ten such alternatives.

The ten alternative communication strategies that follow vary in their degree of departure from reliance on a standard formal technical report. Some strategies suggest how to improve the impact of an existing report (for example, through the use of research briefs or graphics), while others involve the substitution of other forms of communication (for example, hearings or television presentations) for the formal report. These strategies also differ in terms of how the presentation strategy can affect the data collection and analysis phases of the evaluation, from having little influence (stem and leaf displays, policy briefings) to having a great deal of influence (operational network displays, adversary hearings). The selection of an appropriate strategy for a particular study will depend, of course, on such factors as the purpose of the study, audience needs and interests, communication expertise and resources available, and the types of evaluative information to be conveyed.

The ten strategies or techniques that follow fall roughly into two broad categories. The first five strategies might be called *individual techniques* in that a single individual is likely to receive the evaluation communication at any given time. These techniques rely primarily on visual communication, especially written narratives, displays, and graphics. Daniel Macy in "Research Briefs" discusses the use of abstracts, embedded quotes, executive summaries and other supplements to standard reports. Walter Hathaway in "Graphic Display Procedures" summarizes the multiple uses of graphic displays in reporting. Gaea and Samuel Leinhardt in "Stem-and-Leaf Displays" describe the use of stem and leaf diagrams for presenting and summarizing numerical data analyzed using exploratory data analysis procedures. In "Operational Network Displays," Brent Wholeben illustrates the use of operations research modeling procedures in communicating decision alternatives in program evaluation. Finally, Nick Smith in "Geographic Displays" discusses the descriptive and analytical uses of maps in evaluation.

The second five strategies included in Part II could be called *group techniques* in that the evaluation communication is most likely to be shared with several people at one time. These procedures include a combination of visual and auditory elements. In "Oral Policy Briefings," Michael Hendricks describes the use of briefings targeted to small groups of key administrators. Robert Stake and Daniel Balk describe the use of panel presentations in less targeted briefings of ad hoc or loose-knit panels in "Briefing Panel Presentations." Murry Levine, in "Adversary Hearings," illustrates the use of adversarial hearing formats in obtaining public discussion and resolution of evaluative issues, while Norman Stenzel in "Committee Hearings" discusses the use of hearings that involve multiple interest groups and a lack of definite pro/con positions. Finally, Judy Shoemaker, in "Television Presentations," considers the use of video tape in presenting evaluative issues to large public audiences.

All these chapters have been written by individuals with experience in the strategies they discuss. Their presentations include practical suggestions and illustrative case examples, providing a valuable resource of alternative communication approaches.

DANIEL J. MACY
Dallas Independent School District

CHAPTER **5**

Research Briefs

Daniel J. Macy is a Principal Evaluator in the Department of Research and Evaluation in the Dallas Independent School District, Dallas, Texas. His professional responsibility is to direct the research and evaluation effort for the District's special education programs. His major interests include communication within the research community and between researchers and practitioners.

There it sat, the 148-page final research report, and believe me, it was a real honey. Glossy multicolored covers with shiny black plastic spiral binding. Inside, the title page boasted an impressive line-up of top-name research and evaluation people, representing some of the nation's best known research institutions.

I felt really good about this one. It had cost a bundle, but was worth every penny. I flipped a few pages and ran my fingers softly across a bar graph and onto a full-page table. It was exhilarating, like shooting through a snow-banked turn. The F ratios were convincing, the orthogonal rotations superb, and the project description marvelous. I couldn't resist . . . just a few more pages.

I cancelled my calls, propped my feet on the desk, and settled into page one. It was beautiful. Then Jones came along. A real trouble maker. Said there was a meeting in 10 minutes and wanted a research brief. My exhilaration dwindled, and I felt cold and afraid. What was a research brief? Had I missed something? Jones said that real research reporting required at least one brief, and maybe even several.

Jones walked on down the hall, and I was left, the final report sitting across my lap.

Like the above project manager we too might ask: What is a research brief? Do I need one? The dictionary gives many definitions for a brief. These range from an official mandate to short snug underpants. While the latter definition may have ancillary application, let us focus on a more plausible definition, such as a short written document or perhaps a synopsis, a condensed statement or outline. As a verb, brief can mean to give important information.

A research brief is then understood to be a written and condensed statement that gives important information about research. The research brief has four significant characteristics. It: (1) is written, (2) is condensed, (3) gives important information, and (4) is about research.

The first characteristic is that the research brief takes the form of a written statement. Only a written statement can be a brief. This does not preclude a nonwritten replication or presentation, but writing is one prerequisite for a brief.

The second characteristic is that the written statement must be condensed, that is, reduced and more compact than some previous statement. This quality implies the existence of a previous research report, such as a final or interim report, which exists in a nonreduced form. In other words, a research brief cannot be the one and only research report. The definition does not specify the extent of reduction, only that it be less than the previous report, though it would probably be a substantial reduction.

The giving of important information is the third characteristic of the research brief. This quality makes the brief active, rather than passive. In some ways a final research report is passive, since one basic function is to document and present the research conducted. The final report may not assume any responsibility for the reader's response, but the research brief should put information into the possession of another person. The brief strives to make the reader attend to the information.

The definition also limits the brief to the giving of important information, that which is of significance or consequence. Information important to one audience may not be to another, and so the content as well as the style of a brief may well depend on the intended audience. However, the information given should be important to that audience at that time.

The fourth and final characteristic of a research brief is that it is about research. It is not limited necessarily to research outcomes. The brief may announce the initiation of new research, describe applications of research methodology, or report on activities of a research foundation or on a myriad of research-related topics.

Aside from its four significant characteristics, how does one recognize a research brief? Where does it live? What does it look like? The brief may reside in many places, including a briefcase (no pun intended), desk top, newsletter, the human hand (a favorite place), direct sunlight, and within other documents or research reports. Research briefs may take several forms including summaries, memos, news items, and short statements, and these may occur in variable patterns and hues.

Example Research Briefs

The following discusses seven examples of research briefs: report summary, executive summary, memo, google, embedded quotation, news item, and abstract.

Report summary. One of the best known research briefs is probably the summary that appears at the end of most, if not all, final research reports. In fact, the once-exhilarated project manager we met earlier probably had a research brief at the end of that spiffy final report.

The report summary's major strength is that it includes comprehensive information within a small amount of text. Therefore, it gives the reader a fairly complete understanding with minimal investment of time and energy. The summary is applicable to any setting or research report, and audience reception is so great that many authorities would judge a research report without a summary to be incomplete.

Executive summary. A very effective variation of the report summary is the executive summary. This has the same applicability as the simple report summary, but has at least two additional strengths. The first is its placement, which should be immediately after the title page, or at least prior to the table of contents. This placement of the executive summary gives the reader an opportunity for advance mental organization prior to attempting the complete report.

The second and perhaps more powerful strength of the executive summary is that it has "executive appeal." Like sex appeal, executive appeal is extremely desirable. The notion of a special summary written for some select group of executives reinforces executives' view of their importance. Likewise, any "nonexecutive" who spends the time and energy to read an executive summary can feel important, just like an executive. Consequently, the executive summary is particularly effective, since the act of attending to the summary makes the reader feel more important.

Executive summaries appear to have been used most frequently in research reports from settings governed by boards of directors or those involving interagency councils. One example application comes from the final evaluation report from a secondary school social studies project in law in education (Macy, 1972). This executive summary condensed the 52-page final report into 2 pages that described project objectives, evaluation design and results, and recommendations. As such, the summary attempted to give local school board members all the information thought essential for decision-making.

The executive summary can assume several formats. One is a question/answer format, and the following gives examples from research for an academic screening project and from a child find project for handicapped children (Kocsis & Macy, 1977; Gilliam, Kocsis, & Macy, 1979):

Question 1:   How did the percent[age] of students flagged high risk in the project compare to the District's profile by grade, sex, and ethnicity?

Results of the educational screening, health screening, and language screening indicated that the percent[age] of students marked high risk was comparative by grade, sex, and ethnicity to the total number of students screened in the target populations.

Question 2:   Who were the agents making referrals to the child find office?

The majority of the referrals were a result of calls from parents, school personnel and various community agencies.

In many program evaluation studies, the framework for data collection, analysis, and interpretation is the set of evaluation questions. The above question/answer format can make the executive summary more faithful to this framework. However, this format may result in less comprehensive information, since the evaluation questions typically deal with outcomes rather than context and study background. Of course, this information, along with recommendations, could be expressed in a question/answer format.

One of the popular settings for the executive summary has been in public school districts in which research and evaluation departments report extensively to boards of education. In the 1973-1974 school year, the research and evaluation department of the Dallas Independent School

District, Dallas, Texas, presented 81 final research reports to the school board (Department of Research, Evaluation, & Information Systems, 1974). The need for research briefs was obvious, and the use of executive summaries made it possible for board members to be more knowledgeable about a large quantity of information.

Memos. The memo provides a remarkably versatile and effective medium for the research brief. Its format and content can be altered easily to increase visual attraction, heighten interest, and improve mental recall through color and physical layout.

One simple application is the attachment of a single page memo to the top of the research report, as a means of capturing audience attention and introducing the report. The following memo was copied on pink paper and attached to a process evaluation report regarding a program for emotionally disturbed students in a public school.

TO: Project XXXX Management Team
Subject: Process Evaluation Report

The information contained in the attached report relates to the extent to which Project XXXX has been implemented as of January 31, 1979. Although most program objectives have been met, the following items should be noted:

1. Assignment of personnel to implement the program has not been completed. Although most of the project staff were aboard in November 1978, the visiting-teacher was not assigned until January 1979, and the educational diagnostician has not yet been assigned. Only two teacher aides were assigned to the five project teachers. In January 1979, both aides left the project and have not been replaced (see pp. 4 and 5).

2. Building modifications have not yet been begun. The time-out room, "a small enclosed room which permits observation by an adult without interaction," is important for the safety of both students and staff (see p. 7).

In the above example, the project was only six months old at completion of the process evaluation, and accordingly the report dealt with implementation variables. The evaluator used the memo not only to communicate critical findings, but also to educate members of the project management team about the time-out room. Members of management teams do not have equal commitment to nor mental involvement in project management, and the research brief may be the only information to which selected managers attend.

Another effective application is to attach a sequence of memos, with the first giving very easy and superficial information, the next giving more detailed information, and so forth. Sequenced memos may deal also with different content areas. For example, in reporting from a systems analysis of paper-processing in a public school speech and language program, the author used three single-page memos. The first listed the three kinds of information contained in the final report, the second showed simple computations for the cost of the analysis, and the third listed major findings. If readers did not get to the fourth piece of paper, they still possessed a great deal of useful information.

One advantage of the memo is mobility, since it can travel independently and need not be attached to the more cumbersome report. Another advantage is the opportunity to personalize distribution. The memo could be written to Dr. J. Smith with copies to Adams and Brown (designated by "cc" at the end of the memo). Now Smith knows that Adams and Brown ought to know, and vice versa. These applications are particularly useful within organizations and institutions.

Googles. The google is a novel research brief, and the first known application was for nine research and evaluation studies completed for the special education department in the Dallas Independent School District in 1978-1979. Reports from these nine studies totaled more than 350 pages, and dissemination to the more than 500 special education teachers and staff was unrealistic. Googles were developed in response to the need to share research and evaluation outcomes with a large audience whose interest potential varied enormously.

The newsletter announcement of googles was directed primarily to teachers and stated in part:

> We think there is a real need to improve the communication of research and evaluation results, and so we have conjured up the concept of a google. Now you say, what is a google? A google is a one-liner designed to make its owner appear intelligent and well-read. An even moderate supply of googles should enable one to speak intelligently about any of several research and evaluation studies [The Birth of Googles, 1980].

Googles written for one study, the special education computerized data base, were as follows:

(1) Rosters of special education students were printed routinely every six weeks.

(2) Management made 90 ad hoc requests for data base information and rosters.

(3) Computer generation of the annual statistical report to the state was more cost effective than manual production.

(4) Computer terminals were planned for use in special education subdistrict offices during 1979-1980.

Reference for the respective final report was given at the end of each google list.

Audience reaction to googles was not evaluated systematically, but the feedback received was mixed. A major difficulty in composing googles is that the number of things to know and remember rapidly exceeds the reader's capacity and/or desire to remember, especially since many in the target audience may have only remote interest at the outset. One strength of the google is its attention-getting capacity. The eccentric sound of the word likely ensures 100% initial participation. A second strength is dissemination efficiency, since the ratio of production cost to the number of potential readers is very small. Googles can lead also to more comprehensive reporting to an interested subset of the google audience.

Embedded quotations. The embedded quotation is either an abridgment or a direct restatement of a portion of a research report and is set apart within the text of the report. A follow-up study of graduates from early intervention projects for handicapped infants and toddlers provided one occasion for effective use of embedded quotations. The 108-page final report included 36 embedded quotations. The following gives one example quotation:

. . . . percent[age] located was −.04, which indicated no relationship. The absence of a relationship between number attempted for follow-up and the percent[age] located suggested that the number of

> *"RESULTS OF FOLLOWUP SHOWED THAT PERSONNEL WERE ABLE TO LOCATE ABOUT 78% OF THOSE CHILDREN FOR WHOM FOLLOWUP WAS ATTEMPTED . . . 8% HAD MOVED . . . 2% WERE DECEASED . . . 12% WERE UNKNOWN."*

children selected for followup did not affect followup success. Other factors such as accuracy of project records and ambition of staff determined success in locating graduates. The interested reader may consult Table 4 [Macy & Carter, 1980, p. 13].

When first handed a final report, people typically flip pages prior to page-by-page reading. In such cases, the embedded quotation catches the eye and gives the reader a visual and mental foothold in the text of the report. If sufficient interest is present, more comprehensive information is available immediately to the reader in the text adjacent to the quotation.

Another advantage of quotations is that a comprehensive set embedded throughout a report can provide a complete overview, and perusal of embedded quotations could be equivalent to a report summary. In fact, quotations can be used directly or in modified form in several other types of research briefs.

The final report from the followup study of early intervention graduates was the author's first experience with embedded quotations. In addition to being easy to compose, the quotations greatly facilitated the writing of the report summary. Audience reaction was also quite positive.

News items. The news item is similar to the report summary but is more flexible in content and emphasis. News items may appear in newspapers, newsletters, and in news columns or departments in serial publications. The newsletter of the Research on Evaluation Program of the Northwest Regional Educational Laboratory includes a work-in-progress segment for news items about on-going research efforts.[1] *Educational Researcher* occasionally includes a "Research Notes" section, as do several professional journals and newspapers.

One obvious advantage of the news item is that the cost of dissemination is free and easy, since the host publication bears this cost. The host publication also offers a preassembled, readily accessible audience, assuming the news item is appropriate for the audience.

Abstracts. Perhaps the oldest and most venerable research brief is the abstract, commonly seen as a journal abstract, dissertation abstract, or document reproduction service abstract. The major strength of abstracts, especially journal and dissertation abstracts, is the extent of prepublication editing by an independent agent. This frequently results in a very concise, accurate, and informative report summary. In fact, the potential information gained to the reading effort invested ratio may be highest for abstracts. However, one limitation of most abstracts is that they read like minijournals, and they serve only the journal audience. On the other hand, tradition suggests that the abstract has been a highly effective brief for this audience.

Conditions and Limitations

There is one critical condition for the use of research briefs . . . the researcher must believe! Research is one of the essential ways in which humankind moves toward perfection and fulfillment. The researcher must believe in the value of research and believe in sharing it with others. If researchers really believed, would not they share more with the human community? Hence, one's philosophy of research must embrace research briefs.

The message for researchers is simple: "Tell your story." The research brief provides great opportunity to tell at least part of the story to a lot of different people. Given a single research brief, Jones might have told some of the story at that meeting. As it was, Jones failed even to get a copy of the final report.

The traditional avenues for research dissemination have been "scholarly" publications, such as journal articles, conference presentations, and more recently, final reports to funding agencies. Most assuredly, these reach only very limited and parochial audiences. The research brief calls the researcher to break from tradition and to risk rejection by self and by others. What self-respecting, learned, and promising researcher would spend precious time composing a memo to parents of students at Lincoln High School or to the Northampton town meeting? And, really, aren't googles just a tad informal? There is at least one researcher who shows great disbelief and uncontrollable laughter at mere mention of googles.

The Joint Committee on Standards for Educational Evaluation stated, "It is crucial that the evaluators, in cooperation with the client, exert special effort to reach and inform all right-to-know audiences" (Standards for Evaluations, 1981, p. 40). The Committee further cited the need to use reporting formats and approaches appropriate for various audiences. Hence, in education there is legitimacy and potential mandate for research briefs, and in some cases failure to use briefs may constitute professional negligence for the educational evaluator.

One difficulty in developing the research brief is that by definition it is active and gives important information, rather than merely documenting its presence. Of course, briefs succeed in this capacity to varying degrees, but the writer of briefs faces a special challenge. The brief must induce the reader to participation. Jones was too busy or too disinterested to read, or even look at, the whole report, but only a little inducement would have gotten Jones to read a brief.

The research brief offers the possibility of gaining important information with only a small investment of time and effort. The brief must first get the readers' attention and then convince them to read. Consequently, the brief should be visually pleasant, suggest ease of reading, and appear understandable and memorable. Briefs that are complex and tedious in appearance are not likely to entice the reader. These considerations do not preclude the inclusion of technical information, but do imply that the target audience can read such material ably. Variations in color, print, space, and style can contribute to a brief's power of inducement.

The most serious limitation of the brief is brevity; it cannot tell the whole story. Consequently, bias in selecting content for a research brief can result in at least two serious problems. First, the audience could be misled through incomplete information or insufficient qualification. Second, information included in a brief may not have the same importance for the audience as for the researcher, or it may carry more than one message. Research briefs, therefore, require that the researcher be sensitive to the information needs and priorities of the target audience and understand potential audience reactions and interpretations. Too many researchers write for the journal audience or the funding agency. Consider that the typical research journal article fits a school faculty like a bowling ball on a billiard table. The research brief clearly calls the researcher to develop a variety of writing styles suitable for a range of audiences.

Another limitation of research briefs is the absence of empirically validated principles for deciding when and how to use briefs. However, recent research has focused on factors' influencing the effectiveness of evaluation reports (Braskamp, Brown, & Newman, 1978). Thompson, Brown, and Furgason (1981) reported numerous significant interactions among variables influencing the effectiveness of a simulated and abbreviated evaluation report. Such research may lead to an information base for more effective use of research briefs.

Research, yours and mine, is important. It deserves to be heard, and people need to hear it. Final reports and journal articles give us only monophonic reporting, but we can adopt the full range of research briefs and come to multiphonic broadcasting. However, effective use of research briefs involves many factors: cost, time, audience, content, style, purpose, philosophy, to name just a few. Researchers must weigh relative benefits and limits in creating the right brief for the right job.

Note

[1]Newsletter: Research on Evaluation Program, Northwest Regional Educational Laboratory, 300 S.W. Sixth Avenue, Portland, Oregon 97204.

References

Braskamp, L. A., Brown, R. D., & Newman, D. L. The credibility of a local educational program evaluation report: Author source and client audience characteristics. *American Educational Research Journal*, 1978, 15(3), 441-450.

Department of Research, Evaluation, & Information Systems. Abstracts of research and evaluation reports: 1973-1974. Dallas Independent School District, Dallas, November 1974.

Gilliam, D.F.C., Kocsis, J. J., & Macy, D. J. Executive summary: 1978-1979 evaluation of Dallas child find. Research Report No. SP79-417-41-08. Dallas: Dallas Independent School District, Dallas, June 1979.

Kocsis, J. J., & Macy, D. J. Executive summary: Evaluation of the 1976-1977 project HELP screening. Research Report No. SE77-065-4-8. Dallas Independent School District, Dallas, July 1977.

Macy, D. J. Evaluation of the 1971-1972 law in a changing society program, Research Report No. 72-60. Dallas Independent School District, Dallas, July 1972.

Macy, D. J., & Carter, J. L. *Triple t infant followup study.* Dallas: Triple T Infant Consortium, 1980.

Reisman, K. C., Holt, M. A., Kocsis, J. J., & Macy, D. J. Special Education Data Base, Research Report No. SP79-415-31-08. Dallas Independent School District, Dallas, September 1979.

Standards for evaluations of educational programs, projects, and materials (Developed by the Joint Committee on Standards for Educational Evaluation). New York: McGraw-Hill, 1981.

The birth of googles. *Sequel,* Newsletter from the Special Education Component of the Department of Research, Evaluation, & Information Systems. Dallas Independent School District, Dallas, January 1980.

Thompson, P. A., Brown, R. D., & Furgason, J. Jargon and data do make a difference: The impact of report styles on lay and professional evaluation audiences. *Evaluation Review,* 1981, 5(2), 269-279.

WALTER E. HATHAWAY

Portland Public School System

CHAPTER **6**

Graphic Display Procedures

Walter E. Hathaway is currently Director of Research and Evaluation for the Portland, Oregon Public School System. His duties and interests span a wide range of educational research and evaluation concerns affecting the competency and satisfaction of both students and staff and the effectiveness and attractiveness of schools and schooling. He has been afforded the opportunity to review numerous recent research and evaluation reports through chairing the AERA Division H Awards Competition and through his involvement in the Educational Research and Evaluation Director Networks of the Council of Great City Schools and the National Institute of Education.

INCREASINGLY, AS EVALUATION has evolved into a formal, systematic process, evaluators have wondered why more attention is sometimes not paid to the wisdom packed lovingly into our dissertation-like reports.

Author's Note: *The author wishes to express his gratitude to Jay Smith who did the graphic design for this chapter and to Joy Harris who did the typography.*

And we have come up with some pretty good answers to that important question such as:

- "We ask the wrong questions so the findings are irrelevant"; or

- "We get the results there too late to be used"; or

- "We don't get the findings to the people who need to know them."

Recognition of such problems has led to progress toward more deliberateness and involvement in design, greater timeliness in reporting, and more careful identification of intended audiences.

The effort to find ways to improve the usefulness and use of evaluation results, combined with a parallel concern for the usefulness of knowledge gained through research, has led over the last decade to a growing body of research and development at the national, regional, and state levels on:

DISSEMINATION ★ CAPACITY BUILDING
UTILITY ★ UTILIZATION
IMPACT ★ DIFFUSION
FACILITATION, ETC.

Much of this work has helped us toward greater success in timely identification of potential audiences for our findings and in working with them to tailor the evaluation message to their needs. It seems, however, that we have largely neglected a somewhat homely but critical aspect of improving the process of communicating evaluation information, namely, the media through which we convey the message.

A picture of the process of communicating information in general is illustrated in Figure 6.1. This figure helps to illustrate the point that a principal source of failure to successfully and effectively communicate evaluation results may lie not in the lack of timeliness, appropriateness, or clarity of the message nor in the failure to direct it in a personalized way to the appropriate audiences, but simply in not choosing the right vehicles to get the message across to the intended audiences in ways that they can readily grasp it.[1]

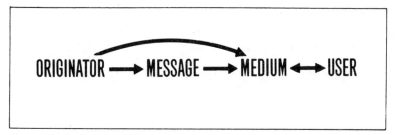

Figure 6.1 The Communication Process

The scheme in Figure 6.1 may usefully be broken down into two subparadigms, depending on whether the purpose of the communication is to help the users gain a body of information (Figure 6.2) or is to assist them in solving a problem or making a decision as is usually the case in evaluation (Figure 6.3). Part of the problem with the communication of evaluation results is that we have been erroneously guided by the paradigm in Figure 6.2. In selecting our media when we should have been following the paradigm in Figure 6.3. The difference is that the latter approach respects the needs of hard-pressed users actively engaged in problem-solving and decision-making, and not necessarily looking our way for help. The use of graphic display procedures is perhaps one small way to capture and focus the attention of those we seek to serve and to share with them in a meaningful way our important messages about:

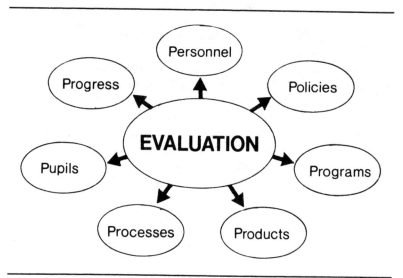

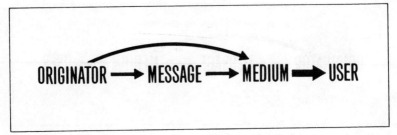

Figure 6.2   Communicating to Share Information

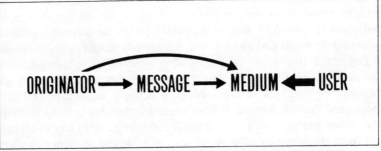

Figure 6.3   Communicating to Facilitate Problem Solving and Decision Making

A symptom of how little attention has been paid to the subject of the medium of communication of evaluation results in general and the use of graphics in particular is that few sources treat these subjects directly. The abundant writing on the theory and practice of evaluation pays scant attention to the reporting phase and even less attention to the medium of reporting. Even the limited literature focused directly on evaluation reports and their characteristics dwells almost exclusively on the content of the message. Sometimes the issue of timely audience identification and adaptation of the message to it is touched upon. There is also an occasional nod in the direction of a requirement for "clarity" of communication. But there is little concern for use of alternatives to the verbal medium of communication. [2] Accordingly, for the brief discussion of the use of graphic technique for evaluation reporting that follows I have drawn primarily upon the literature on graphic design itself and on the rich fields of organizational and business communication.

Graphic Technique

The purpose of graphic design is to get the people in a target group to respond to a visual image. The techniques of graphic designers include typography, symbolism, illustration, and photography.[3]

An obvious first step toward using the techniques of graphic display to improve the reporting of evaluation results is to incorporate them appropriately into the body of our traditional printed evaluation reports in the form of well designed illustrations, graphs, charts, and the like. The next step is to supplement these written reports by other forms of presentation as the needs of audiences and the availability of resources permit. Examples of ways to share the results of evaluations that lend themselves readily to graphic display techniques are exhibits, posters, brochures, overhead transparencies, slide/tape presentations, videotapes, and films.

The application of the design process to evaluation reporting can be as simple as selecting an appropriate color or design for a report cover, or as complex as weaving graphics throughout a complex report and building a series of graphically enriched versions of the report targeted at special audiences. Such versions could range, for example, from a brochure for parents and students to a videotape for a board of education and a school district staff.

The most effective use of graphics in enhancing the usefulness of evaluation reporting requires a partnership between evaluation and graphic design professionals. While we are all designers to some extent and have some skills of graphic design, we have much to learn and gain from colleagues and consultants well trained in graphic design principles and techniques.[4] A sample scenario of an effective way for evaluators to operate as partners in such an association would be to:

Discuss the evaluation and the role of graphic display in it with the graphic designers at the outset.

Seek the graphic designers suggestions at the completion of the evaluation design.

Take a draft of the report(s) and alternative reporting formats to the graphic designers with the evaluator's ideas for use of graphics laid out in the form of notes, preliminary sketches, etc.

Receive, review and revise designer draft copies of all reports, brochures, film scenarios, videotape scripts, etc.

Since much of what we attempt to communicate in evaluation is quantitative or is based upon quantitative results, some special attention needs to be paid to the use of graphic display in reporting numbers. Of course, much effective use is already made in evaluation reports of such

	Use		Misuse
1.	To clarify complex data	1.	May oversimplify data
2.	To emphasize relative magnitudes	2.	May overemphasize quantitative aspects
3.	To help identify trends	3.	May exaggerate trends
4.	To demonstrate relationships	4.	May oversimplify relationships

Figure 6.4 Possible Uses and Misuses of Graphs and Tables

Types	Advantages	Disadvantages
Graphs	Vivid means of presenting data and relationships	A poorly designed or inappropriately chosen graph may hurt more than help; takes time to prepare
Tables	Enhances clarity through logical arrangement and concise description; use of columns and rows facilitates comparisions	Recognition by reader requires familiarity with legends and relationships; difficult to portray trends; some readers shy away

Figure 6.5 Advantages and Disadvantages

techniques as graphs and tables, but Figures 6.4-6.7 provide a simple and useful guide for making even more effective use of these popular measures of presenting data.[5]

Examples of Graphic Display

In spite of the fact that little is being published on the subject of use of graphic display techniques in effectively sharing evaluation results, there is a growing body of practice that can be drawn upon for useful models. During 1981, as chairman for the American Educational Research Association (AERA) Division H awards competition, I had the opportunity to review almost 200 current, outstanding examples of the evaluation craft submitted by evaluators and their institutions. There were 12 major categories of reports including policy analysis, research studies, evaluation studies, test results, district statistical profiles, methodological advances, and cooperative studies. The reports in these categories tended to be

Types	Advantages	Disadvantages
Area	Simply display for non-technical viewers	Difficult to shade for differentiation or to label parts; unsuitable for comparison with like graphs
Bar	Easy single scale comparison of amounts, subdivisions, relations	Limited to single scale; must limit subdivision to avoid confusion
Column	Features two scales; relatively eary comparison of related items having different measurement units	Time needed to prepare; special skills needed to scale relationships of unlike units
Curve	Most flexible; emphasizes and compares trends; illustrates plotted points; can be used for extrapolation	May include too many concepts and distort or misrepresent significance of numerical data
Surface	Most useful for comparing multiple trends	Fewer uses because of limitation in arrangement of elements; screening may confuse reader or create optical illusion

Figure 6.6 Basic Types of Statistical Graphs (each is exemplified in Figure 6.7)

excellent instances of the extensive compilations of verbal and quantitative information with which we are familiar. Some of the reports, however, and especially those receiving awards, paid significant attention to graphic design principles.

A second group of categories provided more scope for some visually exciting entries. This group included guides to interpreting and using test results, executive summaries, study report brochures, and unique reporting techniques. The award winner among the brochures was a special report by Phoenix Union High School, District #210, on a study of "the dropout problem." The report itself was a well designed, multicolored, 85-page in-depth description of the study and its conclusions. The major graphic excitement, however, was contained in a series of four lively brochures aimed at students who might be thinking about dropping out of school. These accessible, 7-page long brochures vividly present the experiences and opinions of district students who had dropped out and who had returned to school. They also give valuable information about the difficulty of

Examples of Graphs

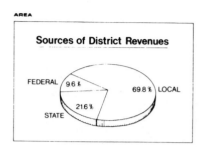

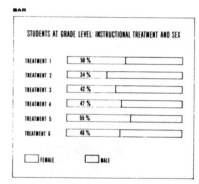

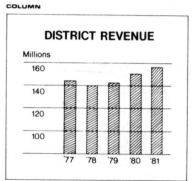

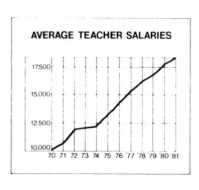

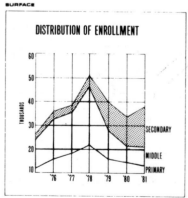

Figure 6.7   Examples of Graphs

Figure 6.8

getting jobs or further training after leaving school. The series also contained encouragement for students considering leaving school to meet with their school counselor. The judges of the awards competition found the combination of the report and the brochure to be a powerful and attractive set of media for sharing the results of this evaluation in an effective

THINKING ABOUT
DROPPING OUT?

BEFORE YOU hang glide over the Grand Canyon....

sign a ten-year contract....

join the Army....

sell your tape deck....

move to North Dakota....

quit your job....

climb Mt. St. Helens....

buy a used car....

AND....

BEFORE YOU drop out of school....

CHECK IT OUT!

The following pages contain comments
from students who dropped out of school,
then came back. You will be interested
in what they have to say. Here are some
of their ideas....

Figure 6.9

way with diverse audiences. The first two pages of the first of the four brochures are included as Figures 6.8 and 6.9.

A second area of evaluation reporting that seems unusually rich in examples of graphic display is that of guides to interpretation and use of test data. Here the challenge is to communicate awareness and under-

Audience	Need/Purpose							
	Orientation	Administration	Interpretation & Use of Scores	Interpretation & Use of Reports	Interpreting Test Scores to Parents	Interpreting Testing Program to Public	Meaning & Interpretation of Standards	Meaning & Interpretation of Gains
Teachers: Elementary Teachers	X	X	X	X	X	X	X	X
H.S. Teachers	X	X	X	X	X	X	X	X
Test Coordinators	X	X	X	X		X	X	
High School Counselors	X	X	X	X	X	X	X	X
High School Administrators	X		X	X		X	X	
Elementary School Principals	X	X	X	X		X	X	X
Area Administrators	X		X	X	X	X	X	X
Central Administrators	X		X	X		X	X	X
Curriculum Personnel	X		X	X		X	X	X
Community Relations	X		X	X	X	X	X	X
School Board	X		X	X		X	X	X

Figure 6.10 Audiences and Needs in the Area of Test Data Interpretation and Use

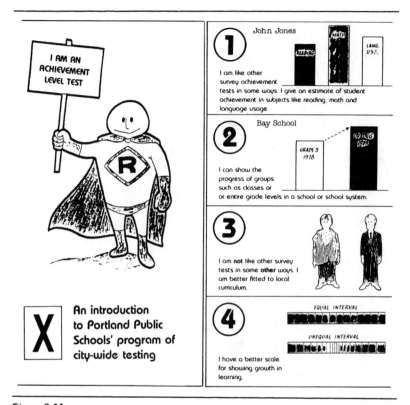

Figure 6.11

standing of complicated and multileveled test reults to diverse audiences. A matrix of these audiences and their needs appears as Figure 6.10.

For the last two years the Division H award in the area of test data interpretation and use has gone to districts who produced a layered set of media to meet the complex information needs of such diverse audiences. These efforts include brochures, orientation manuals, test score and report interpretation manuals, technical manuals, overhead transparency packages, and slide/tape presentations. The Montgomery County (MD) Schools were this year's award winners. The previous year the award went to the Portland (OR) School District. The scope of the material in these offerings is so broad that it makes selecting a small but appropriate and representative sample difficult. Nevertheless I have included as Figures 6.11 and 6.12 selected panels from one of Portland's brochures. This material was also available in one of several slide/tape presentations.

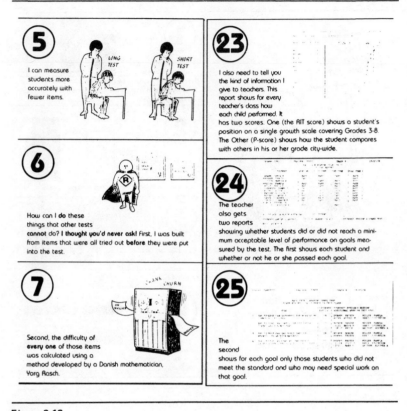

Figure 6.12

Both Portland and Montgomery County report that their work in this area has been helpful in communicating information about testing programs and their results. They and others are engaged in efforts to expand the quality and range of media available for this purpose and the scope and sophistication of their use.

Assessment of Graphic Technique

As school districts, research and development agencies, and universities struggle to communicate the results of evaluations more effectively, a body of techniques is emerging that often includes good use of graphic displays, particularly for awareness and orientation purposes and especially for lay audiences. Such uses can be expected to grow in quantity and quality.

Some difficulties with the use of graphic techniques is that they require more time and more money both for report planning and execution. Also there are few guides to follow as you march into this relatively new territory for evaluators. Those of us fortunate enough to have "in-house" graphic designers would benefit by including them early and often in our evaluation planning sessions. Another potential new ally, especially for typography, can be found in the person of the director of the word processing center if you have one. Alternately, consultants in graphic design can usually be found in any even moderately large community. Business and professional organizations can often be helpful in providing advice and even in sharing capability.

In summary, the attainment of the larger professional goals of evaluators and even our survival (as federal and state requirements and resources for evaluation dwindle) may well depend upon major improvements in our ability to communicate the results of our work more effectively. Appropriate and cost effective use of graphic display techniques is one path to such improvement that is thus far generally not much used. As we continue to ask ourself as a profession, "Where are we going?" we would perhaps do well to consider this path "less traveled by."

Notes

[1]This scheme is traceable back to Shannon's original model of communication systems.

[2]I did, however, find one article on the use of pictorial presentations of research results. It managed, however, to get through a 17-page discussion of its subject without a single nonverbal symbol, picture, or illustration!

[3]Photography is normally viewed as one of the four channels of expression in graphic design along with symbolism, typography, and illustration. Since this topic is addressed in an earlier chapter, no special attention is paid to it here.

[4]A simple test of the proposition that design is better left to designers and evaluation to evaluators would be to switch roles and compare the resultant reports.

[5]The author wishes to acknowledge the inspiration and information used from Vardaman and Vardaman (1973) in designing Figures 6.4-6.7.

References

Alkin, M., Duillak, C., & White, P. *Using evaluation: Does evaluation make a difference?* Beverly Hills, CA: Sage, 1979.

Berryman, G. *Notes on graphic design and visual communication.* Los Altos, CA: William Kaufman, 1979.

Brittain, J. M. *Information and its use.* New York: John Wiley, 1970.

Caplan, N. Factors associated with knowledge use among federal executives. *Policy Studies Journal,* 1976, 4(3), 229-234.

Caplan, N., & Barton, E. Social indicators. In *1973: A study of the power of information and utilization by federal executives.* Ann Arbor, MI: Institute for Social Research, 1976.

Cherry, C. *On human communication* (2nd ed.). Cambridge, MA: MIT Press, 1966.

Cook, T. C., & Pollard, W. E. Guidelines: How to recognize and avoid some common problems of mis-utilization of evaluation research findings. *Evaluation,* 1977, 4, 161-164.

Cooley, W. W., & Lohnes, P. R. How can evaluations influence decisions and policies? *Evaluation research in education: Theory, principals and practice.* New York: John Wiley, 1969.

Crandall, D. P., & Harris, R. C. *Views on the utilization of information by practitioners.* Andover, MA: The Network, 1978.

Guba, E. G. Problems in utilizing the results of evaluation. *Journal of Research and Development in education,* 1975, 8(3), 42-54.

Haenn, J. F. Reasons why evaluations and testing don't inform. Paper presented at the American Educational Research Association Annual Meeting, Boston, Massachusetts, April 1980.

Havelock, R. G., & Lingwood, D. A. *R&D utilizational strategies and functions: An analytical comparison of four systems.* Ann Arbor, MI: Center for Research on Utilization of Scientific Knowledge, 1973.

Hawkins, J. D., Roffman, R. A., & Osborne, P. Decision makers' judgments, the influence of role, evaluative criteria, and information access. *Evaluation Quarterly,* 1978, 2(3), 435-454.

Hood, P. D., & Blackwell, L. *Key educational information users and their styles of information use* (Vol. 1). San Francisco: Far West Laboratory of Educational Research and Development, 1976.

Lange, R. R., & Speiss, M. An empirical study of four providing variables affecting utilization of evaluation. Paper presented at the American Educational Research Association Annual Meeting, Chicago, Illinois, April, 1974.

Loucks, S. F., & Meyers, E. C. Improving the usefulness of R&D information by responding to audience concerns and practices. NTS Research Corporation, September 1978.

Nielsen, V. G. Why evaluation does not improve program effectiveness. *Policy Studies Journal,* 1975, 3(4), 385-390.

Phoenix Union High School. Special report: The dropout problem, 1980.

Shannon, C. E., & Weaver, W. *The mathematical theory of communication.* Urbana: University of Illinois Press, 1949.

Smith, S. The utility and utilization of evaluative information. TEAM Associates, 1976.

Vardaman, G. T., & Vardaman, P. *Black communications in modern organizations.* New York: John Wiley, 1973.

Weick, K. E. Educational organizations as loosely-coupled systems. *Administration Science Quarterly,* 1976, 21, 1-19.

Weiss, C. H. Between the cup and the lip. *Evaluation,* 1973, 1(2), 49-55.

GAEA LEINHARDT
University of Pittsburgh

SAMUEL LEINHARDT
Carnegie-Mellon University

CHAPTER **7**

Stem-and-Leaf Displays

> *Gaea Leinhardt is Research Associate and Director of the Dimensions of Instruction and Learning Project at the Learning Research and Development Center, University of Pittsburgh. Her interests include program evaluation, educational policy, and classroom behavior of teachers. ● Samuel Leinhardt is Professor of Sociology at the School of Urban and Public Affairs, Carnegie-Mellon University. His research interests focus on statistical methods, mathematical models of social systems, and the delivery of human services.*

JOHN W. TUKEY coined the term "exploratory data analysis" to distinguish the exploratory search for patterns in data from traditional statistical inference in which data are used to test hypotheses. Tukey has created a host of very intriguing and useful exploratory procedures. In addition to their data analytic qualities, they possess three features that should make them highly attractive to evaluators engaged in communicating with evaluation audiences. First, they are highly intuitive and do not depend upon knowledge of some elaborate statistical theory for comprehension. Second, many are graphic or semigraphic and thus convey their information content visually rather than numerically. Third, they are based upon the use of the order statistics, such as the median and the quartiles, which are more readily understood by lay audiences than are means and standard deviations. A fourth feature that renders them attractive from a data analyst's perspective is their resistant quality; i.e., they are little effected by the presence of a few highly deviant values.

We have presented a general introduction to Tukey's work elsewhere (Leinhardt & Leinhardt, 1980). In this chapter we will focus on one technique, the stem-and-leaf display which, though only recently introduced (Tukey, 1971, 1972, 1977) has already gained widespread acceptance and is available on many popular statistical computing packages (e.g., MINITAB, BMDP, DAP). We focus on the stem-and-leaf display because it is, in a way, the most basic exploratory data analysis (EDA) tool.

The Stem-and-Leaf Display

The stem-and-leaf display is essentially a technique for rewriting a set of values so as to minimize the numbers used to characterize the values while highlighting some important features of their empirical distribution. It is quite similar to a histogram except that it consists of numerals rather than boxes or bins and is usually displayed vertically rather than horizontally. Because it is constructed of numerals, one or a set assigned to each data value, it retains much more information about the original data than does a histogram, permitting, in most instances, retrieval of an original value by direct interrogation of the display. This feature also permits the determination of summary order statistics. The stem-and-leaf display can be used to display any set of numerical values (we will not pursue its use to display qualitative data; see Tukey, 1977, p. 22) although there are circumstances in which its use may not be convenient. A very large sample, for example, can give rise to a severely elongated or simply big display, one which is not easily rendered on a normal sized sheet of paper. In other cases, highly skewed or spread out values may impose problems of a similar nature. Sampling the values and using more than one display to cover the range of values in the data can usually resolve these difficulties. Another solution is to use some criterion to set aside some high or low values, displaying the remaining values in the stem-and-leaf.

The stem-and-leaf display exploits the fact that numeric values are written using a place-holding convention. That is, when we write the value 1023.78 we are specifying the thousands, hundreds, tens, units, tenths, and hundredths that compose the value. Having long ago adopted the decimal system, we are all quite at ease in using this complex "powers of ten" notation as a way of indicating measurements.

Often, however, and this is especially true when values are basically measuring the same thing, writing down a sample of numeric values is redundant and inefficient. For example, if we are writing down dates within some century, say 1900, then the left two digits of the year are unnecessary as long as we have made note of the century. Thus the set of years 1901, 1924, 1948, 1914, 1943, 1944, 1932, 1917, 1911 could more simply be written 01, 24, 48, 14, 43, 44, 32, 17, 11 with no loss of information. Clearly, if we are noting years within a decade we should be satisfied with one numeral to indicate each year.

A stem-and-leaf display is nothing more than a device for accomplishing this kind of shorthand recording of data values. Its parts consist of a vertical bar that separates a value into left and right portions. On the left of the bar a number is written representing that portion of a data value that is one order of magnitude, i.e., one power of ten, higher than the portion of the value written on the right of the vertical bar. The left portion is called the stem, the right is called the leaf. An ordered column of stems rises (or falls) along the vertical bar and rows of leaves (which may or may not be ordered) move to the right from the bar.

Consider the nine years listed earlier. A simple stem-and-leaf display of the two digit year values consisting of one stem and nine two digit leaves would look like this:

$$19|01, 24, 48, 14, 43, 44, 32, 17, 11$$

The vertical bar separates the 19 (hundred) from the years within the century. Each year appears to the right of the bar. Commas have been used between the pairs of year digits to avoid confusion; they are not necessary when each leaf consists of one digit.

A more informative stem-and-leaf display can be constructed by allowing the stems to refer to decades. We will drop the 19 since it is easy enough to note once on the display that the years fall in the period 1900 to 1999. The stems of this display will be written arbitrarily as running down the page from earlier to later decade:

```
0 |
1 |
2 |
3 |
4 |                century:  19
```

Now we add the leaves. The year 1901 will appear simply as a 1 to the immediate right of the stem 0. The year 1924 will appear as a 4 to the right of stem 2. The procedure is repeated until we get to the year 1943. We have already placed an 8 next to the stem for the year 1948. We would like to place a 3 next to this same stem. And that is essentially what we do but instead of overwriting the 8 we place the 3 to the immediate right of the 8 on the same row. The completed display is:

```
0 | 1
1 | 471
2 | 4
3 | 2
4 | 834           century:  19
```

This small example illustrates the basic features of the stem-and-leaf display and also demonstrates how easy it is to construct, much easier, in fact, than a histogram. The efficiency of the display should be obvious. We have used 16 digits to fully record the information that originally took 36. While in small data sets such economies are not impressive, they quickly become so as the sample size increases. More importantly, we have reduced the numerical information to its essential features, ridding the display of unnecessary and redundant material.

Since each value is represented by a single digit and each digit occupies an equal amount of space, the length of a row of digits is proportional to the frequency of values occurring within the interval established by the stem value. Thus the display contains the same kind of information as does the bar height of a histogram. The differences, of course, rest in the ease of construction of the stem-and-leaf display and the fact that the individual data values have not been lost.

The stem-and-leaf display allows us to get a feeling for the way in which the data values are distributed. By visually examining the shape we can answer questions such as whether the data are unimodal and symmetric about a center or skewed toward one end; we can see if some values are especially common or particularly rare; we can see outlying values or separations in the data; we can determine whether there is one or several modes; we can get a feeling for whether the data cluster tightly or spread out broadly. The shape of the values can be outlined by drawing an easy curve bordering the outer right edge of the leaves:

```
0 | 1
1 | 471
2 | 4
3 | 2
4 | 834
```

Of course, it's hardly necessary for us to add this outline to this particular data set since the multimodal pattern is clear from the display.

Because of its rowlike nature, the display also makes it convenient to count the leaves of each stem:

Count		
1	0	1
3	1	471
1	2	4
1	3	2
3	4	834

We can obtain summary order statistics by using this row-by-row count and the fact that the stem-and-leaf display retains information on each data value. First we *count up* the batch of values by adding a column that sums leaf counts going from lower to higher stem value:

Count up	*Count*		
1	1	0	1
4	3	1	471
5	1	2	4
6	1	3	2
9	3	4	834

An additional column records the *count down,* from higher to lower stem values:

Count down	*Count up*	*Count*		
9	1	1	0	1
8	4	3	1	471
5	5	1	2	4
4	6	1	3	2
3	9	3	4	834

Notice that there is one row on which the count up and the count down are equal: the third stem, that for 1920, with a count up and a count down of 5. This is the midway point in the counting. One half of the values, four of them, are above this midway point and one half are below. This is the stem that contains the median data value and, since there is only one leaf on the stem, we immediately see that the median year is 1924. The median is an effective and quite easily understood summary statistic indicating the general level or centering of the values.

We can replace the three columns of counts with one that indicates the *depth* of the values in toward the center from either end. The combination of the columns *count up* and *count down* will suffice. The rule is simply to take the smaller value of the two on each row but, where the depth corresponding to the row containing the median would appear, we just indicate the row count and, to maintain clarity, place this value between parentheses:

Depth

1	0	1
4	1	471
(1)	2	4
4	3	2
3	4	845

The depths increase as we move from either end of the display toward the center.

The fact that each data value is represented in the display with a numeral allows us to use it to organize the values still further and obtain additional summary statistics. Ordering the values is now a simple exercise. The natural ordering we imposed on the stems accomplishes a partial ordering of the data values. We now need only redraw the display with leaves ordered and all the values will be ordered:

Depth

1	0	1
4	1	147
(1)	2	4
4	3	2
3	4	348

It is now easy to observe that 1901 is the smallest value or the lower extreme and 1948 is the highest value or upper extreme. We have already obtained the median but had there been other values on the stem for 1920 locating the median would not have been as simple as it was. After having ordered the values, however, it is always a straightforward task. We would simply have entered the middle stem and either counted up from the left or down from the right to locate the median value.

We can observe this process by locating the quartiles, the data values falling one quarter of the way into the set of values from either extreme. By convention, in a batch of n values, the median is the value located at depth $(n + 1)/2$ if n is odd and halfway between the values at depths $n/2$ and $(n + 2)/2$ if n is even. In the latter case the two middle data values are averaged to yield the value of the median. A similar rule holds for the quartiles; i.e., if the depth of the median is m, then one simply replaces m for n in the above formula for the location of the median. To avoid dealing with weighted averages that would otherwise occur if n were even and m represented a location halfway between two observed values, Tukey adopts a truncation rule that calls for dropping the fractional portion of a depth. Thus, if n is even, say 10, m is 5.5, i.e., the average of the fifth and sixth ordered values. To obtain the quartiles, drop the .5. This yields $(5 + 1)/2$ or 3 as the quartile depth. Thus, in the years data we locate the third and seventh values and use them as the quartiles. Because of this truncation rule we speak of approximate quartiles or, in Tukey's terminology, "hinges."

The median year of the years data was at depth 5 since n = 9. The hinges will be at depth $(5 + 1)/2$ or 3. Thus we want to find the values at the third and sixth rank order locations. Looking at the stem-and-leaf display we count in from the low end and find leaf 4 on stem 1 for the year 1914, the lower hinge. Operating similarly at the high end yields the year 1943 for the upper hinge.

Together with the extremes, (E), the medians (M) and hinges (H) form what Tukey refers to as a "five number summary." For the years data the five number summary is 1901, 1914, 1924, 1943, 1948. Dropping the 19 and putting the values into a framework to emphasize the middle values, yields 1 [14,24,43] 48.

An analytically more effective display of the five number summary involves use of an inverted "U" design:

Statistic	Depth	Value	
M	5	24	
H	3	14	43
E	1	1	48

The advantage of this structure is that is facilitates computation of the range and the approximate interquartile range through the subtraction of the left value from the right on each row (neglecting the median, of course):

Statistic	Depth	Value		Range
M	5		24	
H	3	14	43	29
E	1	1	48	47

We mentioned in the introduction that Tukey uses order statistics because of their resistant quality. A mean will respond rapidly to even one single deviant value in a sample. If, for an arbitrary set of values, we were to repeatedly increase one value and then recompute the mean, we would see the mean move toward the deviant value in a linear fashion. The median does not possess this feature. It will only change when the deviant value crosses from one side to the other of the median and then only to move one ordered value in the direction of the deviant value. Of course, if the data values are highly discontinuous, such jumps can be sizable, but in general, the movement of the median in response to highly deviant values is rather slight.

Resistance is very important when working with empirical social science data such as that encountered in educational evaluations. Outliers, whether due to contaminated samples, poor measurement, or natural variation, are common and can distort the analyst's impression of the data if nonresistant statistics are relied upon. This refers, of course, not just to the use of means but to all mean-based statistics. It is easy to see what happens to a mean when a single outlier is added to a batch. The lack of resistance of the standard deviation, the usual measure of spread or variability, is somewhat less obvious but no less true. Consequently, the standard deviation can be a very poor indicator of the variability of a sample.

Tukey's remedy is to rely on the hinge spread, the difference between the upper and lower hinges, as a measure of spread or variability. Roughly equivalent to the interquartile range, this statistic is easy to calculate using information obtained from a stem-and-leaf display (see the simple calculation above), readily interpreted, and easily communicated.

The stem-and-leaf display thus provides the evaluator with a basic organizational, descriptive, and analytic tool. It permits quick and efficient organization of data values while putting them into a format that readily conveys their shape and calls attention to special features. By retaining information on individual values it facilitates obtaining the order statistics, which, because of their resistant qualities and interpretability, are often more useful for exploratory and communication purposes than are more traditional summary statistics.

Empirical Example

The ordered stem-and-leaf display below represents values of a variable measuring amount of silent reading (in minutes per 40-minute period). Fifty-three children were observed in an experimental reading program. The leaves are single digits and the unit of the display is .01. Thus, to reconstruct an actual data value one takes a stem, say 0, juxtaposes it with a leaf, say 6 to form 06 then locates the decimal place before the 0 since the 6 is a hundreths place holder. The reconstructed value is .06. Notice the skewed shape of the empirical distribution that is portrayed by the display; the fact that the possible outlier value 1.63 is clearly visible; the presence of several peaks and valleys in the values and the popular value .35 that occurs five times.

Depth		
·2	0	69
10	1	0366677
16	2	035677
(11)	3	22355555688
26	4	2444889
19	5	28
17	6	24699
12	7	57
10	8	0234
6	9	2
5	10	4
4	11	35
2	12	7
	13	
	14	
	15	
1	16	3

n = 53   Leaves are hundreths

Stem-and-leaf display of silent reading variable (from data originally collected by Cooley, Leinhardt, & Zigmond, 1979).

Assessments and Comments------SLUG

The stem-and-leaf display is so easily constructed that most individuals, after seeing one for the first time, find it hard to understand why it has not been around longer than it has. Most audiences have no difficulty comprehending stem-and-leaf displays and are usually able to construct similar displays after only limited instruction. There are some aspects to construction that are not obvious, however, and need to be borne in mind especially when complex data sets are being displayed. First, while the number of stems for a good, i.e., informative and visually pleasing, display can be determined by trial-and-error methods, a rule does exist that can act as a guide. This rule states that the number of stems should be no greater than $10(\log_{10} n)$ where n is the number of observations to be displayed.

Second, when dealing with positive and negative values, two zero stems are needed, one for values between 0 and the first negative stem and one for values between 0 and the first positive stem. To see this, subtract the median year, 1924, from each year of the nine we have been working with. The new set of median-adjusted values is: -23, 0, 24, -10, 19, 20, 8, -7, and -13. If we used a single-0-stemmed display we would get:

$$
\begin{array}{r|l}
-2 & 3 \\
-1 & 03 \\
0 & 08\text{-}7 \\
1 & 9 \\
2 & 40 \\
\end{array}
$$

That is, the values 0, 8, and -7 would appear on the same row presenting a rather confusing display. A double-0-stemmed display solves the problem:

$$
\begin{array}{r|l}
-2 & 3 \\
-1 & 03 \\
-0 & 7 \\
0 & 08 \\
1 & 9 \\
2 & 40 \\
\end{array}
$$

The only remaining difficulty occurring around zero is what to do with hard zeros when they are numerous. Hard zeros are often treated as if they were positive but a better way to handle them as far as stem-and-leaf displays are concerned, is to allocate half to the -0 stem and half to the 0 stem putting the one additional zero, if there is an odd number, in either the -0 or 0 stemmed row, at random.

A third concern arises when one wishes to stretch a display so that values that might normally fall on one row fall on two or more. This would be needed when there are many leaves on each stem but the range of stem values is small. A stem can easily have two rows, one in which one row contains leaf values ranging between 0 and 4 and another containing those with values 5 to 9. Splitting into 5 rows follows the rule of putting 0 and 1 on one row, 2 and 3 on the next, 4 and 5 on the third, 6 and 7 on the fourth, and 8 and 9 on the fifth.

As a final caution we point out that if negative values are being displayed and the leaves of the display are to be ordered, the negative leaf values are ordered in apparently reverse order. That is, the larger magnitude leaves occur to the left of the row so that counting up from the lowest value of the display and counting down from the highest value will be consistent operations.

References

Cooley, W. W., Leinhardt, G., & Zigmond, N. *Explaining reading performance of learning disabled children.* Pittsburgh: University of Pittsburgh Learning Research and Development Center, 1979.

Leinhardt, G., & Leinhardt, S. Exploratory data analysis: New tools for the analysis of empirical data. In C. Berliner (Ed.), *Review of research in education.* American Educational Research Association, 1980.

Tukey, J. W. *Exploratory data analysis* (limited preliminary ed.). Ann Arbor, MI: University Microfilm, 1971.

Tukey, J. W. *Statistical papers in honor of George W. Snedecor.* Ames, IA: State University Press, 1972.

Tukey, J. W. *Exploratory data analysis.* Reading MA Addison-Wesley, 1977.

BRENT E. WHOLEBEN
University of Washington

CHAPTER **8**

Operational Network Displays

Brent E. Wholeben is Associate Director of the Bureau of School Service and Research and Assistant Professor of Educational Administration at the University of Washington. Considered a pioneer in the application of mathematical modeling techniques to evaluation and decision-making in education, Dr. Wholeben has published a book on modeling techniques for school closures; has recently completed a major technical research study on the application of these techniques for determining fiscal roll-backs; and is currently writing a new book on the further utilization of mathematical modeling techniques within the educational milieu.

> *net·work (net'wurk') n. 2(c) a group, system, etc. of interconnected or cooperating individuals; (Websters New World Dictionary, 2nd College Edition, 1978).*

Operation systems—collections of related and/or mutual activities to accomplish a common goal—have provided the evaluator with the most complex challenge to successful assessment of their mission, content, process, and outcome. The challenge to evaluation stems almost entirely from the simultaneous need to view and understand the dynamics of each such activity and its contribution to total system performance, while measuring the interactive relationship between the ongoing operations and their interconnected or cooperative impacts upon each other in accomplishing the stated goal or mission. This need to view both main and interactive effects existent within an operating system is relevant at all levels of the system hierarchy: *from* the system level as a collection of interconnected systematic programs, *through* the program level as a group of cooperating goals and objectives, *to* the objectives level as an array of interacting activities and/or tasks. The evaluation of operation systems is therefore complex—but not insurmountable.

The Network Approach to Operations Modeling

Parallel to the idea that the major part of evaluation is contained within the detailed planning for that evaluation—the critical need in evaluating systematic operations is to utilize a form of content and process representation that provides two main ends: (1) a representation of the criteria utilized in the evaluation and their concomitant effect upon the various operations being evaluated; and (2) a representation of the methodology that will guide the use of these criterion-referenced effects in formulating the required evaluative conclusions. The key to successfully fulfilling these two outcomes lies in viewing operation systems' modeling as a network approach.

The network is viewed most often as a one-to-one classification scheme, where two variables are matched or related in order to demonstrate some aspect of the system. For example, time-flow analysis methodologies such as CPM (critical path method) and PERT (program evaluation review technique) connect specific activities to certain chronological periods of time; operations research techniques similarly connect potential solution alternatives to competing criterion indicators via quantitative measures of those criteria for each program alternative. This latter example best reflects the usefulness of the network approach as a form of representation for the evaluation of operational systems and their components.

The network approach views operations evaluation as a system of multiple, competing programs (goals, objectives, activities, and the like) to be "valued" across specified, defined criterion-referenced points:

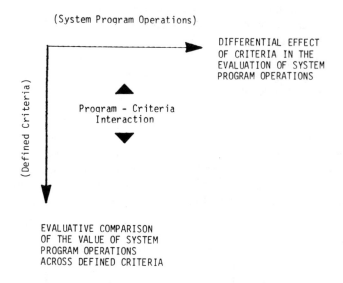

(System Program Operations)

DIFFERENTIAL EFFECT OF CRITERIA IN THE EVALUATION OF SYSTEM PROGRAM OPERATIONS

(Defined Criteria)

Program - Criteria Interaction

EVALUATIVE COMPARISON OF THE VALUE OF SYSTEM PROGRAM OPERATIONS ACROSS DEFINED CRITERIA

Thus, in order to adequately represent the context and application of evaluation within operation systems' modeling, a network display must not only be demonstrative of content and process (as previously specified), but must in addition be indicative of both the *direction* of each "system" subcomponent in fulfilling overall system mission and the *extent* to which this mission is impacted and satisfied. This is the substantive role of defined performance criteria.

Performance Criteria for Initial Modeling Formulation

Figure 8.1 represents the generic range of criterion categories that must be addressed when building an operation systems' evaluation model; that is, measures of (1) effectiveness, (2) efficiency, (3) satisfaction, and (4) expenditure are required wherever appropriate for each of the operational subsystem components being evaluated. The orientation of any particular criterion can be toward measuring desirable impact (such as positive effect) or not-so-desirable impact (such as negative effect). The evaluator, in the "valuing" of each component across the various criteria, will most certainly be watching for those subsystem items that *maximize* the aspects of the total system as defined by the stated "positive" criteria, and concomitantly *minimize* those aspects defined by the stated "negative" criteria.

While the quantitative values that reflect the criterion-associated measures may take many forms, a suggested format is to employ an 11-point interval-based scale. This illustrates the full range of low-to-high measures for each specified criterion and arithmetically associates a measure of both magnitude and direction to each criterion indicator. For the purposes of illustrating the examples to follow in this chapter, the 11-point scale is assumed.

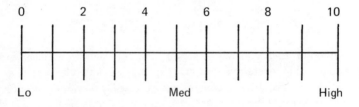

Three Approaches to Operational Network Modeling

To modify the demands of a network approach to system evaluation, the initial step of specifying the "system" as a collection of "interconnected or cooperating" parts must be accomplished—that is, the delineation of the system into programs, programs into goals, goals into activities, ad nauseaum . . . depending upon the depth of evaluation desired. The criteria must then be defined, and subsequently measured against each of the delineated subsystem components.

Three frameworks are available to collectively represent the results of this exercise in delineation, measurement, and assignment. The first approach (and the most simplistic) is the *descriptive model*; the major goal of this approach is to concisely describe the nature of each program individually across the specified criteria. Loosely speaking, such a model is representative of a main-effects orientation. The second approach or

FOCUS	CRITERIA	ORIENTATION	OBJECTIVE
EFFECTIVENESS	EFFEC 1	POSITIVE	MAXIMIZE
	$\vdots$		
	EFFEC i		
	EFFEC i+1	NEGATIVE	MINIMIZE
	$\vdots$		
	EFFEC m		
EFFICIENCY	EFFIC 1	POSITIVE	MAXIMIZE
	$\vdots$		
	EFFIC j		
	EFFIC j+1	NEGATIVE	MINIMIZE
	$\vdots$		
	EFFIC n		
SATISFACTION	SATIS 1	POSITIVE	MAXIMIZE
	$\vdots$		
	SATIS k		
	SATIS k+1	NEGATIVE	MINIMIZE
	$\vdots$		
	SATIS p		
EXPENDITURE	EXPEN 1	POSITIVE	MAXIMIZE
	$\vdots$		
	EXPEN r		
	EXPEN r+1	NEGATIVE	MINIMIZE
	$\vdots$		
	EXPEN s		

Figure 8.1 Development of Program Performance Criteria for Operational Systems' Network Modeling

co-relational model seeks to compare or co-relate the field of subsystem components across all criteria. The overriding goal is one of visual cohesiveness and generalized understanding of the overall impact of all criteria, across all programs, upon the system.

The third and most interesting approach is the *experimental model.* While accomplishing the primary ends of both the descriptive and correlational models, the experimental model provides a generalized diagnostic-prescriptive function for system evaluation; it allows for system simulation (experimentation) to evaluate "suggested" changes and/or "variable" impact. Each of these orientations will be depicted in the following sections, utilizing the same data base for comparative purposes.

Descriptive Modeling: The Histographic Approach

The descriptive approach is best implemented utilizing the histographic aspects of the familiar statistics-based histogram. Such a histographic approach easily denotes both the magnitude and direction of the criterion-referenced impact upon each program of the operation system, while indicating the generalized content and process of the evaluation strategy itself. Figure 8.2 provides an example of this descriptive modeling approach.

Recall that the orientation of the various generic criteria can be both positive as well as negative; that is, a value of 8 on POS-1 indicates a measure of high *positive* impact, while a corresponding value of 8 on NEG-4 indicates a measure of high *negative* impact. Thus, a program is viewed as "beneficially contributory" to system mission to the extent that: (1) high values exist on "positive" criteria; and (2) low values exist on "negative" criteria.

Recall also that the primary requisite of the descriptive-histographic orientation is to describe each program, individually, by its impact upon the system via criterion measures. Thus the major limitation to this model is its lack of generalizability to collective system functioning.

Correlational Modeling: The Dimensional Approach

The correlational model takes the implied third dimension of the descriptive approach, and makes the dimension explicit. The major goal of a correlational-dimensional strategy is to provide a representation of the total system, via each program delineation and the associated criteria measures. Figure 8.3 depicts the network display for this approach.

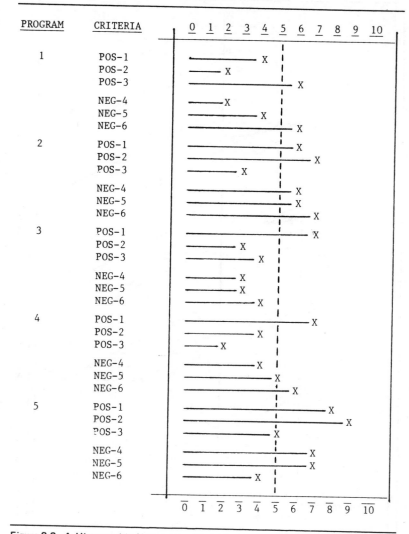

Figure 8.2 A Histographic Networking Model for Representing Performance Characteristics of System Subprograms

This model better describes the trends existent within each program, and their assumed impact upon the system as a whole. Moreover, the three-dimensional graphic display can be easily "color-overlay" designed, as demonstrated by the diagonal shading(s) depicting high-positive with

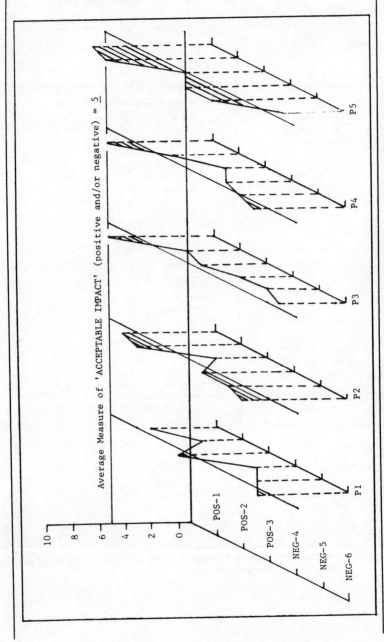

Figure 8.3 A Dimensional Networking Model for Representing Performance Characteristics of System Subprograms

228

CRITERIA	OPERATIONAL PROGRAMS					CONDITONS		INTERPRETATION		
FOC N	P1	P2	P3	P4	P5	DIR	LIM	SUM	DIFF	EVL
POS 1	4	6	7	7	8	≥	25	32	+7	+
POS 2	2	7	3	4	9	≥	25	25	0	0
POS 3	6	3	4	2	5	≥	25	20	-5	-
NEG 4	2	6	3	4	7	≤	25	22	+3	+
NEG 5	4	6	3	5	7	≤	25	25	0	0
NEG 6	6	7	4	6	4	≤	25	27	-2	-

Figure 8.4 An Operations' Network Design Model for Representing Performance Characteristics of System Subprograms

high-negative interaction. While the dimensional-approach better addresses the stated limitation of the first model—a lack of generalizability to collective system functioning—the need to assist the decision-making requirements for planned change usually associated with evaluation is not immediately satisfied via this orientation.

Experimental Modeling: The Decision-Matrix Approach

Providing an operations research orientation to the representation of evaluation results for operational network modeling is the diagnostic-perspective feature of the experimental modeling approach, as shown in Figure 8.4. While not as graphic or (seemingly) useful to the novice evaluator, the seasoned specialist will easily see the decisional orientation of this matrix format, and its application to system simulation needs.

Each program's measures access the positive impact and negative impact are entered via a matrix design; in this case, a 6 x 5 dimensional matrix. With an 11-point scale as the measuring device, the value 5 is considered "average" and multiplied by 5, representing the expected average impact upon the five programs of the system. The resulting value of 25 is entered as a conditional limit (LIM). Since the positive criteria are desirable (and the negative, not), the evaluator will wish to maximize any positive impact upon the system, and minimize any negative effect. That is, the programs will be evaluated to see to what extent their collective positive impact exceeds system expectations (sum of POS - i $\geqslant$ 25); and to what extent the collective negative impact is reduced (sum of NEG - j $\leqslant$ 25).

The actual sums (SUM) can then be compared arithmetically with the arbitrary limit of 25, and summarized for decisional interpretation of system functioning (DIFF). A resulting gross evaluation of impact [(+) = exceeds requirements; (0) = meets requirements; (-) = fails to meet requirements] can also be made (EVL).

The experimental model not only provides a ready reference for viewing current system operational functioning, but also allows a quantitative paradigm for exploring the potential impact of decisions made via a structural formative evaluation for program improvement. If the "programs" are redefined as "goals" or "objectives," then a new and useful paradigm exists for operationalizing a summative evaluation strategy.

One Step Beyond
Experimental Modeling

This chapter has limited its discussion to an operational networking approach to evaluation representation and has presented three very useful techniques for displaying operation subsystem criterion measures across systematic programs. It has further been stressed that the term "program" is generic to this discussion and that the program could realistically represent not only actual program entities, but also goals, objectives, activities, tasks, or even individual responsibilities—to cite a few. This cannot be overemphasized. Operational network displays can be subjected to any criterion-based evaluation need.

However, the author would be remiss in not addressing a further use of this model, that is, the evaluation of programs across criteria, as a way of deciding which programs should be maintained due to their "positive" effects, and which programs must be modified or abandoned due to their resulting "negative" influence. This is a form of decisioning (sic) that has revolutionized the idea of operational modeling and its impact upon the use of predictive evaluation techniques for evaluating (validating) potential decisions and their impact.

The Future for Employing
Operational Modeling

Since "operation" is a highly generic term that could represent any entity from program through individual, the use of an operations modeling approach in evaluation is diverse. Defining "operation" as *schools* in school-closure decisions, *budgets* in fiscal roll-back decisions, *teachers* in reduction-in-force decisions, or *instructional activities* in curriculum development decisions—functional knowledge of the operation's modeling technique is most useful.

Useful also, of course, is a methodology in which a complete display of data, options, and their interaction can be visualized. Network displays provide such flexibility. In addition, the display of data within a network configuration can provide the evaluator/decision maker with the incomprehensibly powerful tool of simulating potential future actions and therefore "testing" their presumed effects upon the total operating system.

Finally, networking the relationship between "operations" and "criteria" illustrates the new, emerging role of the evaluator. As more complex problems face the administrator day-to-day—problems that have no historical perspective with regards to solution—the evaluator's role becomes one of a *decisional scientist*. In this fashion, the evaluator can seek to better foresee and understand today's decisions upon tomorrow's operations.

NICK L. SMITH
Northwest Regional Educational Laboratory

C H A P T E R *9*

Geographic Displays

Nick L. Smith is Director of the Research on Evaluation Program at the Northwest Regional Educational Laboratory in Portland, Oregon. His primary interest is in the methodology of evaluation and field research, and he has edited several recent volumes on alternative methods of evaluation.

GEOGRAPHIC DISPLAYS provide a concise and readily understood means of sharing evaluative information with a variety of audiences, from technical specialists to high-level administrators to the general public. Although maps and other forms of geographic displays commonly appear on television, in popular magazines, and occasionally in newspapers; they are infrequently used in evaluation reporting.

The purpose of this chapter is to review briefly some of the ways in which maps can be, and have been, employed in evaluation, and to encourage their wider use. Before providing a number of examples of the use of maps in evaluation, I would like to provide some background by addressing the variety of geographic questions that can arise in evaluation, and by summarizing three analytic techniques that can be used to answer those questions. The majority of the chapter will then be devoted to illustrations of the use of maps.

Geographic Questions and
Analysis Techniques

Perhaps one reason that evaluators use geographic displays less often than they might is that they are unaware of the range of geographic questions that are relevant in evaluation work. In an earlier article (Smith, 1979, p. 119), I provided the following sample list of evaluation problems that are geographic in nature:

- What is the distribution of academic achievement throughout a state or region?
- What is the relationship between the quality of health care and the distribution of medical clinics in an urban setting?
- What is the regional distribution of patterns of school funding?
- What is the relationship between policy implementation and the geographic accessibility of the policy-making body?
- What geographic conditions influence questions of school busing and school consolidation?
- What is the relationship between the incidence of crime and the distribution of law enforcement resources?

The common element among these questions is that the geographic location, setting, or place is important in understanding the events or behaviors of interest. To identify geographic questions of importance in a particular study, evaluators should ask themselves, their clients, and audiences such questions as:

- Where are the people, events, or conditions of interest?
- What else is at that location too?
- Does it make a difference where these people, events, or conditions are?
- How are these people, events, or conditions related to others in different places? (See Monk & Hastings, 1981)

Any time the spatial distribution of some element of the program under study is meaningful and important in assessing the value of the program, evaluators ought to consider a geographic study of that element.

There are a number of analytic strategies available for the treatment of geographic data. As an introduction, I will summarize three such techniques: geocode analysis, trend surface analysis, and social area analysis. These techniques all involve the assignment of a geographic location to each datum so that the data can be represented on geographic maps. These maps are similar to the contour maps used to indicate earth elevations in atlases and weather fronts on television weather shows. Quantitative analysis procedures can then be used to analyze the spatial relationships illustrated by the maps. (See Smith, 1979, for a more detailed presentation of these techniques, including references that present basic procedures and illustrate applications.)

Geocode Analysis

Geocode analysis is a procedure for aggregating individual data over a geographic area by using symbolic codes (e.g., street addresses or census tract numbers) to denote geographic locations. By plotting information, for example, the occurrence of an armed robbery, at the geographic location of the event, it is possible to display the concentration or density of similar events throughout a region. One could, for example, produce computer printer plots that used shading or contour lines to show area distributions of armed robberies within a large city.

In conducting a geocode analysis of, for example, an educational program, one:

(1) compiles an Address Coding Guide (e.g., address of each student);
(2) builds an Individual Characteristics Data File (e.g., student achievement scores);
(3) merges the Address Coding Guide with the Individual Characteristics Data File; and
(4) produces computer grids, plots, and contour maps of individual characteristics by geographic location (Smith, 1979, p. 120).

These procedures have been employed in studies of school redistricting, the identification of Title I students, projections of school enrollments, and comparative reading evaluations. They are particularly useful in settings that have preexisting data files and geographically defined service areas, such as state departments of education and community mental health centers.

Trend Surface Analysis

Instead of plotting individual data points on a grid as is done in Geocode Analysis, Trend Surface Analysis uses statistical procedures to estimate data that appear at irregular intervals (such as the distribution of emergency medical centers) to produce contour maps. Because Trend Surface Analysis is a statistical estimation procedure, it is less costly than Geocode Analysis, but results in less detailed information.

Conducting a Trend Surface Analysis involves:

(1) selecting points in a geographic region to represent that region (for example, an elementary school);

(2) assigning three values to each point (two coordinate values to establish the point's geographic location and the value of the study variable of interest; for example, the number of bilingual children at that school);

(3) using statistical modeling procedures to produce a surface equation;

(4) constructing a contour map using the surface equation;

(5) using regression analysis and analysis of variance to determine local trends, regional trends, and how well the model fits the data; and

(6) overlaying multiple surface maps to illustrate the geographic interactions between variables of interest (for example, concentrations of bilingual children and children with below-grade-level achievement test scores).

These procedures have been used in studies of school board elections, dissemination of educational innovations, statewide educational needs, financial support for schools, reading test scores, community mental health delivery, and law enforcement.

Social Area Analysis

Social Area Analysis (also called Ecological Analysis in sociology) is an approach from epidemiology that focuses on groups not as collections of individuals but as organized wholes that can be characterized by their patterns of behaviors and attributes. Social Area Analysis is not a discrete procedure, but a collection of techniques used to study characteristics of groups within defined geographic areas. The purpose of Social Area Analysis is to differentiate between subpopulations, using demographic characteristics that are predictive of other behaviors or characteristics of interest (for example, the use of family socioeconomic indicators to predict children's learning difficulties).

A complete Social Area Analysis might involve such steps as:

(1) definition of the geographic region or catchment areas of interest and the collection of relevant demographic data;

(2) through factor analysis or cluster analysis, the development of theoretically meaningful and psychometrically stable indices of catchment area characteristics;

(3) through profile analysis, the identification of similar catchment areas;

(4) the collection of data on conditions, behaviors, or characteristics of interest and the study of relationships between these variables and catchment area indices through multiple regression; and

(5) the verification of apparent relationships through direct inquiries of group members, experimentally controlled studies of treatment interventions, or time series designs (Smith, 1979, pp. 123-124).

These procedures have been used to study the geographic distribution of veterinarians, relationships between census tract characteristics and health problems, between hospital performance and community characteristics, and in studies of deviant behavior, voting behavior, and looting during blackouts. Social Area Analysis is increasingly being used as a needs assessment device (see, for example, Piasecki & Kamis-Gould, 1981, and the entire Volume 4, Number 1, 1981, issue of *Evaluation and Program Planning*).

Geocode Analysis, Trend Surface Analysis, and Social Area Analysis are three highly technical procedures for the analysis of geographic data. These procedures require access to computers, statistical programs, and mechanized plotting facilities. But, of course, all this high technology is not essential in using maps to display evaluation results. Let us now turn our attention to the simpler, more straightforward use of maps in evaluation using facilities generally available to everyone.

Cartography in Evaluation

Maps can be used to present descriptive information or as a basis for more complicated analysis. I illustrate these two uses below, followed by a few words of caution concerning the preparation and interpretation of maps.

Descriptive Use of Maps

Maps can be used to provide information on geographic setting, to orient the evaluation reader, and to summarize descriptive information. Complicated geographic patterns, although difficult to describe verbally or in writing, can be readily understood when presented on a map or other visual representation.

Consider, for example, Figures 9.1 and 9.2. Figure 9.1 illustrates the 16 western states that participated in a mail survey study of school board

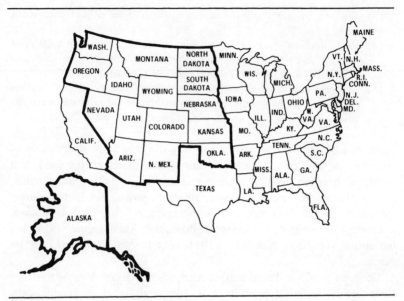

Figure 9.1   States Participating in a Survey Study

involvement in accreditation evaluations (Smith, 1978). Instead of using a map, one might describe this sample by saying: "The 16 westernmost states participated in this study, including Alaska but excluding Hawaii, California, and Texas," or one could simply list the 16 states. The visual representation conveys this information more clearly than such verbal descriptions, however. Imagine the difficulty of describing the ten service areas portrayed in Figure 9.2 in words.

Maps are also used to provide public information on the location of service facilities. For example, some large school districts publish maps identifying the location of administrative offices, schools, and support facilities. The Evaluation Department of the Portland, Oregon, Public Schools has employed this use of maps in its evaluation of individual schools. An evaluation report (e.g., Hathaway, 1978) might include (a) pictures of the school buildings and grounds, (b) a copy of the school district map with the school site highlighted, (c) a detailed street map with the school boundaries indicated, and (d) a diagram of the school building floor plan. These illustrations, along with verbal descriptions, provide a general orientation to the setting within which the school operates. Such an orientation is especially useful in a large school district like Portland's,

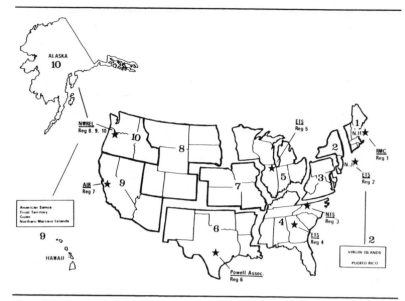

Figure 9.2 Service Areas of Title I Technical Assistance Centers

where school board members, school administrators, and the public who are audiences of the evaluation report may not be familiar with each school in the district.

Maps do not have to be expertly drawn or highly precise to convey valuable information to the reader. Consider, for example, Figures 9.3 and 9.4, which come from an evaluation of migrant education projects (Savard, 1980). Figure 9.3 illustrates in an approximate but effective way the general distribution of migrant education projects in the State of Oregon in 1979-1980. Figure 9.4 is more complicated but serves to give the reader a basic orientation to the migration patterns which are resulting in the need for the educational programs. Note how the following text from the evaluation report complements and further clarifies the visual display:

> The problems of migrant education cannot be appreciated without an understanding of the migration patterns involved and the agricultural factors which induce that migration. The map which follows depicts the major migration patterns for 1979-1980. The map also indicates the numbers of interstate, intrastate, and settled-in migrants, the major crops the migrants work in, and the estimated

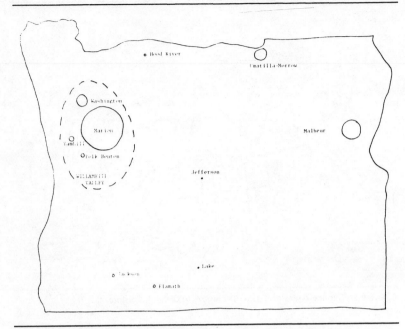

Figure 9.3 Locations and Relative Size of Oregon Migrant Education Projects, 1979-1980, Regular Term

NOTE: Areas of circles are approximately proportionate to percentage of total children.

importance of the area as a home base. In general the patterns have not changed much since last year with the exceptions of certain differences in Malheur, Umatilla-Morrow and Jackson Counties.

The number and types of migrants, interstate, intrastate and settled-in, give some idea of the magnitude of the Project and the severity of movement-induced educational problems. The list of major crops in the area suggests the economic importance of the farm labor provided by the migrants. The estimated importance of the area as a home base suggests the demand for social and general educational (non-project) services which may exist. This is a factor which has a subtle but important effect upon the acceptability of the Project in the eyes of the schools and the general popution.

One major pattern is the interstate movement from South Texas to the Willamette Valley and Malheur Area. South Texas is an impor-

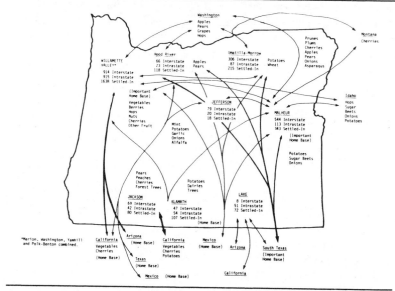

Figure 9.4   Location of Students by Migrant Type and Major Migration Patterns and Crops, Regular Term, 1979-1980

tant home base but more and more of these migrants are settling in the Willamette and Malheur Areas.

Another major pattern is the traffic between the Willamette Valley and California with a minor branch to Arizona and New Mexico [Savard, 1980, p. 3, 5].

Analytic Use of Maps

The preceding discussion of analytic procedures such as Geocode Analysis, Trend Surface Analysis, and Social Area Analysis provided an introduction into what might be called "high technology" analytic uses of maps. It is important to note, however, that rather complex problems can be solved with the aid of a map, but without the need for highly sophisticated procedures. The following single example will suffice to illustrate the point.

Several years ago, I worked at a university computer center that had five major computer stations on campus in addition to its main facility. At that time, it cost approximately $2000 a month to operate each of the stations which were geographically spread around the campus. The computer center billed the university departments for computer use and each station was to have sufficient use, or was to generate sufficient charges, to support its operation and maintenance. However, some stations were being used very little while others were very busy. The following question therefore arose as part of our evaluation of the computer service delivery system: "Is there sufficient potential business at each station to warrant maintaining it or are some stations placed in campus areas of low need?" If sufficient potential use could not be demonstrated for a station, then that station would have to be removed. (Note that this is a basic needs assessment service delivery question calling for a kind of market analysis.) I was able to answer this question, in part, through the use of a campus map.

In addressing this service delivery question, I did the following (see Figure 9.5).

(1) I plotted the location of each station and of the main center on a campus map.
(2) I assumed that computer users would logically prefer to use the closest station, other things being equal, and sectioned off the campus into service areas (a service area being simply the region closest to each station).
(3) I assumed that the "location" of each user was that user's academic department office so that all the computer charges for, let's say, the staff of the agriculture department, could be plotted at the departmental office.
(4) By plotting the departmental computer charges, I could determine the amount of computer funds being spent within each service area and which funds logically should have been spent at the service area's station (this was the "potential market revenue" for computer services in that area).
(5) By comparing actual revenue generated by the station with the potential market revenue, I was able to determine that:
   (a) there was sufficient market to maintain each station if all users went to the geographically closest station, and
   (b) some stations were generating more than their share, others less.
(6) Using a series of maps such as Figure 9.5 (the analysis was a bit more complicated than summarized here), I was able to communicate the results to computer center administration and station managers who could then move on to the next phase of the evaluation: determining what was drawing some users away from their most geographically convenient facilities.

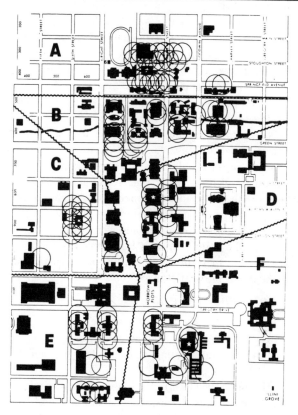

Station	Percent Potential Use	Percent Actual Use
A (Main Facility)	25	39
B	22	8
C	13	17
D	13	20
E	14	6
F	12	11

◯ = 1% of total revenues for research computer use

Figure 9.5 Campus Market Areas for Computer Services

Similar problem analyses could be performed with basic client use data and maps for a variety of evaluation applications. One does not need high technology or expert graphics skills to make effective use of geographic displays, unless large amounts of data are involved. One final example follows which illustrates both analytic and descriptive uses of maps with a large data base (53,000 students).

During 1981 the Portland Public School District conducted a series of studies in order to decide which of its 128 schools to close or to consolidate (Portland Public Schools, 1981). Geocode analysis was used to assess the impact of various possible school closures or consolidations and geographic data were analyzed using linear programming techniques to minimize student travel time. Geographic scattergrams such as Figure 9.6 were used to show the distribution of minority and handicapped students. A series of maps such as Figure 9.7 were used to illustrate the numerous closures and consolidations considered and were instrumental in obtaining public reaction to the various options (see Table 9.1 for analysis). Clear understanding of the variety of options would have been extremely difficult without the use of the district maps.

Cautions in Preparing and Interpreting Maps

Monk and Hastings (1981) provide an excellent summary of the problems of preparing and interpreting maps. A few of their major points follow.

Monk and Hastings (1981) warn that maps, like statistical tables, can be very misleading to unfamiliar users. They urge that care be taken in the selection of the scale of a map. The scale (technically the ratio of the distance on the map to the distance on the ground) affects the amount of detail possible in the map, the effectiveness of certain symbols, and the inferences that can be drawn from the map. Finer scales, for example, make greater inferences possible but reduce either the scope or legibility of the map.

One must also take care in selecting the symbolism and the grouping of data into categories for representation to avoid information overload. Further, although certain symbols can be used to indicate correlations in data, one must take care that readers do not necessarily equate surface area with amount of effect or importance.

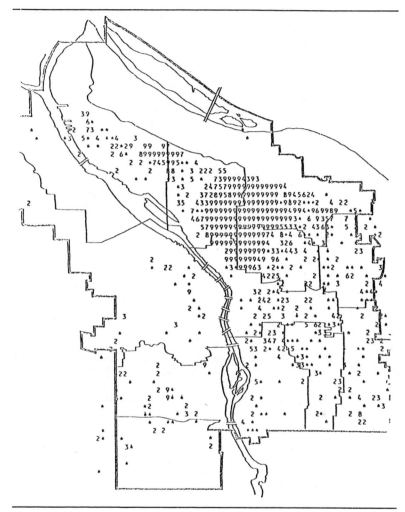

Figure 9.6 Geographic Distribution of Black Students

NOTE: This computer scattergram shows the geographic distribution of Black students enrolled currently in the Portland Public Schools. A star represents one student. Digits 1 through 8 represent the corresponding number of students. The digit 9 means that nine or more students reside at that location. This is the greatest resolution of this distribution we can achieve with current software. An attempt was made to overlay the computer printed distribution on a District map showing **current** high school boundaries. The scaling and orientation of this overlay was done by hand, but is relatively precise.

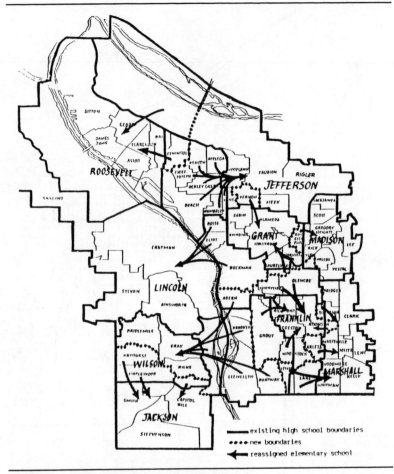

Figure 9.7   School Closure/Consolidation Option 1a

Monk and Hastings (1981) stress that

The purpose of the map and the inherent nature of the data are
important criteria in decision making. . . . It is thus essential to
recognize that while a map can reveal some generalizations, it must
usually be accompanied by qualifying commentary and must be
interpreted with knowledge of the data base [p. 161, 162].

TABLE 9.1 Force Field Analysis

Option: Adams, Cleveland, Washington/Monroe

Criteria	Advantages	Disadvantages
Program	• Enrollment of over 1,400 permits provision of all programs/services	• Those schools with an enrollment less than 1,350 would have a potentially seriously deficient program
Fiscal/Facility	• Space utilization improvements: Madison 75% - 80% Lincoln 77% - 96% Franklin 73% - 81% Jackson 65% - 86% Marshall 55% - 84% Wilson 73% - 97%	• Space utilization: Grant 89% - 103% Roosevelt 73% - 75% • Jefferson underutilized
Neighborhood Integrity	• Breaks down east/west demographic/geographic barriers	• All high school attendance boundaries affected • Redefines some traditional neighborhoods
Student Services	• Student enrollment guarantees insure continuation of maximum levels of student services (e.g., counseling, guidance, etc.)	• Insufficient space Adams site for both Special Education and ESL
Desegregation	• Provides greater evidence of fairness to all communities regardless of socio-economic or racial considerations • Improved socioeconomic mix of student population	• Special demands in graining Black community support of new Jefferson High School site • There would not be enough space at Jefferson at Adams to accommodate all assigned students
Cost Savings	• $1,417,388	

The reader interested in using maps accurately and effectively is urged to read the Monk and Hastings chapter (1981) and to study the 12 examples they provide before proceeding.

Conclusion

Maps are forceful and effective communication devices that appeal to, and are readily understood by, a variety of audiences. They can be used simply to illustrate spatial relations or to provide a basis of complex statistical analysis. They add variety to a report, quickly provide spatial orientation to the reader, and can be produced with a minimum of expense and technical expertise. Sometimes, information that cannot be adequately portrayed in words, numbers, or graphic displays, can be clearly represented through maps. Surely such a versatile and powerful tool should be used more widely in the reporting of evaluation results.

References

Hathaway, W. E. Lane school. School Evaluation Studies No. 64. Portland Public Schools Evaluation Department, Portland, Oregon, April 1978.

Monk, J. J., & Hastings, J. T. Geography. In N. L. Smith (Ed.), *Metaphors for evaluation: Sources of new methods.* Beverly Hills, CA: Sage, 1981.

Piasecki, J. R., & Kamis-Gould, E. Social area analysis in program evaluation and planning. *Evaluation and program planning,* 1981, 4(1), 3-14.

Portland Public Schools. *School closures/consolidations: Superintendents' report.* Portland, Oregon, April 1981.

Savard, W. G. Title I-M ESEA Oregon migrant education program: Educational impact report. Final report submitted to Oregon Department of Education, November 1980.

Smith, N. L. Role of school boards in school self-study evaluations. Final report submitted to National Study of School Evaluation, August 1978.

Smith, N. L. Techniques for the analysis of geographic data in evaluation. *Evaluation and Program Planning,* 1979, 2(2), 119-126.

MICHAEL HENDRICKS
Office of the Inspector General
U.S. Department of Health and Human Services

CHAPTER *10*

Oral Policy Briefings

Michael Hendricks is the Assistant Director, Office of Service Delivery Assessment, U.S. Department of Health and Human Services. His academic training includes postdoctoral study in methodology and evaluation research at Northwestern University. Qualitative evaluation techniques, especially the areas of sampling and analysis, are his main current professional interests.

ON AUGUST 21, 1980, a remarkable meeting took place in the Hubert H. Humphrey Building headquarters of the U.S. Department of Health and Human Services. Into the sixth floor conference room of then Secretary Patricia Roberts Harris gathered the entire top management of the department to hear an oral policy briefing on the results of a recent evaluation study. In addition to Secretary Harris, the audience was composed of the Under Secretary, both Deputy Under Secretaries, the Inspector General, the Assistant Secretaries for Planning and Evaluation, Legislation, and Management and Budget, the Director of the Office for Civil Rights, the Administrators of the Public Health Service, the Social

Author's Note: *The author wishes to thank Bud Fick, Lis Handley, Terry Hedrick, Ron Schwartz, and Jane Tebbutt for their helpful comments on an earlier version of this chapter.*

Security Administration, the Office for Human Development Services, and the Health Care Financing Administration (which administers the Medicare and Medicaid programs), and the heads of the specific programs evaluated. In effect, the highest echelons of the department were assembled in one room for the sole purpose of hearing the results of a single evaluation study.

This event, both extremely gratifying and exremely unusual to program evaluators, was the culmination of a Service Delivery Assessment (SDA) of restricted patient admittance to nursing homes. For approximately one hour, the presenter described and discussed the SDA's findings and conclusions with this audience. Interrupted occasionally for a question or comment, the presenter described nursing home admission policies at the local level, drew appropriate comparisons to provide perspective on the descriptions, and provided a personal, subjective interpretation of the findings. The formal presentation lasted about 20 minutes, after which there were questions and answers and a general discussion of future options. Following this discussion, several actions were assigned by the secretary and the briefing was completed.

While remarkable as a single event, this briefing was only one of approximately 40 such briefings that have been presented by the Office of Service Delivery Assessment (SDA) to Secretaries Califano, Harris, and Schweiker over the past four years. Service Delivery Assessment is an innovative form of program evaluation, created in 1977 in the Department of Health and Human Services, which provides timely, policy-relevant information on conditions and activities, problems, and best practices at the service delivery level. SDA is quite unlike traditional program evaluation, basic research, fiscal auditing, program monitoring, compliance reviews, investigations, or management analysis. Instead, it is more analogous to investigative reporting and relies heavily on intensive observations and discussions during site visits to local settings (see Hendricks, 1981).

Small teams of SDA staff spend several weeks at local sites throughout the country. While on site, these staff observe conditions and activities, attend previously scheduled meetings, examine documents, and contact a wide variety of persons involved in the delivery of services. Typical respondents include clients, front-line providers, local-level administrators, involved and knowledgeable third parties (e.g., judges, advocacy groups, professional organizations, related service providers), and local, state, and federal program officials. After analyzing the wealth of qualitative information from these visits, the SDA leaders prepare and present the type of briefing described above.

Based on four years of experience with oral policy briefings (called "briefings" in this chapter), we in SDA have learned several lessons for creating a successful presentation. The remainder of this chapter outlines these lessons regarding (1) planning the briefing, (2) setting the stage, (3) presenting the briefing, and (4) following up. A final section discusses some of the advantages and disadvantages of using an oral policy briefing to present evaluation findings. While many of these lessons are applicable to all evaluations and all briefings, other lessons may be idiosyncratic to SDA and may need modification in other circumstances.

Planning the Briefing

A successful briefing must be carefully planned far in advance of the actual briefing date. Part of this planning is substantive, such as selecting which information to present. Every evaluation produces more information than could be presented in a reasonable briefing, and it is important to choose the material to include very carefully. Helpful questions to ask include: Is this information necessary to understanding the program evaluation or services? Does this information cut across organizational or reporting lines? Does this information indicate major consequences for services? Are there major cost implications of this information? Can the audience do anything with this information? As a rule, it is also important to include unexpected findings and findings that validate or refute the existence of suspected problems.

Once selected, this information must be incorporated into an outline of the briefing. This outline must provide a logical, flowing presentation of findings, yet be sufficiently flexible to allow diversions when questions are raised by the audience. While in some situations (e.g., a large audience or unusually formal structure to the briefing) it may be desirable to discourage or even prohibit interruptions, SDA briefings deliberately encourage questions at any time. These questions often spark the most effective and exciting interactions of the entire briefing, but only an outline that is flexible can accommodate them.

Once the briefing material has been selected and outlined, planning of a more practical nature is required. For example, who will present the briefing? One single presenter is most effective by far, but this presenter must possess several rare traits. First, the presenter must have a complete substantive knowledge of the topic, since questions may address any aspect of the findings and since credibility is often an all-or-nothing proposition. One erroneous or uncertain answer can easily undermine the perceived validity of the entire briefing. In addition, the presenter must also possess sufficient dynamism to capture the audience's attention, an effective speaking voice, the interpersonal skills to relate to the audience, and the confidence and poise to handle the distractions that inevitably occur.

Credibility and poise can both be developed by practicing the briefing as many times as possible before a wide variety of audiences. Practice briefings help in at least two ways. First, the presentation is polished during repeated practices and thus the presenter becomes more comfortable and more poised. Second, the questions asked by different audiences indicate the likely reactions from program experts, policy makers, and evaluators and thus point out aspects of the briefing that need further thought or a different presentation. For both these reasons, we encourage extensive and varied practice briefings as early as possible.

Practice briefings also allow the presenter to test and refine audio-visual aids. Most audiences, especially high-level officials, are extremely busy and deal with numerous issues during a typical day (see Mintzberg, 1973). It is difficult to capture their undivided attention for one hour, but effective audio-visual aids can help enormously. The goal is to stop the unrelenting pace of their day and to focus their attention on the briefing. Short videotapes, films, or slides are especially effective, since they require a darkening of the room and undivided attention of all audience members. Also effective are graphic displays of trends, maps of sites visited or service settings, and representative samples of literature or materials used in the program(s).

One visual aid that should accompany every briefing is a set of large, high-quality briefing charts. Placed conspicuously at the front of the room, these charts can be used by the presenter as he or she works through the briefing and can essentially provide a summary of the findings for the audience. It is important that each chart provide information and not just an outline (e.g., "services are improving" instead of "services") yet not appear cluttered or confusing. A side benefit of briefing charts is that, by lightly penciling reminders at the appropriate places on the charts, the presenter can dispense with a script or extensive notes and still have information invisible to the audience.

A related visual aid that must be planned in advance is a letter-sized handout of these briefing charts. Graphics specialists can photograph each chart and create exact duplicates to be given to the audience at the beginning of the briefing. Thus, all audience members can follow the briefing charts regardless of their seating or eyesight, notes can be written at the appropriate point, and each audience member leaves the briefing with a professional and appropriate reminder and summary of the briefing.

Setting the Stage

Once the briefing is planned, there are several important steps that should be taken to set the stage for the actual briefing. Too often these steps, which can make or break a briefing, are not given enough attention. The first is to determine the participants, both among the presenters and the audience. In addition to the single presenter, one or more key staff who conducted the evaluation should attend, since they can assist with questions or reactions. This staff person, especially if sitting near the presenter and armed with back-up information such as computer printouts or supplemental analyses, can also enhance the overall credibility of the study. If the presenter is momentarily taken aback, this staff person can often respond and avoid an embarrassing silence or error.

The selection of an appropriate audience is also critical. Ideally, this audience is kept to a small, select group of persons with the ability to act on the findings. Otherwise the briefing will be viewed as a background session or staff meeting. It is important to enlist early the attendance of the highest possible ranking audience member, since this person's attendance will attract the attendance of other high-level officials. In addition, however, several key staff must attend the briefing, since they will be able to provide detailed knowledge of issues raised and will be responsible for following up any actions coming from the briefing.

Bridging the presenter and the audience, it is necessary to have a high-ranking liaison, since the presenter is almost always of lower rank than those in the audience. This discrepancy of ranks can lead to awkward or even embarrassing moments unless a liaison can defend or protect the presenter in critical situations. In SDA this liaison is the Inspector General, who manages the SDA process for the secretary and who is a strong supporter at briefings.

A second way to set the stage for the briefing is to provide advance briefing materials to each audience member. These materials are important, since they often determine the audience's predisposition and questions. A full set of briefing materials in SDA includes an agenda, a summary of the presentation, and an attached copy of the full draft report.

The agenda deserves special attention, since it determines the structure of the briefing. Following an initial introduction of the issues and the presenter by the liaison, it is wise to limit the formal presentation to no more than one-third the allotted time for the briefing. The goal of an evaluation briefing is to provide the information of most interest to the audience, and often this cannot be completely determined in advance. Only by presenting a fairly broad overview of the findings and then leaving sufficient time for questions and discussion can the audience participants discuss their own concerns. An added advantage of extensive general discussion is the opportunity for the presenter to show the wide range of expertise not reflected in the formal presentation.

A second lesson regarding the briefing agenda is to explicitly allot a brief time for the program to respond to the presentation. In SDA, this 5-minute reaction accomplishes at least two purposes. First, it allows the audience to note agreements or disagreements with the SDA briefing; this allows the secretary to better assess the information presented. The second utility of the program reaction is the dialogue thus created among the presenter, the program, and the audience. The remainder of the discussion often becomes a three-way discussion of various options for action and their possible impact on services.

Briefing materials should be distributed several days prior to the actual briefing, since many audience members will receive their own preliminary briefings from their own staff. As the briefing date approaches, however, a few final touches can enhance the overall presentation by arranging the briefing room for maximum impact. The goal of the seating arrangement is to place the presenter as close as possible to the highest-ranking audience members, all of whom are seated closely together. This highlights the presenter, minimizes distractions from others, and increases the presenter's visibility once discussion begins. This physical proximity also eliminates the need for a microphone and speakers, thus creating a more intimate, personal atmosphere.

Lighting can also be used to highlight the presenter and to minimize distractions. If possible, additional lighting on the presenter and the charts and/or slightly reduced lighting on the audience can help focus attention. If videotapes, films, or slides are used, the lighting can be dimmed completely for these aids and then raised only halfway for the remainder of the presentation. Full lighting can then be used to encourage general discussion after the presentation.

Presenting the Briefing

Once the briefing is planned and the stage has been set, it is time for the actual briefing. Following the introduction by the liaison, the presenter outlines the specifics of the briefing by summarizing the issues addressed, how the study was conducted, by whom, when, in what locations, and who was contacted. Next the presenter grabs the attention of the audience, usually by audio-visual aids discussed above. This is also a good time to humanize and personalize the briefing by using case studies, anecdotes, or personal examples to portray the reality of the briefing issues. These techniques aim at bringing the briefing materials to life and to capture the interest of often-isolated managers and officials.

Once the audience's interest has been captured, the presenter must provide three basic types of information: (1) a *description* of the program, especially of actual conditions and activities at the service delivery level, (2) a *comparison* of this information with appropriate other information to provide perspective, and (3) any *interpretations* of the findings and their implications.

Describing the program generally has two components: describing program activities and describing conditions in which the program operates. The first is relatively straightforward and involves such questions as: What are the goals and objectives of the program? What is the budget for the program? What services does the program deliver? What changes are occurring in the program? However, services are not delivered in a vacuum, so it is also necessary to describe conditions in which the program operates. This includes answering questions such as: What are clients like? What are conditions like at service delivery sites? What relationships exist with other programs? What does the community think of the program?

But describing the program is not sufficient, since information must be placed into perspective to be useful. Accordingly, the presenter must draw appropriate comparisons between the program as observed and appropriate standards. However, the exact comparisons will vary with each evaluation and each briefing. For example, it may be informative to compare a program to legislated or ideal performance standards, to its own past performance or performance in different conditions, or to other programs, either hypothetical or actual.

Finally, the briefing must include interpretations of the findings, although it is vitally important that interpretations be clearly distinguished from findings lest the audience view the presenter as biased. While the audience may not agree with all interpretations, the presenter is obligated to provide an informed judgment for their consideration. Interpretations take a variety of forms and often include judgments of strengths and weaknesses of service delivery, barriers to better performance, best operating practices, relationships between findings, operational problems that need attention, and issues requiring further analysis.

Important to conveying these three types of information is the style of the presenter. The presenter must aim to be *informative* and to convey the findings accurately and completely. This goal can be achieved during the planning stage, when the briefing material is selected and the briefing is practiced. The presenter also aims to be *understandable* and thus avoids technical jargon, involved discussions of obscure issues, or complex statistics. Instead, the presenter relies on simple language (the *New Yorker* style), commonly understood terms, and graphic yet straightforward discussions of the issues. (Brown, Braskamp, and Newman [1978] show that evaluator credibility is not diminished by using jargon-free reporting styles.)

The presenter also aims to be *realistic* in the sense of conveying the real-life implications of the information. Audio-visual aids such as discussed above are very effective in retaining and presenting this "humanization," as are direct quotes and illustrations from situations encountered. Finally, the presenter aims to be *objective* and not distort findings to present only one ideology or viewpoint. Labeling interpretations explicitly, selecting examples and quotations to reflect the full range of experiences, and admitting imperfections in the information obtained during the evaluation are the types of steps that both insure and reflect objectivity.

Following Up

An evaluation can produce a number of beneficial results, including early warning of problems, immediate program improvements, more focused policy analysis, improved program administration, better monitoring of new programs, better design of projected programs, more informed legislative submissions, dissemination of best operating practices, and more informed decision makers. Often a briefing can crystallize a number of follow-up actions that are appropriate and that would produce one or more of these beneficial results.

However, several ingredients are needed for best follow-up. First, the assignments need to be defined clearly and completely. An off-hand remark by an audience member needs to be pursued by the liaison to see if a specific action should be taken. Second, responsibility for each action needs to be assigned to a specific individual. Third, staff must be assigned the responsibility of tracking the assigned task and its completion. By necessity, these staff must work for a high-ranking member of the audience lest their efforts to complete the assignment be ignored. Fourth, unless the evaluator wishes to avoid follow-up involvement, it is necessary for the formal assignment to include a specific role for the evaluator. This role may simply include being informed of the final actions. On the other hand, it may involve reviewing or even participating in the follow-up actions from the briefing. Finally and ideally, a penalty should be established for failure to follow up the actions as assigned.

Conclusions

There are several disadvantages to using an oral briefing to present the findings of an evaluation study. The presentation is transitory and not lasting, and thus is open to misinterpretation or misrepresentation by audience members. The presentation is almost entirely dependent on the personal abilities of the single presenter. Similarly, the mood of the audience members influences their receptivity to the briefing, and a crisis in the morning can easily disrupt their attention to a briefing in the afternoon. Scheduling difficulties, more severe with more senior staff, can greatly reduce the timeliness of a briefing. Finally, the nature of a briefing requires omission of much useful information from the presentation.

However, these disadvantages are heavily outweighed by the considerable advantages of briefings as a technique for presenting information. Briefings are visible events involving several persons and thus possess an impact that is difficult to ignore. They also provide timely information, especially if the briefing is an early presentation of findings that have not yet been finalized in written form. A briefing is a personal interaction between evaluator and audience, not the more impersonal exchange of a written report. Accordingly, a briefing allows an exchange of ideas and comments that is vital to reaching consensus on future actions.

But the most important advantage of an oral policy briefing is its congruence with the normal style of operating among program officials. Managers and information users in general receive their important information from personal contacts in an oral form (see Mintzberg, 1972; Hawkins, Roffman, & Osborne, 1978; Cox, 1977). It is unrealistic to expect managers to change their ways of receiving information during the occasional moments when they are receiving evaluation information. Instead, evaluators must present information in the audience's preferred style. Some evaluators call for all evaluation findings to be presented in an oral briefing (Boruch & Cordray, 1980). We can offer no better advice than to echo that call.

References

Boruch, R. F., & Cordray, D. S. (Eds.). An appraisal of educational program evaluations: Federal, state, and local agencies. Report submitted to the U.S. Department of Education. Psychology Department, Northwestern University, Evanston, Illinois, 1980. To be published by Cambridge University Press.

Brown, R. D., Braskamp, L. A., & Newman, D. L. Evaluator credibility as a function of report style: Do jargon and data make a difference? *Evaluation Quarterly,* 1978, 2(2), 331-341.

Cox, G. B. Managerial style: Implications for the utilization of program evaluation information. *Evaluation Quarterly,* 1977, 1(3), 499-508.

Hawkins, J. D., Roffman, R. A., & Osborne, P. Decision makers' judgments: The influence of role, evaluative criteria, and information access. *Evaluation Quarterly,* 1978, 2(3), 435-454.

Hendricks, M. Service delivery assessment: Qualitative evaluations at the Cabinet level. In N. Smith (Ed.), *New directions for program evaluation: Federal efforts to develop new evaluation methods.* San Francisco: Jossey-Bass, 1981.

Mintzberg, H. *The nature of managerial work.* New York: Harper & Row, 1973.

ROBERT E. STAKE
University of Illinois

DAVID E. BALK
University of Illinois

CHAPTER **11**

Briefing Panel Presentations

Robert E. Stake is Director of CIRCE, the Center for Instructional Research and Curriculum Evaluation, a unit of the College of Education of the University of Illinois. He has been active in the conceptualization of methods for evaluating educational programs and has directed various national evaluation studies, particularly one resulting in Case Studies in Science Education. • *David E. Balk is visiting Research Associate at the University of Illinois at Urbana-Champaign, where he received his Ph.D. Prior to dectoral studies, he directed the Research and Evaluation Department at Phoenix South Community Mental Health Center.*

PROGRAM EVALUATORS, particularly those who make naturalistic observations and use unstructured interviews, find it difficult to encapsulate their descriptions and confine their reports to a suitable size for readers. One remedial ploy is to use a "briefing panel." This chapter describes one particular use of such a panel and the methodological issues considered.

We are using the term "briefing panel" to identify a group of people, perhaps a project's advisory committee, called together to hear a compressed presentation of project activities and findings. Its members raise questions, discuss issues, and perhaps offer additional interpretations and recommendations. The panel might role-play a policy board or sponsor or management team, but need not. The burden on the evaluators is to devise more pungent presentations, anticipate data needs, and incorporate reactions. Content more suitable for footnoting, appendices, and omission can be identified and a superior organization of written materials may be effected.

The information explosion in western technological society presents a booming, buzzing confusion to many leaders expected to make policy and decisions based on judicious use of information. How can busy people read the many materials pertinent to policy formation and program development? How can busy persons discern which portions of an entire report are paramount?

Time constraints on leaders and project directors present a dilemma to evaluators. Evaluators need to get their attention if reports are to be of service. How can evaluators provide information that will be of use, not ignored or misunderstood? The time and costs of careful evaluation planning, data-gathering, analysis, and write-up are surely wasteful if the final evaluation product cannot get time on the decision maker's agenda.

The terms "briefing" and "debriefing" are in common use in program administration, and will be discussed later. First we will focus on a procedure the evaluator arranges so as to parallel and anticipate the actual informing of administrators and other audience members.

The PDHDS Briefing Panel

We at the Center for Instructional Research and Curriculum Evaluation (CIRCE), University of Illinois, have set up panels, briefed them, and then had them inform us as to how to better inform others. One CIRCE briefing panel was assembled a cold day in March 1981. CIRCE had accumulated numerous written reports, mostly from site visitors to secondary schools. These 45 schools had been selected nationally to participate for 18 months in a teacher in-service program, the Program for the Development of Humanities Disciplines within the Schools (PDHDS), sponsored by the National Humanities Faculty (NHF).

Unlike many administrative debriefings at which briefers and panel members are provided questions to be answered, the CIRCE panel review was highly unstructured. The CIRCE project was approaching an interim reporting deadline, following a plan and schedule originally proposed to NHF.

Five individuals with expertise in pedagogy and humanities education were brought together to be briefed. The two professors of educational philosophy knew each other well, and one of them knew the professor of secondary education (literature), but the language arts teacher and the professor of curriculum (and theatre arts) knew none of the others. An effort to get them all acquainted the previous evening fell victim to a snowstorm. Each of them knew at least one of the four evaluators; two knew all of them.

The panelists were charged:

(1) to consider specifically the strengths and shortcomings of PDHDS strategy to upgrade humanities teaching and learning in the schools (both public and private) and to consider more generally the various strategies and obstacles to such improvement; and

(2) to discuss philosophy, methods, and results to date of the PDHDS project, giving particular attention to alternative ways of assisting school classes to include humanistic education.

The panel members were provided some materials ahead of time. When interviewed six months later the panelists said they had read these materials thoroughly. At the actual proceedings the panel was provided with additional written reports, a not unusual phenomenon for panel reviews. CIRCE staff explained the purpose of the day's proceedings, introduced the panel members to persons in attendance at the review, and instructed the panel members to be themselves rather than to play a role.

The physical arrangements for the proceedings were the large dining area of the University's Faculty Club, with seating as shown:

```
                    evaluators
                     X  X  X
              X
   panel       X                    X
              X                    X    witnesses
             X  X
            X  X  X  X  X  X  X
                   observers
```

Proceedings began at 9 a.m. with an hour set aside for CIRCE evaluators and witnesses. At 10 a.m. the panelists were asked to break an imposed silence and to indicate questions or topics on which they would like more information, which they got. As previously arranged, at 11 a.m. the panelists were asked to take charge and to proceed in any way they chose. They were asked to spend at least an hour on their task. They were separated for a lunch break and encouraged to return after lunch for up to a two-hour session if they felt it warranted. The sessions lasted until 3 p.m. They were taped and a transcript was later prepared. The issues raised, the alternative ideas for assistance to teachers, and a few verbatim statements were included in the interim report submitted to NHF.

A scanning of that report, however, shows that the panel contributions were not treated as if of major significance. And there was a feeling of disappointment—noted more by panelists and observers (many of whom were evaluation specialists) than by the CIRCE evaluators. Why was that? Was the briefing ineffective? Did the briefing successfully impart lots of field data to a small group of persons, enabling them to use that information without loss in meaning?

During their discussion, the panel members, as would be expected, drew greatly on their general knowledge of the humanities and education in the public schools. In the words of one panel member, they used the CIRCE reports as "pretexts rather than texts." In opening remarks the panelists had been encouraged to draw upon their personal experience and not to be concerned about how little they knew about the present projects. They used their time after 11 a.m. to ask for additional details of the administration of the program and of individual schools, but they moved fairly quickly to the more general consideration of humanities education and teacher in-service education expected of them. The briefing then did not appear to be unsuccessful.

But perhaps the issues of the PDHDS project were of less interest to them than some of their own, or than some of the issues the program evaluators apparently enjoyed discussing. An issue recurrently discussed was whether a specific humanities content is needed to impart that which comprises the humanities. In some persons' minds this discussion was germane and helpful to the overview of PDHDS projects in secondary schools.

The panel members revealed some fundamental disagreement, not only on what constitutes the humanities, but also on how to impart such knowledge. These recurrent themes, embedded in the panel members' general knowledge but applied to PDHDS specifics reported by CIRCE briefers, added usefully to the evaluation of the PDHDS projects; as one panel member said in an interview six months later, this recurrent discussion provided "criticism of the notion that the NHF projects were concerned with the humanities."

It did not seem that closure was achieved regarding what comprises the humanities and how to impart that knowledge. An observer of the panel presentation said such an issue proves nettlesome to full discussion but that the discussion "brought to the surface assumptions guiding conversations about the humanities." One panel member believed closure would have been achieved if the panel had been expected to "produce a written document summarizing our discussion and views." As it was, this panel member summarized the panel's accomplishment by saying "some consensus [was achieved] about the usefulness of the PDHDS approach to curriculum change."

A CIRCE member's major criticism of the presentation was that the panel did not stay with any one topic long enough to explore it sufficiently. This outcome could not be attributed in justice to the briefing but rather, in his opinion, the conversation wandered partly because the panel lacked a group identity. "People unfamiliar with the context they are in become hesitant to ask probing questions, tough questions of each other."

Interviews with persons six months later regarding the proceedings of this panel review uncovered numerous uncertainties. Panel members, some CIRCE participants, and some observers indicated they felt confused about what the panel was supposed to do and what other persons were to do. A panel member said, "I couldn't figure out whether we were being held to a specific agenda." An observer said that it seemed the charge given the panel was "so nebulous the panel remained unsure what they were supposed to do." This same person said the panel, however, did come up with germane comments helpful during later work engaged in by CIRCE to evaluate the PDHDS projects. A panel member said the panel had been chosen deliberately for diverse views, but this person had remained unsure if the panel was advisory or evaluative and said his function and the panel's at the proceedings had never become clear for him.

The lack of structure at the proceedings became the single theme commented on freely by everyone interviewed. While many persons believed this lack of structure permitted "a lot of good things to emerge" the reaction of most was that the proceedings would have been improved with more structure.

One observer explained the lack of an emerging structure at the proceedings by referring to the dynamics of interaction. It had been hoped that, once the briefing occurred, the panel members would engage themselves in a conversation regarding their deep concern about in-service and humanities education, would draw on each other's rich experience, and now and then refer to the specific PDHDS projects for illustration. However, what transpired was something else. The CIRCE people never could divest themselves of the dominant presence they seemed to exert. Panelists talked more to evaluators than to fellow panelists. One panel member regularly turned to talk to the large group of people supposedly there as unobtrusive observers. A CIRCE staff member also seemed to be directed more to the audience than to the panel.

The physical arrangements have been faulted. It has been suggested that interaction among panel members would have been promoted by reseating the panel at 11 a.m. around the table, to face themselves rather than the evaluators. One panel member suggested in hindsight that panel interaction would have been enhanced had the panel members been placed in a small room with a TV camera beaming proceedings to observers.

Perhaps because the CIRCE people assembled the panel, served as the expert witnesses, and remained much in evidence during the proceedings, it was difficult for the panel *as a panel* to review critically the CIRCE reports and the PDHDS projects. Each panel member remained an individual, commenting as an individual.

According to the recollections of participants and observers, the PDHDS briefing panel should be considered less than highly successful. The panelists wanted to be helpful, but felt they were not. But what was the contribution to the preparation of the interim report?

The director of the evaluation project said:

> What we got out of it turned out to be more a result of preparing for the briefing, and participating in it, less in getting feedback from it. It was a more real task anticipating the needs and interests of these five panelists. But of course their interests may not have been those of the NHF people.

Staff people at the National Humanities Faculty expressed a considerable satisfaction with the interim report and indicated it was well received by their funding agency, the National Endowment for the Humanities, when NHF applied for continuation funding.

Formal Briefings

It is reasonable to suppose that evaluators could utilize briefing panels more effectively by knowing about the technical use of administrative briefings. Procedures commonly call for a brief, accurate, and clear oral communication of specific objectives, tasks, or information to one or more persons, for instance, a program manager, a board of directors, or a panel of experts (Gore, 1969). Briefings have been employed in varied contexts. The U.S. Air Force has used briefings for many years as an efficient method for communicating reports to project managers (Gore, 1969); British industrial firms use briefings in order to explain company decisions and the reasons behind them to employees at all levels (Industrial Society, 1970); the Service Delivery Assessment (SDA) was established by Joseph A. Califano at the Department of Health, Education, and Welfare in January, 1977, to provide oral policy briefings to the Secretary on a routine basis lest he remain uninformed of activities and conditions pertinent to local health care, social services, income maintenance, and education (Hendricks, 1981; see also his contribution to this volume).

These varied sources use briefings typically in a highly structured fashion. The SDA format is not only highly structured but routinized. In this case, problems are specified by the Secretary, who is indisputably the decision maker and key target of the briefings. Data are presented and issues raised in face-to-face sessions, with specific rather than general policy ramifications in mind. Briefers can prepare their oral reports from familiarity with the Secretary's conceptual framework and with the constraints that the Secretary would impose clearly in mind.

The gains arising from oral briefings to leaders include extended face-to-face communication between the researchers (the briefers) and their primary audience. Because the researchers are present, the decision maker(s) can raise questions pertinent to extrapolating future program policies and decisions. The briefing can be likened to a prospecting endeavor. The data's "lode of meaning" can be mined through personal talk rather than remain uncovered in the depths of a written report. Biases and personal values that color data and their interpretation can be brought to the surface for assaying and scrutinizing. New shafts can be opened and explored as the presenters and their audience interact regarding the evaluation report. It is contended that brief, accurate, and clear oral presentations permit and facilitate efficient and effective use of decision makers' time and evaluators' experience.

Strengths of the panel review are summarized by evaluators at Northwest Regional Educational Laboratory (Owens, Haenn, & Fehrenbacher, 1976). External experts can apply a fresh perspective in interactions with program-related personnel, provide multidisciplinary expertise in project reviews, and permit use of nationally known talents that would be too expensive on an extended basis.

Two types of panels are typically employed: investigative panels and advisory panels. A Senate subcommittee hearing would be an example of an investigative panel. The National Science Foundation (NSF) panels that evaluated the many precollege curriculum development projects (National

Science Foundation, 1976) illustrate advisory panels. Usually, panels follow highly structured formats. For instance, NSF charged its panels of experts with answering 10 evaluative questions and a set of subquestions. Senate hearings follow specified time limits for obtaining testimony and indicate who will engage in these activities; protocol is directed by committee rules.

As a result of the use of the CIRCE briefing panels and a consideration of this literature, the major questions for the evaluator considering a briefing panel seem to be:

(1) Who should be on the panel? Those similar to ultimate readers? Stakeholders? Fellow evaluators? People with distinguished reputations?
(2) How great a diversity of panelists should be sought?
(3) Is it important to create an identity, a group bond, among the panelists? How can relationships to the evaluators be minimized? How can the evaluators' frames of reference be exceeded?
(4) How much should their task be structured? How much of the evaluator's task should they know? And assume?
(5) How much material should they get in advance? How much of the opening sessions should be spent purely in informing?
(6) Should they be asked to prepare statements? Individual or consensus? Should they be invited to make program recommendations?

We believe answers to these questions will vary with the situation. We believe that more structure to the sessions and coherence in the panel will expedite what the evaluators could do for themselves, but that less structure and more diversity will help evaluators discover what they otherwise would overlook.

Briefings are simplifications, often likely to be oversimplifications. Distant administrators use them not only because they are busy, but because by omitting much of context and detail they make intolerably complex problems more tolerable.

It would reflect well on evaluators to resist the many exercises in simplification for which they are employed. They cannot resist most. They must reduce complex phenomena to simple representations. The costs of simplification should be worried about. The experience of briefing panels is one that can assist an evaluator in deciding what information deserves priority plus what simplifications are not just encapsulations—but in fact are falsifications.

References

Gore, J. B. Briefing as a method for communicating reports to project management: A thesis. Unpublished masters thesis, Ohio State University, May 1969. Available from ERIC, ED 039 627.

Hendricks, M. Service delivery assessment: Qualitative evaluations at the cabinet level. In N. L. Smith (Ed.), *New directions for program evaluation: Federal efforts to develop new evaluation methods.* San Francisco: Jossey-Bass, 1981.

Industrial Society. Systematic communication by briefing groups. Industrial Society, London, May 1970. Available from ERIC, ED 052 407.

National Science Foundation. Panel evaluation of 19 pre-college curriculum development projects, December 8-12, 1975. National Science Foundation Directorate for Science Education, Washington, D.C., 1976. Available from ERIC, ED 125 160.

Owens, T. R., Haenn, J. F., & Fehrenbacher, H. L. The use of multiple strategies in evaluating an experience-based career education program. *Research, Evaluation, and Development Paper Series* No. 9. Northwest Regional Educational Laboratory, Portland, Oregon, 1976. Available from ERIC, ED 137 325.

Stake, R. E., & House, E. R. *An interim evaluation report of PDHDS.* Champaign, IL: Center for Instructional Research and Curriculum Evaluation, March 1981.

MURRAY LEVINE
State University of New York, Buffalo

CHAPTER *12*

Adversary Hearings

Murray Levine is Professor of Psychology at SUNY Buffalo. He is currently interested in the relationship between social science and law, and he is interested in qualitative methods of research. He has published a case study of organizational change in a mental hospital, and is the author of a volume on the history and politics of community mental health.

THE ADVERSARIAL CONCEPT of evaluation is grounded in the observation that applications of social science technology have encountered major problems as consequences of the embeddedness of human service programs in complex, political, social, and value contexts (Campbell, 1979; Levine & Levine, 1977). Even within the scientific model, the choice of perspective and the selection of measurements reflect value decisions about what is important to study, and from whose perspective. In an educational program, the perspectives of child, teacher, school administrator, central administrator, school board member, union official, mayor, city councilman, state educational authority member, parent, and citizen-at-large are not necessarily the same. Objectives salient for one group may not be those valued or salient for another. The sponsorship of research has important impact in defining the problem (Gouldner, 1968; Levine &

Author's Note: *This report was prepared while the author held a Foundations Fund for Research in Psychiatry Fellowship, 1981-1982.*

Graziano, 1972), but the aura of objectivity lent by quantification and research design may obscure the value and perspective problems that emerge only later in battles about the significance of evaluation results.

Objective and quantitative methods that exclude the use of "softer" subjective and anecdotal reports, or which require respondents to reduce rich experiences to the arid abstractions of rating scales or questionnaires present other problems (Levine, 1980a). High-constraint research designs may further preclude an examination of unanticipated negative or positive consequences of a program. Scriven (1972) has recommended a "goal free" approach to overcome these problems. The recognition of the many issues in applying social science technology to applied problems has stimulated the search for alternatives.

An adversary model and its variants, hold some promise for remedying some of the deficiencies. In essence, the adversarial model operates with the assumption that truth emerges from a hard, but fair fight, in which opposing sides, after agreeing upon the issues in contention, present evidence in support of each side. The fight is refereed by a neutral figure, and all the relevant evidence is weighed by a neutral person or body to arrive at a fair result. The adversarial approach, in comparison to other legal models for fact-finding and dispute resolution, has a cultural reputation as a fair method. Participants report the greatest satisfaction with the process of party presentation (Thibaut & Walker, 1975). Adversary approaches provide a disciplined method for introducing and testing qualitative testimony. Cross-examination provides a form of control to reveal the limits of any bit of testimony to support a proposition. The systematic review of evidence of a variety of kinds allows for a weighting of evidence in arriving at a conclusion. The model is less restricted to conclusions based on statistically derived p values, allowing a more Bayesian approach in integrating information from diverse sources (Perkins, Note 1).

The Legislative Phase

In the legal system, a dispute may arise only when there is a rule of law to provide the standards against which an act or series of events may be evaluated. The rule of law states the rights and responsibilities, the obligations and duties, which when violated give rise to a cause of action. Laws are written prospectively by legislatures in the form of statutes, by administrative agencies in the form of regulations, or they evolve in the common law through judicial decisions reflecting the community's efforts to solve recurrent problems. In theory, the emergent law represents a concensus on standards, values, and norms of conduct.

The analog of law in program evaluation is a statement of the goals and objectives of a program. This analogy directs the evaluator to confront the political, social, and value issues, and not to ignore those as unfortunate "noise in the system." The analogy tells us that in order to achieve concensus, the statements of goals and purposes, (the law) should reflect the interests of the "constituencies" concerned with the program under evaluation. No dispute can be settled unless the underlying standards reflect some concensus.

Experiments using the adversary model have approached the problem of the underlying "law" differently. Wolf (1975) used an elaborate dragnet to garner complaints in a phase he called "issue generation," followed by an "issue selection" phase. A panel composed of a cross-section of various constituencies of the program under study (i.e., faculty, students, and administrators) reviewed the issues for relevancy and put them in final form. Wolf's evaluative teams used the issues as the bases for developing their cases in the next phase, the prehearing period. In the prehearing phase, existing evaluations were reviewed, witnesses interviewed, and other relevant evidence identified. Owens and Hiscox (Note 2) and Braithwaite (Note 3) used comparable methods.

Levine, Brown, Fitzgerald, Goplerud, Gordon, Jayne-Lazarus, Rosenberg, and Slater (1978) followed the legal analogy more closely. They held a day long, open "legislative hearing." The managing group invited testimony from some knowledgeable individuals, but the hearing was open to anyone who wished to testify concerning the goals and standards the educational program under evaluation ought to have met. Following the hearing, the managing group condensed all of the material into a statement of goals and standards for the program in question and submitted it to the official faculty-student body "legislatively" responsible for modifications in the program. They were asked to read, debate, amend, and then ratify the statement. The process proved a useful exercise in value and goal clarification.

Pretrial Process

Projects have followed different steps in further delimiting the issues for the later hearing. Wolf (1975) turned over the task of issue delimitation to two teams of evaluators, one of which presented the case for the existing program, and the other the case for alternatives. Owens and Hiscox (Note 2) said only that "a great deal of effort" went into selecting the most important issues for trial. Levine et al. (1978) adhered more closely to a legal model. Once the statute was adopted, two teams of adversaries were appointed to conduct an investigation whose purpose was to determine which specific aspects of the program allegedly violated the program's own law—its statement of goals and standards. The plaintiff team then wrote a formal complaint, alleging four specific program failures to live up to its law. After conducting its own investigation, the defendant team wrote a reply either denying the allegations or otherwise answering them. The complaint and the reply served to delimit the issues for trial.

The pretrial process was helpful in itself. First, it forced a focus on the specifics of a relevant complaint. It did not allow any complaint, only those which alleged a violation of the program's goals and standards as written in the statute. Second, the process helped clarify issues for the group affected by the program. Each adversary team interviewed the same prospective witnesses. The fledgling attorneys were not only interested in obtaining information, but also in probing the quality of testimony to be offered by each prospective witness. The interviews tended to be searching. Many participants reported that the experience of being interviewed by advocates of different positions forced them to clarify their own thinking.

One reply to a formal complaint (a demurrer in an older legal terminology) may ask the judge to dismiss it for failure to state a complaint for which relief can be granted. Such an approach could be very useful in testing a decision maker's interest in proceding with an evaluation. Following the legal analogy, one would take the specific complaints, and an estimate of what might be proven to the sponsor or to the relevant decision maker with this question: "If the following allegations were proven at trial, would you modify the program accordingly?" If the answer to that question is "No," then we have the equivalent of the failure to state a complaint for which relief can be granted. The process could stop at that point.

The decision maker and the program participants would have had the benefit of the clarification emerging from the legislative and pretrial phases. The decision maker would have a clearer idea of the nature of complaints about the program, and their force. The answer "No" to the question "Would you modify the program?" is a clear, unambiguous operational definition of the weight the decision maker places on the issues. Coming after a preliminary investigation, participants may feel they have a more precise view of the issues than they had had before.

The Trial or Hearing

The open trial is a vehicle for high drama. However, as any experienced observer of the legal scene knows, in all but the most publicized and sensational of trials, most courtrooms are bereft of spectators. Few have the time or interest to sit through a drawn-out trial, reducing its potential to educate members of a program's constituencies as to its merits and deficiencies.

In our trial (Levine et al., 1978), few stayed for the entire two-day event. Braithwaite (Note 3) reported that 64 interested persons registered, but few stayed through the full two-day hearing. Those who attended both days rated the experience as interesting, informative, understandable, and useful. The trial or hearing itself may not be the best method for reaching a large concerned constituency. Carefully edited videotapes, acceptable to plaintiffs and defendants, reducing the key testimony on the major issues to an hour, may be the best way to present the trial to those concerned with its outcome [Editor's Note: see Chapter 14 on television presentations].

An adversarial approach may be useful in presenting and evaluating the results of more conventional research. The Science Court, advocated by Kantrowitz (1967, 1975; Task Force, 1976) suggested another method for dealing with complex data in an adversarial format. Experts for each side can exchange position papers, citing studies and presenting data. Through exchanging such papers, the points of scientific agreement and disagreement can be identified, and the time allotted in a trial or a hearing to working through complex information reduced substantially.

The controversy about scientific data at Love Canal suggests the usefulness of an adversarial approach. Residents affected by the toxic waste dump site near their homes developed a mistrust of government scientists. In an effort to restore trust, the Governor of New York appointed a prestigious commission to review and evaluate all studies done at Love Canal. The prestigious commission issued a widely cited report. However, knowledgeable observers were able to point to serious omissions, overstatements, and statements for which no evidence existed. Had those studies been reviewed in an open adversarial proceeding, a very different report would have resulted (A. Levine, 1982).

Stake and Gjerde (Note 4) conducted a program evaluation in which the final report contained an advocate's statement summarizing the most favorable data and arguments, and an adversary's summarizing the most damaging criticism. The reader was invited to weigh and resolve the differences. Stake's (Note 5) report on Project City Science also included a summary of favorable and unfavorable features. Levine (Note 6) conducted an external evaluation of a crisis service for inmates recently released from a county penitentiary. The contract with program personnel contained an agreement that a draft of the report would be submitted to the project for review before release to the sponsor. It was understood that the evaluator would retain final editorial control. If project personnel demonstrated factual errors, these would be changed. If there were irreconcilable differences of interpretation, then the evaluator agreed to publish the project director's comments as inserts in the report at the page where the disputed point appeared. Levine (1980b) followed a similar rule in conducting a case study of a changing psychiatric hospital.

The Jury or the Panel

It is a problem to select a fair panel and to settle the panel's role and mode of operation. Wolf (1975) selected highly qualified professionals representing a variety of viewpoints on the program in question. Braithwaite (Note 3) convened a seven-person panel of "policy makers, citizens and informed stakeholders." Although he pointed out that their selection was crucial, he did not specify principles for selection. Levine et al. (1978) selected a jury randomly from a panel made up of faculty members and graduate students in doctoral programs in departments other than the one housing the program under study. Wolf (personal communication) once selected a jury made of critics of a program in order to educate them to its merits. The selection process warrants creative thought.

Each project followed somewhat different rules in allowing the panelists or jurors to participate actively in the questioning of witnesses. Wolf (1975) allowed panelists to ask questions (see Arnstein, 1975). Braithwaite (Note 3) allowed panelists to ask questions immediately following each witness's testimony. Wolf and Braithwaite point out that their panelists were selected for their knowledge, and were impatient with more passive roles. Levine et al. (1978) made some provision for jurors to submit written questions through the judge. Few of the jurors exercised that option.

The Panel's Charge

The charge, or the question offered for resolution, sets the panel's task in deliberating and also the relevance of evidence. In an ordinary jury trial, the judge charges the jury. It is the jury's task to find the facts within the framework of law specified by the judge. The judge's charge settles the value framework and other aspects of the charge define the jury's "work" (Levine, Farrell, & Perrotta, 1981). Arnstein (1975) described the difficulties of an open-ended charge presented to the panel. It spent a great deal of time trying to decide what and how it was going to decide. The "sides" were not always clear either.

Braithwaite (Note 3) presented two questions to his panel. Both required a judgment as to the "future promise" of two approaches. His panelists said the issues were not well defined, and not nearly as dichotomous as they had been presented during the hearing. Popham and Carlson (1977) described similar problems in framing questions in a manner suitable for adversary resolution.

Levine et al. (1978) wrote out a detailed charge requesting a special verdict from their jury. The four questions could be answered yes or no, but the jury was also requested to specify the most compelling points of evidence for their verdict on each question, and they were encouraged to include such recommendations as they felt would be useful. The charge did seem to structure the jury's work (Levine, Farrell, & Perrotta, 1981). The charge not only helped to produce a task-oriented group, but it was helpful in resolving internal conflicts.

Popham and Carlson (1977) found that it was difficult to pose questions that were amenable to adversary evaluation. Advocates and witnesses expressed ambivalence about presenting only one side of a complex question. Braithwaite (Note 3) made similar observations about witness' testimony. Arnstein (1975) also noted that each side's testimony was not necessarily favorable to the position the advocate was supporting. Few people were happy about presenting less than a full picture.

A major problem for the future is learning how to specify the issues and to write the charge to the jury or panel in such a way that the questions are amenable to resolution by an adversarial procedure. Although panels or juries must work with time limits for practical reasons, and although the time limits might affect the deliberative process adversely, Levine et al. (1978) and Braithwaite (Note 3) both reported that careful structuring of the charge, and careful socialization of the panelists into their roles, can result in satisfactory products despite arbitrary time limits.

The Decisions and Their Aftermaths

None of the studies of adversary evaluation presently in the literature reported the effect of the panel verdict on the subsequent development of the program under study. Levine et al. (1978) presented the jury's written verdict to the "legislative" body responsible for the graduate program. Because the program had been found "not guilty" on all counts, the need to modify it was reduced considerably. However, the jury's written verdict and recommendations did lead to some minor adjustments in the program's procedures. The conflict that had propelled the trial largely dissipated by the end of the trial. In the several years after the trial, the issues

that were settled have not occupied the legislative body's time and attention to the degree that they did before the trial.

The Present Status of the Model

The adversarial process, as it has been used so far, is time-consuming,
expensive, and cumbersome. A body of critical literature depicting deficiencies and limits is cumulating (see Arnstein, 1975; Popham & Carlson,
1977; Levine et al., 1978; Wolf, 1979; Braithwaite, Note 3; West, Note 7).
To date, no adversary evaluation has been carried out in a volatile situation
with a great deal at stake. Most of the experimental work has taken place
in relatively friendly settings. A few administrators with whom I have
discussed the approach, have expressed leeriness of engaging in an open
process with the potential for getting out of control.

Despite all the difficulties, one should not overlook the merits of the
concept. Much of scientific method depends on an adversarial approach to
the determination of what will be accepted as the conventional scientific
widsom (Levine, 1974). The adversarial approach in essence requires a
delimitation of the issues, so that relevance can be defined. It requires
some form of party presentation, and it requires the opportunity for
cross-examination. Those key elements can be created in forms other than
the trial or a hearing. Aside from its usefulness as a full-scale evaluative
method, the concept may be useful in thinking about how research with
important social implications may be presented publicly.

In normal science, peer review, independent criticism, and replication
guarantee that unstable or fluke results will be weeded out. In policy-
oriented research or in evaluation, where the outcome may depend on a
single study conducted from a single perspective by a single group, there is
grave danger that decisions will be based on either inadequate or seriously
biased information, no matter the technical competence of the single piece
of research. The need for adversarial review at several stages of research
with policy implications is critical as we enter an age of large-scale,
centrally funded research. Such studies, probably conducted by prestigious
agencies or centers will be hailed as definitive and no one else will have the
resources to undertake replications. An adversarial approach, in which a
variety of perspectives is represented, may be essential in an age of big
science and government control, especially if those claiming the mantle of
science desire to maintain public trust. The need to develop fair methods
of fact-finding and dispute resolution, and convincing methods of pre-

senting controversial findings is as important as the need to develop more powerful or efficient research methods.

Reference Notes

[1] Perkins, D. V. Bayesian inference from qualitative and quantitative data in program evaluation. Unpublished paper, Department of Psychology, SUNY Buffalo, 1980.

[2] Owens, T. R., & Hiscox, M. D. Alternative models for adversary evaluation: Variations on a theme. Paper presented at the American Educational Research Association Annual Meeting, New York, 1977.

[3] Braithwaite, R. L. A case study and judicial evaluation of CETA/Education linkages and their transferability. Final Report from Hampton Institute Educational Resources Center, to Office of Research, Evaluation, and Consultation. November 1980.

[4] Stake, R., & Gjerde, C. An evaluation of TCITY, the Twin City Institute for Talented Youth. CIRCE, University of Illinois, 1971.

[5] Stake R. Evaluation Report, 1975 of Project City Science. CIRCE, University of Illinois, 1975.

[6] Levine, M. The offender crisis service. An evaluative study. Department of Psychology SUNY Buffalo, 1974.

[7] West, A. S. An adversarial model of evaluation. Report to NSF. Denver Research Institute, University of Denver, 1976.

References

Arnstein, G. E. Trial by jury: A new evaluation method. II. The Outcome. *Phi Delta Kappan,* 1975, 57 188-190.

Campbell, D. T. Assessing the impact of planned social change. *Evaluation and Program Planning,* 1979, 2, 67-90.

Gouldner, A. W. The sociologist as partisan: Sociology and the welfare state. *American Sociologist,* 1968, 3, 103-116.

Kantrowitz, A. Proposal for an institution for scientific judgment. *Science,* 1967, 156, 763-764.

Kantrowitz, A. Controlling technology democratically. *American Scientist,* 1975, 63, 505-509.

Levine, A. *The Love Canal: Science, politics, people.* Lexington, MA: D. C. Heath, 1982.

Levine, A., & Levine, M. The social context of evaluative research. A case study. *Evaluation Quarterly,* 1977, 1, 515-542.

Levine, M. Scientific method and the adversary model. Some preliminary thoughts. *American Psychologist,* 1974, 29, 661-677.

Levine, M. Investigative reporting as a research method. An analysis of Bernstein and Woodward's *All the President's Men. American Psychologist,* 1980, 35, 626-638. (a)

Levine, M. *From state hospital to psychiatric center.* Lexington, MA: D. C. Heath, 1980. (b)

Levine, M., Brown, E., Fitzgerald, C., Goplerud, E., Gordon, M. E., Jayne-Lazarus, C., Rosenberg, N., & Slater, J. Adapting the jury trial for program evaluation: A report of an experience. *Evaluation and Program Planning,* 1978, 1, 177-186.

Levine, M., Farrell, M. P., & Perrotta, P. The impact of rules of jury deliberation on group developmental processes. In B. D. Sales (Ed.), *The trial process. Perspectives in law and psychology* (Vol 2). New York: Plenum, 1981.

Levine, M., & Graziano, A. M. Intervention programs in elementary schools. In S. E. Golann & C. Eisdorfer (Eds.), *Handbook of community mental health.* New York: Appleton-Century-Crofts, 1972.

Nadler, B., & Shore, K. Evaluating educational programs. An experience with the judicial evaluation model. *Education,* 1979, 99, 387-391.

Popham, J. W., & Carlson, D. Deep dark deficits of the adversary evaluation model. *Educational Researcher,* 1977, 6, 3-6.

Scriven, M. Evaluation perspectives and procedures. In J. W. Popham (Ed.), *Evaluation in education.* Berkeley, CA: McCutcham, 1972.

Task Force Presidential Advisory Group on Anticipated Advances in Science and Technology. The science court experiment. *Science,* 1976, 193, 653-656.

Thibaut, J., & Walker, L. *Procedural justice.* Hillsdale, NJ: Erlbaum, 1975.

Wolf, R. Trial by jury. A new evaluation method. I. The process. *Phi Delta Kappan,* 1975, 57, 185-187.

Wolf, R. The use of judicial evaluation methods in the formulation of educational policy. *Educational Evaluation and Policy Analysis,* 1979, 1, 19-28.

NORMAN STENZEL
Illinois State Board of Education

C H A P T E R *13*

Committee Hearings

Norman Stenzel is a program evaluator with the Illinois State Board of Education. His current interests are techniques for technical assistance to schools, limited budget evaluations, and nontesting assessment of students. In recent work he has implemented goal-free evaluation, naturalistic observation, and research on evaluation.

A COMMON LAMENT of evaluators is that their works are set aside to gather dust instead of being used. In order to correct this problem emphasis has been placed on what the evaluator can do. Timely reporting, audience identification, report clarity, and evaluation impact, for example, are topics in the recent *Standards for Evaluations of Educational Programs, Projects, and Materials* (Joint Committee, 1981). But these are general statements and many specifics are simply assumed. One strategy that can provide specifics for each of these concerns is a committee hearing approach in reporting evaluative results.

Using a Congressional Select Committee as a metaphor, evaluators can craft variations suitable for many settings. There is no doubt that committees and committee-like structures are common features in many program evaluation settings, so why not use them for evaluative purposes? This chapter provides an introduction to the use of the committee hearings format. Included here are two examples of applications of the committee hearings in evaluation, identification of purposes best served through the approach, considerations in selecting a committee, and discussion of some procedural tactics.

Examples of Committee Hearings

Two applications of committees in evaluation illustrate some of the diversity possible in the use of committees. One was an elaborate public hearing focusing on a state-wide evaluation of regional projects in special education. The second example took place in a high school district where a committee of history teachers used the approach in their textbook selection process.

The special education evaluation, sponsored by the Illinois State Office of Education, commissioned third-party evaluators to assess the effectiveness of regional projects designed to provide service to low-incidence handicapped students. Although the evaluators had anticipated providing a traditional report, a series of events led to their agreement to participate in a presentation of their work before a committee of stakeholders. Included on the committee were state office staff, regional project personnel, and various advocacy groups. Each was to represent a "constituency" of similar groups and was "advised" by other persons representing their constituency. The hearing was chaired by a deputy superintendent in the state office.

The purpose of the hearing was to examine the evaluative procedures, test the conclusions reached, and examine the recommendations offered. The evaluators had an opportunity to make a verbal presentation of their work to supplement the written report. Once that was accomplished, committee members had two opportunities to ask questions. The first round of questions was used to initiate areas of inquiry, and the second round was used for clarification and elaboration. The product of the hearing was a set of position statements from each of the committee members. These statements were submitted to the State Office of Education administrators as perspectives on the evaluation.

The textbook evaluation was conducted in a committee hearing format in order to accommodate the contending value perspectives present among the history teachers faced with selecting a new textbook. The teachers disagreed about what history is and what students should learn as a result of their educational experience.

This committee was chaired by one of the teachers selected by the other committee members. The committee engaged both in the investigative processes and provided testimony before their own committee on their assigned investigative tasks. Information presented before the committee was also provided by teachers from nearby schools where the contending textbook choices were used.

The scope of the information presented to the committee included readability information, pilot test results, and testimony from users. The persons presenting the information were interrogated from a variety of value perspectives. The result, after intense committee deliberation, was a single recommended text for board adoption supported by the teachers and documented in a written summary and analysis of the data.

Purposes for Committees

These two examples illustrate two different purposes that may be undertaken through the committee approach—meta-evaluation and valuation. Having a purpose in mind will be useful in determining if a committee tactic is appropriate; it can serve as a guide to determining committee membership; and it will provide cues for the organization and operation of the committee.

Meta-Evaluation

Meta-evaluation is generally defined as evaluating evaluations. The special education example illustrates how a committee approach can add a meta-evaluative dimension to an evaluation.

In traditional approaches to evaluation, examination of the evaluation itself is not often considered to be part of the processes contemporary to the work. Any test of the strength of evaluations is typically left to intellectual sparring after the results are presented. This is most likely to occur where the stakes of the evaluation are high and where the results have some visibility. The national Follow Through evaluation was just such an event.

Using a committee hearing to review an evaluative report can afford an opportunity to add a test of the strength of the evaluative process and products at a time most critical to making decisions. The results of a hearing could be distributed either in a single volume or conjointly with the evaluation report.

In reviewing the processes, the focus of the study can be questioned; data collection and analyses can be reviewed; links of data to judgment and recommendations be probed; and the communicative quality examined. Is this what should have been done? Is this how it should have been done? Is this justified? Is it clear, understandable, and unambiguous?

Meta-evaluation can also check for bias. In his article on the control of bias, Scriven (1975) suggested that persons subjected to an evaluation should have an opportunity to review and respond to the evaluation. The committee format can allow just such an opportunity. Under such a rubric not only the application of processes may be examined, but also the influence of the evaluator's perspectives.

Valuation

Valuation here is meant to be the assignment of merit or worth through the evaluative process. Indeed, it is the value in evaluation.

It would be difficult to find a setting in which evaluation results are viewed in the same way by members of relevant audiences. Evaluation takes place in settings reflective of our pluralistic society. The committee format can bring together persons representing diverse value perspectives to hear evidence and to provide conclusions and recommendations based on the evidence. This was the case in the textbook evaluation example.

A variation of this purpose could be a "trial balloon" approach. In highly politicized settings the committee tactic can provide a systematic approach to inform the public about the evaluation with the deliberate intent of attending to public reaction.

Another purpose of a committee hearing as an evaluation report can be the involvement of decision makers in active review of the evaluative results. In the special education evaluation, that purpose was an important feature in convincing the evaluators to participate in the hearing when it had not been a part of their original contractual agreement.

Although the purposes proposed so far may be appealing, an additional consideration should be made prior to deciding upon the use of a committee approach: Will the committee have primary or shared power in any way, or will it serve only in an advisory capacity? Reflecting upon the answers to those issues should lead to a statement to be included in a "charge" to the committee. The extent of the authority vested in the committee should be clearly specified to prevent any misunderstandings.

Committee Selection

Reflections on the function of a committee will provide some of the background for making decisions about the personnel to serve on an evaluative committee. It is quite possible that an existing committee can serve in a committee hearing. School boards, textbook committees, curriculum committees, advisory panels, faculty committees, and executive committees may be used. If a new committee is to be established, the strategies used to form the committee revolve around the issue of how inclusive or exclusive the committee will be.

Formulation of an exclusive committee would likely incorporate only the immediate decision makers who would have the authority to use the results of the evaluation. A slightly less restrictive tactic could consider other executives or staff whose knowledge, skills, or attitudes could be useful in examining the matters of concern.

Strategies for committee composition may be devised to obtain membership that is more inclusive than those listed above. The special education evaluation deliberately sought to include a wide variety of stakeholders, but it could have been broader yet. In a broad sense, stakeholders include beneficiaries or recipients of service. Organizing a committee solely composed of clients in review of an evaluation of service delivery would certainly provide an important test of results from a relevant value perspective.

Membership on committees could also be determined by identifying what kind of expertise would provide an adequate examination of data treatment and interpretations. One type of expertise that is often overlooked, however, is simply the ability to frame questions or build a case (Wolf, 1975). Another skill to be considered is the ability to develop an argument (House, 1977). When committees are composed of nonexperts, adding a person with just these skills as "counsel" to the committee is a tactic to consider.

Committee Operation

Much has to be done once it is decided to use a committee approach in reporting evaluation results. Some variation in activity will reflect the identified purpose of the committee, and some will reflect the composition of the committee. A general description of some of the roles that can be incorporated into the committee, some guidelines for the operation of the committee, and some aspects of the stages of operation will be useful to have in mind.

Roles

The workings of a committee can be assisted by definition of roles suggested by the Congressional Select Committee metaphor. It should be noted, however, that the metaphor should not be inflexible and should not be used to censor common sense.

A committee chairperson was utilized in both of the hearings summarized here. Of course, the chair serves as director of the hearing and is responsible for administration of any agreed upon rules of operation. The gate-keeper functions of keeping the committee on task, maintaining orderly procedure, and attending to time considerations are features which, although mundane, are important.

As was noted in these examples, the designation of a chair can take place through election or appointment. The dynamics of committee composition in the two applications is worth noting at this point. The first-among-equals strategy was used in circumstances where the persons on the committee knew each other and felt they had a stake in how the committee was organized. It is likely that in other circumstances where the committee is composed either of colleagues or persons who have worked together, committee selection of a chair is feasible with a minimum of effort.

The designated appointment of the chair was used where the members of the committee did not necessarily know one another (Wolf, 1975) and where the hierarchical structure of the sponsoring organization needed to be taken into consideration (the special education hearing). Certainly, it is politic to accommodate organizational structure in the committee operations if hierarchy and status are dominant features.

Another role that is suggested by the select committee metaphor is that of committee counsel. In the congressional setting there may even be chief and minority counsels; however, for evaluative purposes multiple counsels may not be necessary if the purpose of the counsel to provide service to all of the committee members is emphasized.

The role of a committee counsel in evaluation would not be as legalistic as the term suggests. In the evaluative committee the counsel can be selected with the purposes of the committee effort in mind. For example, if the committee is to serve as a recipient of the results of an investigation (as in the special education evaluation), the counsel could be a person with methodological expertise. The counsel could then advise nonexperts on ways to frame questions. If the committee is to examine data in order to provide recommendations, the functions of the counsel could be performed by the chief evaluator. The evaluator would help to organize the hearing, prepare the order of testimony, suggest the types of witnesses, and brief the committee on the scope of the testimony that could be provided by each of the witnesses.

In complex situations, having a person available to spend time attending to details while the committee members are engaged in their own daily regimen may be a necessary approach. The counsel then could prepare drafts of rules, memos, or other communiques to apprise committee members about progress; brief the committee prior to hearing activities; and assist in obtaining the best possible testimony from witnesses.

Other roles in elaborate committee settings might include clerical staff in support of the effort. Even personal staff for committee members might help sift through information prior to the hearing and suggest fruitful lines of questioning.

Guidelines

Well considered guidelines can serve to shape the conduct of the committee and provide a set of expectations for prospective witnesses. The committee may even want to formalize the guidelines as rules of the committee. In this latter form the underlying principle for many of the procedures is that of fair play for persons involved.

Witnesses should be notified well in advance of a hearing. In a case when the evaluators will supply the necessary testimony as part of the reporting mechanism, this poses little difficulty. On the other hand, if other persons are to be included, their voluntary participation will be facilitated by an ample amount of lead time.

Witnesses should be informed of the purposes of the hearing, and the role their testimony is expected to play. If there are particular technical issues with which witnesses will be expected to deal, the issues should be identified in advance to the witnesses so that preparations can be made prior to testimony.

The witness could be allowed to provide prepared testimony prior to submitting to questioning. The witness could also be allowed to make a brief final statement to provide additional thoughts from their point of view.

Witnesses might even be permitted to bring advisers or support staff to assist in providing information. This may be necessary in particularly complex areas. The committee counsel should check with each witness to determine the extent to which advisers of this sort would be included. The evaluators serving as witnesses in the special education hearing felt that they could benefit from counsel of their own if matters of contract were broached. They brought an adviser for that specific purpose. Such concerns could be the subject of advance agreement between contractors and evaluators, especially in instances of meta-evaluation.

Questioning should be guided by the purpose of the hearing. Committee guidelines should allow the chair to serve as a gate keeper by challenging committee questions on the basis of relevance when necessary. Provision might also be made for witnesses to challenge the relevance of questions.

Questioning could begin with the counsel asking background questions to establish the parameters of potential testimony from that witness. Committee members would then ask questions to establish their areas of interest. As second round of questioning can serve to elaborate and clarify points previously initiated.

Time considerations can also be incorporated in the guidelines. Determining how much time each questioner will have is an obvious decision. In the committee process, one questioner may be allowed to yield time to another questioner and procedures for such an eventuality should be specified in advance.

Stages of Operation

Even though a hearing will serve as a reporting device in itself, there will still need to be preparations in advance of the event. The committee membership should have a role in preparing guidelines and in selecting witnesses or identifying the type of witnesses they would like to make presentations at the hearing. The general principle involved in the selection of witnesses is to seek to obtain the best available person to provide testimony. Another consideration at that point could be to identify how many persons should be called to provide testimony in regard to the same point.

Some thought about the preparations necessary for the witnesses should also be made—especially where the witnesses are not members of a team conducting the evaluation. Witnesses should be familiarized with the general format of the hearing, who the committee members are, who other witnesses are likely to be, what the issues are, and what the rules and guidelines are. If they are to provide an initial statement and a summary statement, suggested parameters of those presentations should be made clear.

Preparation of the committee prior to the hearing should include review of the purpose, clarification of the issues, depiction of the testimony or point of view available via each witness, delimitation of rules and guidelines, establishment of the roles of the chair and the counsel, and committee obligations regarding outcomes. The committee also should review relevant existing materials, discuss the implications of those materials, agree to any stipulations possible, and explore possible division of lines of questioning among members.

The hearing should begin with some opening statement delimiting the purpose of the activity, identifying committee organization, and outlining general procedures. The unstated structure of the hearing will reflect the nature of the information to be elicited through the testimonial process. In the special education e.aluation, the process began with a general overview and proceeded more and more specifically. In the textbook evaluation, specifics were obtained from all of the witnesses with the broad picture intended to be a sum of the particulars. It focused on particular topics or issues one at a time. A variation of the particularistic approach could focus on obtaining testimony related to each proposed recommendation or possible recommendations.

The final phase of the committee work is that of summary. In addition to the verbal setting of the hearing, a written document may be desirable. The written document can be considered to be an attachment to any report by the evaluators, or as a product of the hearing in itself. The committee should attempt to agree on the nature of an overview of their results including points that are generally agreed to. Failing this, the report may contain individual statements of perspective from each of the committee members. The document can also include the prepared statements presented by persons providing testimony. These can include a summary of additional testimony if there is a means to record it. The final section of the written report would include recommendations if they were called for.

Summary

The use of committees to review evaluative data for evaluation reports is not an idea foreign to education. Adding some features of a congressional hearing can enhance the evaluation process. Committees can serve a meta-evaluative function at a point in time when that information can inform decision makers, or they can serve to test and examine data, and make judgments from particular value perspectives.

The cases where this approach has been implemented demonstrate that although the process can be elaborate, it also can be modest and manageable within a constricted timeframe and with virtually a nonexistent budget. In each setting, one can craft a process that is manageable in that instance.

References

House, E. R. *The logic of evaluative argument.* Los Angeles: Center for the Study of Evaluation, UCLA Graduate School of Education, 1977.

The Joint Committee on Standards for Educational Evaluation. *Standards for evaluations of educational programs, projects, and materials.* New York: McGraw-Hill, 1981.

Scriven, M. An introduction to meta-evaluation. In P. A. Taylor & D. M. Cowley (Eds.), *Readings in curriculum evaluation.* Dubuque: Brown, 1972.

Scriven, M. Evaluation bias and its control. Occasional Paper 4. Western Michigan University Evaluation Center, Kalamazoo, Michigan, 1975.

Wolf, R. L. Trial by jury: A new evaluation method. *Phi Delta Kappan,* 1975, 57(3), 185-187.

JUDITH S. SHOEMAKER
U.S. Department of Education

CHAPTER **14**

Television Presentations

Judith S. Shoemaker is a Senior Associate and team leader for the research program on educational testing at the National Institute of Education (NIE), U.S. Department of Education. At NIE she has primary responsibility for designing and implementing a program of research, development, and dissemination on educational testing, focusing on the improvement of current testing practices in the schools. Her professional interests include minimum competency testing, politics in educational testing, test use in the schools, and research management.

"Who's Keeping Score?"

In the Fall of 1981, public television stations broadcast a four-part mini-series sponsored by the National Institute of Education (NIE) called "Who's Keeping Score?" This series explores the pros and cons of minimum competency testing and is the unique product of an evaluation study designed to provide information to state and local decision makers. The study is unique for two reasons; first, it used a nontraditional evaluation

---

Author's Note: *This chapter was written by the author in her private capacity. No official endorsement by the U.S. Department of Education is intended or should be inferred.*

technique based on the judicial evaluation model and, second, it used broadcast television to disseminate the results.

Overview of the Study

NIE has a history of producing research and evaluation reports read by only a few. These reports typically reach only other researchers and rarely influence state and local policy decisions. The major purpose of NIE's research efforts in the area of minimum competency testing was to provide high-quality information to those who were making decisions and implementing programs. An earlier study (Gorth & Perkins, 1979) of minimum competency testing programs in the United States funded by NIE found that practices differed greatly from state to state and that most programs had not been in operation very long. It was also found that policy and program issues tended to polarize groups and individuals. The controversial nature of minimum competency testing plus the newness and diversity of programs led NIE to select a nontraditional evaluation design with the major purpose of providing information and clarifying issues—not to judge or to rate individual programs. The framework adopted was based on judicial procedures with two teams presenting testimony on opposite sides of the same issues (Herndon, 1980; Shoemaker, 1981; Thurston & House, 1981). W. James Popham of the University of California at Los Angeles led the team presenting the case in favor of minimum competency testing and George Madaus of Boston University led the team against minimum competency testing. A summary of their cases can be found in the October 1981 issue of *Phi Delta Kappan* (Popham, 1981; Madaus, 1981).

The Major Event

The study culminated in a three-day hearing held in Washington, D.C. on July 8-10, 1981. In all, 57 witnesses testified at the hearing—including U.S. Representative Shirley Chisholm, consumer advocate Ralph Nader, U.S. Commissioner on Civil Rights Mary Berry, newspaper columnist William Raspberry, educators Ralph Tyler, Ralph Turlington, Joseph Cronin, Art Wise, Robert Ebel, and Michael Scriven, plus other school administrators, teachers, parents, and school board members. The hearing officer, Barbara Jordan, former U.S. Representative from Texas, now with the University of Texas at Austin, explained initially that the hearing was designed to serve an educational function by providing a public forum for discussion of a controversial topic from different and often competing perspectives. The hearing was not intended to result in a victory for one side or the other. There was no jury present to render a final judgment and all decisions were left to the viewing audience.

Rationale for Using Television

The primary audience for the hearing was state and local decision makers—school board members, legislators, administrators, and parents—most of whom would not be able to attend the hearing. Therefore, it was decided that the dissemination plan for the study would include video-tapes of the entire proceedings, with copies distributed around the United States to state and local education agencies. The Southern Educational Communications Association (SECA), in association with Maryland Instructional Television, was awarded a grant to produce the videotapes. SECA suggested that the hearings be edited into three 60-minute tapes presenting the highlights of each of the three days of hearings, plus a 60-minute documentary to introduce the viewer to minimum competency testing, which could then be made available for broadcast on public television. Such a broadcast would easily reach decision makers who typically never read a research report, but who do watch television frequently.

NIE's agreement with SECA had one unique feature. While SECA holds and maintains the copyright on the entire series, they agreed to grant unlimited off-air recording rights for educational (noncommercial) use. According to the trade newsletter *The Videoplay Report,* the result of this agreement is a television series which "represents an outstanding example of what school and library video media professionals have long sought . . . topical materials for local use provided by free broadcast delivery" (1981, p. 1). The report concluded that "NIE has gone further than any other public agency in its use of off-air recording as a means of furthering widespread discussion and consideration of program content" (p. 1). The dissemination of the videotapes is supplemented by a printed user's guide which, together with the 800-page transcript of the entire three-day hearing, is available through NIE to encourage additional study and use (Herndon & Shoemaker, 1981).

The Use of Television in Education

The use of television in education has consistently lagged behind its use in business and industry. Education is an institution historically opposed to change and the use of television is no exception—despite volumes of research demonstrating that students can and do learn from television (e.g., Chu & Schramm, 1967; Hilliard & Field, 1976; Costello & Gordon, 1965; Comstock, Chaffee, Katzman, McCombs, & Roberts, 1978; Myer & Nissen, 1979). Most of the early teacher opposition to instructional television has disappeared; it seems that their initial fears of being person-ally replaced by television sets were unfounded. Although most teachers now think of television (broadcast, closed circuit, or videocassettes) as just another audio-visual teaching tool, fewer than 1% of the school districts in the United States use television as part of the regular instructional program (Hilliard & Field, 1976).

The U.S. Department of Education has long recognized the power of television to teach and, since so many hours are spent viewing by the average child (e.g., about 3 hours per day for the average 9-year-old [Comstock et al., 1978]), has tried to improve children's programming by sponsoring television programs such as "Sesame Street," "The Electric Company," "Villa Allegre," and "Freestyle."

The use of television to inform and influence educational decision makers has been largely ignored, despite research that demonstrates the influence of television on voters and consumers (Comstock et al., 1978). However, a few cases do exist in addition to "Who's Keeping Score?" The most notable example was the evaluation of Hawaii's Three-on-Two Pro-gram conducted by the Northwest Regional Educational Laboratory (1977) which also used an adversarial process. In that study, the major findings of the pro and con teams were televised to inform parents and community members of the results of the study. Robert Wolf of Indiana University has videotaped judicial evaluation proceedings and produced a one-hour videocassette that teaches others how to use the judicial evalua-tion model. Another example, provided by Walter Hathaway during a 1981 NIE presentation, was the videotape of a panel of experts discussing what made their schools effective before the Portland, Oregon school board. The Charleston, South Carolina school district produced a televised annual report to inform the community about the progress of their schools (Cone, 1978).

What can television do that other media cannot do? How does televi-sion compare to other media? Table 14.1 summarizes some of the relevant characteristics of different media types.

Advantages of television. There are many things that television can do well. For example, as a communication tool, television can:

- record an event with very little distortion; it can transmit reality with high fidelity (e.g., panel meetings, hearings, classroom in opera-tion)

TABLE 14.1 Instructional Media Stimulus Relationships to Learning Objectives

Instructional Media Type	Learning Factual Information	Learning Visual Identifications	Learning Principles, Concepts, and Rules	Learning Procedures	Performing Skilled Perceptual Motor Acts	Developing Desirable Attitudes, Opinions & Motivations
Still Pictures	Medium	HIGH	Medium	Medium	low	low
Motion Pictures	Medium	HIGH	HIGH	HIGH	Medium	Medium
Television	Medium	Medium	HIGH	Medium	low	Medium
3-D Objects	low	HIGH	low	low	low	low
Audio Recordings	Medium	low	low	Medium	low	Medium
Programmed Instruction	Medium	Medium	Medium	HIGH	low	Medium
Demonstration	low	Medium	low	HIGH	Medium	Medium
Printed Textbooks	Medium	low	Medium	Medium	Medium	Medium
Oral Presentation	Medium	low	Medium	Medium	low	Medium

SOURCE: Chu & Schramm, 1967, p. 96.

- be used repeatedly to reach large and scattered audiences (e.g., policy makers across the country, parents who cannot attend school meetings)
- create a mood or show an emotion using pictures, music and words (e.g., discipline problems in a classroom, a child's excitement in succeeding with a difficult task)
- transport the viewer to a scene (classroom) or gain access to an individual (politician, celebrity) not normally accessible to the viewer
- make complex ideas and abstractions more concrete through the use of examples or demonstrations
- multiply the effect of the message (e.g., a multimedia approach)

Disadvantages of television. Television has certain limitations and drawbacks that may reduce its usefulness. For example:

- Personal face-to-face interactions (questions and answers) between viewer and communicator are eliminated, thus depersonalizing the communication.
- The presence of television to record an event may distort the event itself (that is, students and teachers may "act" for the camera in the classroom).
- Reality can be misrepresented through selective reporting and editing (e.g., deleting disruptive student behavior from classroom scenes, focusing on isolated and nonrepresentative events such as school break-ins or isolated acts of student violence).
- Costs of production and equipment repair are usually much higher than those for other media, particularly print media.
- Complex phenomena, requiring long verbal explanations, statistical data, or specialized knowledge, may be difficult to portray visually (e.g., many scientists criticized the oversimplistic script of the television series "Cosmos").

Unanticipated effects. It should be noted here that the use of television in the NIE minimum competency testing study did create some unanticipated effects. On the positive side, the use of television seemed to heighten the importance of the entire project, not only for the researchers in the study, but also for NIE and the U.S. Department of Education as well. The national broadcast gave additional importance to deadlines, to project monitoring and to internal communications. The study came to the attention of the Secretary of Education and additional resources needed for the study were obtained with minimum difficulty. On the negative side, at times the technical details associated with television, rather than the research issues, became the focus of everyone's energies. For example, some of the data-sharing meetings between the team leaders turned into long discussions of production techniques, set design, and wardrobe. Selection of witnesses was done keeping television in mind. Who would photograph well? With whom would viewers identify most (or least)? Even when selecting exerpts from the hearing for the three one-hour programs, both teams considered how the testimony "looked" on the television monitor, as well as the substance of what was said. While it is difficult to sort out the media effects in this study, it is clear that the presence of television had a definite effect on what was presented at the hearing and on videotape (Popham, 1982; Madaus, 1982).

When Television Might Be Used Most Effectively

Based on the list of its advantages and limitations as given above, plus our experiences with "Who's Keeping Score," television seems best suited to evaluation studies in which the mode of inquiry is naturalistic as opposed to traditional as defined by Smith (1981). That is, where statistical data, experimental designs, and achievement testing take a back seat to a more descriptive, case-study approach that analyzes programs and their features *in situ*. If the purpose of the evaluation is to tell a story, to describe a dynamic, complex program in operation, to trace patterns of decision-making, or to ascertain people's attitudes and opinions, television seems an ideal medium for reporting evaluation results.

Since television is ultimately just a tool for communicating, it is ideal for client-centered evaluation studies, as opposed to those that seek to advance knowledge or to conduct research, as defined by Smith (1981). Television forces the evaluator to think how the audience will receive the televised message, thus keeping the evaluation focused on the clients and how they will use the information. Television is not a particularly good medium—as was discovered with "Who's Keeping Score?"—for conveying statistical information or research results. Most research tends to be too technical and too complex to convey to a general audience in a short time. However, written technical material could be made available to supplement a visual presentation of the major findings.

Television is also ideally suited to studies which conclude with an "event"—such as the NIE hearings on minimum competency testing, or a panel discussion of the significance of the results, or a legislative hearing, or a phone-in question-and-answer session with the superintendent of

schools. Such "events" are usually more typical of nontraditional evaluation methods rather than traditional ones. Any event that has people doing
things or talking to each other would be appropriate for television. A
visual record of the event, on videotape, could then be reproduced and
distributed to a wide range of audiences throughout the district, state, or
nation. Distribution of videotapes can also bring the event into the homes
and offices of those who might not have been able to attend the event due
to transportation costs. For example, NIE's videotapes of the minimum
competency testing hearing have been distributed across the United States
so that decision makers can see and hear the experiences of others.

Thus, the use of television would be best suited to evaluation studies
with these characteristics:

- naturalistic mode of inquiry
- client-centered
- widely scattered audience
- culminating event or public forum, usually based on a nontraditional
  evaluation technique

Uses of Television by an Evaluator

Described below are different ways in which television might be used
by an evaluator.

Documenting the evaluation process. This approach was used by Robert
Wolf of Indiana University who used videotapes to document how the
judicial evaluation process was used to evaluate a school of education
program. The one-hour videotape explains the nature of judicial evaluation, lists its key features, and then follows the work of two teams as they
collect information and prepare testimony. The tape also shows the
judicial evaluation in process, followed by a debriefing segment in which
key participants share their views on the success of the project.

A similar record-keeping format could be used in other studies, to train
graduate students or other evaluators how to conduct similar evaluations,
or to show clients how their study was conducted. Segments might show
initial planning meetings with advisers and consultants, needs assessment
techniques such as door-to-door canvassing or survey work, data collection
methods (students taking tests, evaluators conducting interviews), methods
of data analyses, and report preparation.

Enhancing formative evaluations. Television techniques could be used
extensively during the formative stages of program development. For

example, a demonstration of a new teaching technique or new teaching materials could be used to introduce teachers and administrators to new programs. A videotape of a program in operation elsewhere could be used throughout program implementation at a new site, to maintain fidelity throughout the process. Videotapes of individual teachers could be used to improve delivery and style of presentation. Videotapes of entire classrooms could be analyzed by teachers and administrators to determine program modifications. In a formative evaluation, television could be an additional tool for providing feedback to teachers and administrators. However, the evaluator would have to make sure that the presence of television was indeed *enhancing,* rather than *distorting,* the instructional program. A classroom with a television camera—no matter how unobtrusive—is almost always different from one without a camera. This effect could possibly be reduced by concealing the camera (e.g., using a two-way mirror) or by reducing the novelty of the camera through widespread use.

Collecting data. Television could also be used strictly as a data collection technique; it has the power to record human interactions and dynamic events with high fidelity. Such scenes then could be analyzed to generate hypotheses, to count specific behaviors, or to characterize human interactions. For example, classroom scenes could be used to determine the nature and frequency of out-of-seat behavior or to characterize the reinforcement techniques of the teacher. A videotape has the advantage of stop-action, plus repeat action, that is impossible under live conditions. Thus, the reliability of the evaluator's observations could be determined.

Evaluations that use interview data could add the visual to the usual audio tape recording. Videotape can add the extra dimension—the depth of feeling and range of emotion—so often missing when audio tapes are transcribed and put into written reports.

Reporting evaluation results. The major purpose of "Who's Keeping Score?" was to report to the public the results of an 18-month research and evaluation study. The study culminated in a three-day "event," modeled after a courtroom hearing, that was ideally suited to television. Taping an event and then editing the results into a single program or a series designed to inform policy makers is one way television may be used to report evaluation results.

For more traditional evaluations that do not conclude in a major event, the following scenario could be used. Begin by introducing the program, describing its major features, and showing the program in operation in several classrooms. Use charts or other graphics to explain the purpose of the evaluation and the questions it addressed. Show how important audiences for the evaluation were involved in the planning and implementation of the study (show panel meetings or advisory groups). Explain briefly the data collection techniques used (students taking tests, evaluators conducting interviews) and analysis techniques (computer at work, evaluators discussing the findings and drawing path diagrams to explain behavior). List each of the major findings in chart form (one per frame) followed by an illustration of that finding. For example, if students read better, show a student reading aloud. Or if a teacher's professional image was improved, interview a teacher to find out what that has meant to the teacher personally. Show what students can and cannot do as a result of the instructional program.

The television segment could end there or could continue with policy and program recommendations, depending on the purpose of the evaluation. The videotape itself could lead to a discussion by viewers of implications for their school district. In "Who's Keeping Score?" for example, there are no conclusions or recommendations; no panel or jury rendered a final verdict. Rather, the viewers were encouraged to form their own conclusions, based on their own community's needs and values. One of the suggested activities in the user's guide recommended that the local community continue the discussion using a similar adversarial format (Herndon & Shoemaker, 1981).

If the evaluator is asked to include policy recommendations, this could be illustrated through interviews with outside experts or school administrators. Another technique would be to videotape a school board meeting or a study panel as they deliberate on the meaning of the results for their schools.

A videotape such as the one described, beginning with program description and ending with policy recommendations, could become a complete record of an evaluation study, its findings, and its impact on decision makers. This videotape could be shown to repeated audiences to inform the public—parents and community leaders—about what is happening in the schools. Perhaps one day the Joint Dissemination and Review Panel of the U.S. Department of Education may accept such a videotape as evidence in deciding whether or not an educational program should be disseminated nationwide.

Presenting annual school reports. An additional responsibility of many evaluation offices is to prepare and distribute an annual report. One way to inform the public and to gain their support is to prepare a television program. This format has been used for a number of years by the Charleston, South Carolina schools (Cone, 1978). Their experience has shown that a televised annual report can reach many more taxpayers than a published report; it is a good vehicle for explaining charts and graphs usually found in annual reports; it can transport taxpayers into the classrooms, answer questions important to parents and the community, and emphasize the importance of community support and involvement in the schools. In Charleston, the annual report program begins with a short talk by the superintendent of schools, who indicates the progress made over the last year. Progress is indicated variously through test scores, building reports, or efforts on behalf of special groups of students. The next segment shows schools and classrooms in operation, followed by a question-and-answer session with the superintendent.

Needed Resources

Resources needed to produce a program can range from a few thousand dollars to hundreds of thousands, depending on the size and scope of the program. As with all technology, it is best to involve professionals who know how to produce and direct educational television programs. However, it is possible to produce a program with the following basic equipment (costs based on prices of Sony equipment in Virginia, October 1981).

(1) single-lens camera with pause and zoom features ($1100.00)
(2) videocassette recorder for half-inch tapes with slow motion, variable speed recorder, and programming capability ($1200.00)
(3) portable television set with remote control switch ($600.00)

This equipment, plus blank cassettes at $20.00 each, could easily form the basis of a school television unit. One camera is often sufficient for most uses. For tape-editing capabilities and fancy production techniques, additional equipment would be needed.

When purchasing equipment, be sure to ask for an educational discount; some businesses will reduce prices for schools. In addition, many sales offices offer service contracts with their equipment which could greatly reduce the cost of repair in case of breakdowns.

Another method is to contract the production work with an independent producer. For NIE's program "Who's Keeping Score?" the entire production was paid for with a grant at a cost of $200,000. Services on the grant included:

- rental of mobile recording van, five cameras, lights, and scaffolding during the hearing; rental of editing equipment and studios for postproduction
- rental of the site for the hearing plus purchase of props used at the hearing
- purchase of high-quality video and audio tapes
- costs associated with the host of the series
- make-up and wardrobe services
- cassette-editing services
- use of a graphics artist and graphics production
- security for equipment on site during the three days of hearings
- personnel costs for producer, director, writers, camera operators, engineers, and their assistants
- per diem costs and travel expenses for personnel

A similar agreement could be designed by a school to obtain production services under contract. Independent producers are numerous and can be found through trade journals or the yellow pages of the telephone book.

There are many sources of additional information on television equipment, production techniques, and programming. One way to become more familiar with equipment is to attend trade shows, such as the annual Los Angeles Professional Video Show. Trade shows include seminars and exhibits, plus a chance to see demonstrations of new equipment and to talk with media professionals. Professional journals in the area of educational television include: *Educational and Industrial Television, AV Communications Review, Educational Technology, Journal of Broadcasting, Journal of Communication, Journal of Educational Technology Systems, Journal of Technological Horizons in Education,* and *Journal of Educational Television and Other Media.* Many of these journals are indexed by the ERIC system and would be included under descriptors such as "instructional television."

A good place to start is Taggart's (1975) *A Guide to Sources in Educational Media and Technology* which begins with the history of the audiovisual movement in education and provides an annotated bibliography for topics such as instructional film and television, media research, selection of media, and aspects of change.

The Video Handbook published by Media Horizons (1972) and *The Video Source Book* (Reed, 1980) describe the world of nonbroadcast television, including facilities and equipment, production techniques, distribution, and a glossary of video terms. *The Video Guide* (Bensinger, 1979) covers more technical information but is directed specifically toward educational issues of video. Another helpful book is *Introducing the Single-Camera VTR System: A Layman's Guide to Videotape Recording* (Mattingly & Smith, 1973) which shows production techniques for a small video system. *Videocassette Technology in American Education* (Gordon & Falk, 1972) covers some of the philosophical problems that accompany change in education, a theme often discussed in articles in *Educational Technology,* and gives examples of how videocassettes have been used in the high school and for adult education.

Additional information can be obtained from clearinghouses, some of which are listed in Table 14.2. For information on funding sources, see *The A-V Connection: The Guide to Federal Funds for Audio-Visual Programs* (National Audio-Visual Association, 1979).

Assessing the Utility of Television in Evaluation

NIE is currently in the process of evaluating the success of "Who's Keeping Score?" NIE is interested in the value of the information presented for decision-making at the local level and in the potential of the adversarial process for other controversial research topics. The Northwest Regional Educational Laboratory is assisting NIE in evaluating the study and will be trying out videocassettes and the user's guide with key decision makers in several states. In addition, NIE has developed a network of "local reporters" who are reporting to NIE on the impact of the broadcast in their area, on whether or not any local activities followed, and on how the media covered the broadcast. As of Fall 1981, early returns show a very favorable response from school administrators, researchers, parents, and others who have seen parts of the televised programs. Additionally, the idea of using videotape as a reporting technique has been very favorably received internally at NIE. As a result, several conferences, including one examining methodological issues raised by three studies on private versus public education, have been videotaped.

According to Smith (1981), the value of any new technique, such as the use of television in evaluation studies, must be assessed against three criteria—its effectiveness, its feasibility, and its compatability. So far, our experience with "Who's Keeping Score?" shows that the broadcast and further distribution of the videotapes and user's guide is an effective

TABLE 14.2   Clearinghouses for Information on Educational Television

Children's Television International
One Skyline Place Suite 1207
5205 Leesburg Pike
Falls Church, Virginia 22041

National Information Center for Educational Media
University of Southern California
University Park
Los Angeles, California 9007

National Video Clearinghouse
100 LaFayette Drive
Syosset, New York 11791

National Audio Visual Center
National Archives and Record Service
General Services Administration
Washington, D.C. 20409

National Audio Visual Association
3150 Spring Street
Fairfax, Virginia 22031

The Agency for Instructional Television
Box A
Bloomington, Indiana 47402

ERIC Clearinghouse on Information Resources
Syracuse University
School of Education
Syracuse, New York 13210

Great Plains National Instructional Television Library
1800 North 33rd Street
Lincoln, Nebraska 68583

technique for providing information to educational decision makers, many of whom would never read an NIE report. It was feasible, although costly, to produce the four-part series. Other educational agencies could spend more, or less, depending on resources available. If a school system is already comfortable with television, if it uses television for instruction, staff development, and communication, then the use of television for evaluation purposes will be quite compatible with the school program. However, it would not be very compatible with school programs that never use television, think of it only as a frill, and do not have the time or resources to produce high quality programs.

Conclusion

New advances in technology, such as videodiscs and cable television, plus the increased availability of personal-use video equipment may make the use of television in evaluations much more feasible. As more and more schools take advantage of the growing number of prerecorded education videocassettes, television may become just another communication tool for the evaluator.

References

Bensinger, C. *The video guide* (2nd ed.). Santa Barbara, CA: Video-Info Publications, 1979.

Chu, G. C., & Schramm, W. *Learning from television: What the research says.* Washington, DC: National Association of Educational Broadcasters, 1967.

Comstock, G., Chaffee, S., Katzman, N., McCombs, M., & Roberts, D. *Television and human behavior.* New York: Columbia University Press, 1978.

Cone, J. C. A televised annual report of your schools may be easier to arrange—and win higher ratings—than you think. *American School Board Journal,* 1978, 165(4), 29.

Costello, L. F., & Gordon, G. N. *Teach with television* (2nd ed.). New York: Hastings House, 1965.

Gordon, G. N., & Falk, I. A. *Videocassette technology in American education.* Englewood Cliffs, NJ: Educational Technology, 1972.

Gorth, W. P., & Perkins, M. R. *A study of minimum competency testing programs: Final summary and analysis report.* Amherst, MA: National Evaluation Systems, 1979.

Herndon, E. B. *NIE's study of minimum competency testing: A process for the clarification of issues.* Washington, DC: National Institute of Education, 1980.

——— and Shoemaker, J. A. *A user's guide to videotapes and transcripts: "Who's Keeping Score."* Washington, DC: McLeod Corp., 1981.

Hilliard, R. L., & Field, H. H. *Television and the teacher.* New York: Hastings House, 1976.

Insider's view. *The Videoplay Report,* 1981, 11(20), 1-4.

Madaus, G. F. NIE clarification hearing: The negative team's case. *Phi Delta Kappan,* 1981, 63(2), 92-94.

——— The clarification hearings: A personal view of the process. *Educational Researcher,* 1982, 11(1), 4, 6-11.

Mattingly, G., & Smith, W. *Introducing the single-camera VTR system: A layman's guide to videotape recording.* New York: Scribner, 1973.

Media Horizons. *The video handbook.* New York: author, 1972.

Meyer, M., & Nissen, U. *Effects and functions of television: Children and adolescents, A bibliography of selected research literature 1970-1978.* New York: K. G. Saur, 1979.

National Audio-Visual Association. *The a-v connection: The guide to federal funds for audio-visual programs* (3rd ed.). Fairfax, VA: author, 1979.

Northwest Regional Educational Laboratory. *3 on 2 evaluation report, 1976-77.* Vol.

I, Technical report. Portland, OR: author, 1977.

Popham, W. J. The case for minimum competency testing. *Phi Delta Kappan,* 1981, 63(2), 89-91.

––– Melvin Belli, beware! *Educational Researcher,* 1982, 11(1), 5, 11-15.

Reed, M. (Ed.). *The video source book.* Syosset, NY: National Video Clearinghouse, 1980.

Shoemaker, J. S. Minimum competency clarification hearings. *National Council on Measurement in Education News,* 1981, 24(4), 3-4, 12.

Smith, N. L. (Ed.). *Metaphors for evaluation: Sources of new methods.* Beverly Hills, CA: Sage, 1981.

Taggart, D. T. *A guide to sources in educational media and technology.* Metuchen, NJ: Scarecrow, 1975.

Thurston, P., & House, E. R. The NIE adversary hearing on minimum competency testing. *Phi Delta Kappan,* 1981, 63(2), 87-89.